Anti-Slavery P
Songs of Labor and Reform

(Volume III)
Of The Works of John Greenleaf Whittier

John Greenleaf Whittier

Alpha Editions

This edition published in 2024

ISBN : 9789367241295

Design and Setting By
Alpha Editions
www.alphaedis.com
Email - info@alphaedis.com

As per information held with us this book is in Public Domain.
This book is a reproduction of an important historical work. Alpha Editions uses the best technology to reproduce historical work in the same manner it was first published to preserve its original nature. Any marks or number seen are left intentionally to preserve its true form.

ANTI-SLAVERY POEMS

TO WILLIAM LLOYD GARRISON

CHAMPION of those who groan beneath
Oppression's iron hand
In view of penury, hate, and death,
I see thee fearless stand.
Still bearing up thy lofty brow,
In the steadfast strength of truth,
In manhood sealing well the vow
And promise of thy youth.

Go on, for thou hast chosen well;
On in the strength of God!
Long as one human heart shall swell
Beneath the tyrant's rod.
Speak in a slumbering nation's ear,
As thou hast ever spoken,
Until the dead in sin shall hear,
The fetter's link be broken!

I love thee with a brother's love,
I feel my pulses thrill,
To mark thy spirit soar above
The cloud of human ill.
My heart hath leaped to answer thine,
And echo back thy words,

As leaps the warrior's at the shine
    And flash of kindred swords!

They tell me thou art rash and vain,
    A searcher after fame;
That thou art striving but to gain
    A long-enduring name;
That thou hast nerved the Afric's hand
    And steeled the Afric's heart,
To shake aloft his vengeful brand,
    And rend his chain apart.

Have I not known thee well, and read
    Thy mighty purpose long?
And watched the trials which have made
    Thy human spirit strong?
And shall the slanderer's demon breath
    Avail with one like me,
To dim the sunshine of my faith
    And earnest trust in thee?

Go on, the dagger's point may glare
    Amid thy pathway's gloom;
The fate which sternly threatens there
    Is glorious martyrdom
Then onward with a martyr's zeal;
    And wait thy sure reward

When man to man no more shall kneel,
  And God alone be Lord!

  1832.

TOUSSAINT L'OUVERTURE.

Toussaint L'Ouverture, the black chieftain of Hayti, was a slave on the plantation "de Libertas," belonging to M. Bayou. When the rising of the negroes took place, in 1791, Toussaint refused to join them until he had aided M. Bayou and his family to escape to Baltimore. The white man had discovered in Toussaint many noble qualities, and had instructed him in some of the first branches of education; and the preservation of his life was owing to the negro's gratitude for this kindness. In 1797, Toussaint L'Ouverture was appointed, by the French government, General-in-Chief of the armies of St. Domingo, and, as such, signed the Convention with General Maitland for the evacuation of the island by the British. From this period, until 1801, the island, under the government of Toussaint, was happy, tranquil, and prosperous. The miserable attempt of Napoleon to re-establish slavery in St. Domingo, although it failed of its intended object, proved fatal to the negro chieftain. Treacherously seized by Leclerc, he was hurried on board a vessel by night, and conveyed to France, where he was confined in a cold subterranean dungeon, at Besancon, where, in April, 1803, he died. The treatment of Toussaint finds a parallel only in the murder of the Duke D'Enghien. It was the remark of Godwin, in his Lectures, that the West India Islands, since their first discovery by Columbus, could not boast of a single name which deserves comparison with that of Toussaint L'Ouverture.

> 'T WAS night. The tranquil moonlight smile
> With which Heaven dreams of Earth, shed down
> Its beauty on the Indian isle,—
> On broad green field and white-walled town;
> And inland waste of rock and wood,
> In searching sunshine, wild and rude,
> Rose, mellowed through the silver gleam,
> Soft as the landscape of a dream.
> All motionless and dewy wet,
> Tree, vine, and flower in shadow met
> The myrtle with its snowy bloom,
> Crossing the nightshade's solemn gloom,—
> The white cecropia's silver rind
> Relieved by deeper green behind,

The orange with its fruit of gold,
The lithe paullinia's verdant fold,
The passion-flower, with symbol holy,
Twining its tendrils long and lowly,
The rhexias dark, and cassia tall,
And proudly rising over all,
The kingly palm's imperial stem,
Crowned with its leafy diadem,
Star-like, beneath whose sombre shade,
The fiery-winged cucullo played!

How lovely was thine aspect, then,
Fair island of the Western Sea
Lavish of beauty, even when
Thy brutes were happier than thy men,
For they, at least, were free!
Regardless of thy glorious clime,
Unmindful of thy soil of flowers,
The toiling negro sighed, that Time
No faster sped his hours.
For, by the dewy moonlight still,
He fed the weary-turning mill,
Or bent him in the chill morass,
To pluck the long and tangled grass,
And hear above his scar-worn back
The heavy slave-whip's frequent crack
While in his heart one evil thought
In solitary madness wrought,
One baleful fire surviving still

The quenching of the immortal mind,
One sterner passion of his kind,
Which even fetters could not kill,
The savage hope, to deal, erelong,
A vengeance bitterer than his wrong!

Hark to that cry! long, loud, and shrill,
From field and forest, rock and hill,
Thrilling and horrible it rang,
Around, beneath, above;
The wild beast from his cavern sprang,
The wild bird from her grove!
Nor fear, nor joy, nor agony
Were mingled in that midnight cry;
But like the lion's growl of wrath,
When falls that hunter in his path
Whose barbed arrow, deeply set,
Is rankling in his bosom yet,
It told of hate, full, deep, and strong,
Of vengeance kindling out of wrong;
It was as if the crimes of years—
The unrequited toil, the tears,
The shame and hate, which liken well
Earth's garden to the nether hell—
Had found in nature's self a tongue,
On which the gathered horror hung;
As if from cliff, and stream, and glen
Burst on the' startled ears of men
That voice which rises unto God,

Solemn and stern,—the cry of blood!
It ceased, and all was still once more,
Save ocean chafing on his shore,
The sighing of the wind between
The broad banana's leaves of green,
Or bough by restless plumage shook,
Or murmuring voice of mountain brook.
Brief was the silence. Once again
Pealed to the skies that frantic yell,
Glowed on the heavens a fiery stain,
And flashes rose and fell;
And painted on the blood-red sky,
Dark, naked arms were tossed on high;
And, round the white man's lordly hall,
Trod, fierce and free, the brute he made;
And those who crept along the wall,
And answered to his lightest call
With more than spaniel dread,
The creatures of his lawless beck,
Were trampling on his very neck
And on the night-air, wild and clear,
Rose woman's shriek of more than fear;
For bloodied arms were round her thrown,
And dark cheeks pressed against her own!
Where then was he whose fiery zeal
Had taught the trampled heart to feel,
Until despair itself grew strong,
And vengeance fed its torch from wrong?
Now, when the thunderbolt is speeding;

Now, when oppression's heart is bleeding;
Now, when the latent curse of Time
Is raining down in fire and blood,
That curse which, through long years of crime,
Has gathered, drop by drop, its flood,—
Why strikes he not, the foremost one,
Where murder's sternest deeds are done?

He stood the aged palms beneath,
That shadowed o'er his humble door,
Listening, with half-suspended breath,
To the wild sounds of fear and death,
Toussaint L'Ouverture!
What marvel that his heart beat high!
The blow for freedom had been given,
And blood had answered to the cry
Which Earth sent up to Heaven!
What marvel that a fierce delight
Smiled grimly o'er his brow of night,
As groan and shout and bursting flame
Told where the midnight tempest came,
With blood and fire along its van,
And death behind! he was a Man!

Yes, dark-souled chieftain! if the light
Of mild Religion's heavenly ray
Unveiled not to thy mental sight
The lowlier and the purer way,

In which the Holy Sufferer trod,
  Meekly amidst the sons of crime;
  That calm reliance upon God
  For justice in His own good time;
  That gentleness to which belongs
  Forgiveness for its many wrongs,
  Even as the primal martyr, kneeling
  For mercy on the evil-dealing;
  Let not the favored white man name
  Thy stern appeal, with words of blame.
  Then, injured Afric! for the shame
  Of thy own daughters, vengeance came
  Full on the scornful hearts of those,
  Who mocked thee in thy nameless woes,
  And to thy hapless children gave
  One choice,—pollution or the grave!

  Has he not, with the light of heaven
  Broadly around him, made the same?
  Yea, on his thousand war-fields striven,
  And gloried in his ghastly shame?
  Kneeling amidst his brother's blood,
  To offer mockery unto God,
  As if the High and Holy One
  Could smile on deeds of murder done!
  As if a human sacrifice
  Were purer in His holy eyes,
  Though offered up by Christian hands,

Than the foul rites of Pagan lands!

. . . .

Sternly, amidst his household band,
His carbine grasped within his hand,
The white man stood, prepared and still,
Waiting the shock of maddened men,
Unchained, and fierce as tigers, when
The horn winds through their caverned hill.
And one was weeping in his sight,
The sweetest flower of all the isle,
The bride who seemed but yesternight
Love's fair embodied smile.
And, clinging to her trembling knee,
Looked up the form of infancy,
With tearful glance in either face
The secret of its fear to trace.

"Ha! stand or die!" The white man's eye
His steady musket gleamed along,
As a tall Negro hastened nigh,
With fearless step and strong.
"What, ho, Toussaint!" A moment more,
His shadow crossed the lighted floor.
"Away!" he shouted; "fly with me,
The white man's bark is on the sea;
Her sails must catch the seaward wind,
For sudden vengeance sweeps behind.

Our brethren from their graves have spoken,
The yoke is spurned, the chain is broken;
On all the hills our fires are glowing,
Through all the vales red blood is flowing
No more the mocking White shall rest
His foot upon the Negro's breast;
No more, at morn or eve, shall drip
The warm blood from the driver's whip
Yet, though Toussaint has vengeance sworn
For all the wrongs his race have borne,
Though for each drop of Negro blood
The white man's veins shall pour a flood;
Not all alone the sense of ill
Around his heart is lingering still,
Nor deeper can the white man feel
The generous warmth of grateful zeal.
Friends of the Negro! fly with me,
The path is open to the sea:
Away, for life!" He spoke, and pressed
The young child to his manly breast,
As, headlong, through the cracking cane,
Down swept the dark insurgent train,
Drunken and grim, with shout and yell
Howled through the dark, like sounds from hell.

Far out, in peace, the white man's sail
Swayed free before the sunrise gale.
Cloud-like that island hung afar,
Along the bright horizon's verge,

O'er which the curse of servile war
Rolled its red torrent, surge on surge;
And he, the Negro champion, where
In the fierce tumult struggled he?
Go trace him by the fiery glare
Of dwellings in the midnight air,
The yells of triumph and despair,
The streams that crimson to the sea!

Sleep calmly in thy dungeon-tomb,
Beneath Besancon's alien sky,
Dark Haytien! for the time shall come,
Yea, even now is nigh,
When, everywhere, thy name shall be
Redeemed from color's infamy;
And men shall learn to speak of thee
As one of earth's great spirits, born
In servitude, and nursed in scorn,
Casting aside the weary weight
And fetters of its low estate,
In that strong majesty of soul
Which knows no color, tongue, or clime,
Which still hath spurned the base control
Of tyrants through all time!
Far other hands than mine may wreathe
The laurel round thy brow of death,
And speak thy praise, as one whose word
A thousand fiery spirits stirred,
Who crushed his foeman as a worm,

Whose step on human hearts fell firm:

Be mine the better task to find
A tribute for thy lofty mind,
Amidst whose gloomy vengeance shone
Some milder virtues all thine own,
Some gleams of feeling pure and warm,
Like sunshine on a sky of storm,
Proofs that the Negro's heart retains
Some nobleness amid its chains,—
That kindness to the wronged is never
Without its excellent reward,
Holy to human-kind and ever
Acceptable to God.

1833.

THE SLAVE-SHIPS.

"That fatal, that perfidious bark,

Built I' the eclipse, and rigged with curses dark."

MILTON'S Lycidas.

"The French ship Le Rodeur, with a crew of twenty-two men, and with one hundred and sixty negro slaves, sailed from Bonny, in Africa, April, 1819. On approaching the line, a terrible malady broke out,—an obstinate disease of the eyes,—contagious, and altogether beyond the resources of medicine. It was aggravated by the scarcity of water among the slaves (only half a wine-glass per day being allowed to an individual), and by the extreme impurity of the air in which they breathed. By the advice of the physician, they were brought upon deck occasionally; but some of the poor wretches, locking themselves in each other's arms, leaped overboard, in the hope, which so universally prevails among them, of being swiftly transported to their own homes in Africa. To check this, the captain ordered several who were stopped in the attempt to be shot, or hanged, before their companions. The disease extended to the crew; and one after another were smitten with it, until only one remained unaffected. Yet even this dreadful condition did not preclude calculation: to save the expense of supporting slaves rendered unsalable, and to obtain grounds for a claim against the underwriters, thirty-six of the negroes, having become blind, were thrown into the sea and drowned!" Speech of M. Benjamin Constant, in the French Chamber of Deputies, June 17, 1820.

In the midst of their dreadful fears lest the solitary individual, whose sight remained unaffected, should also be seized with the malady, a sail was discovered. It was the Spanish slaver, Leon. The same disease had been there; and, horrible to tell, all the crew had become blind! Unable to assist each other, the vessels parted. The Spanish ship has never since been heard of. The Rodeur reached Guadaloupe on the 21st of June; the only man who had escaped the disease, and had thus been enabled to steer the slaver into port, caught it in three days after its arrival.— Bibliotheque Ophthalmologique for November, 1819.

"ALL ready?" cried the captain;

"Ay, ay!" the seamen said;

"Heave up the worthless lubbers,—

The dying and the dead."

Up from the slave-ship's prison
Fierce, bearded heads were thrust:
"Now let the sharks look to it,—
Toss up the dead ones first!"

Corpse after corpse came up,
Death had been busy there;
Where every blow is mercy,
Why should the spoiler spare?
Corpse after corpse they cast
Sullenly from the ship,
Yet bloody with the traces
Of fetter-link and whip.

Gloomily stood the captain,
With his arms upon his breast,
With his cold brow sternly knotted,
And his iron lip compressed.

"Are all the dead dogs over?"
Growled through that matted lip;
"The blind ones are no better,
Let's lighten the good ship."

Hark! from the ship's dark bosom,
The very sounds of hell!
The ringing clank of iron,
The maniac's short, sharp yell!
The hoarse, low curse, throat-stifled;

The starving infant's moan,
The horror of a breaking heart
Poured through a mother's groan.

Up from that loathsome prison
The stricken blind ones cane
Below, had all been darkness,
Above, was still the same.
Yet the holy breath of heaven
Was sweetly breathing there,
And the heated brow of fever
Cooled in the soft sea air.
"Overboard with them, shipmates!"
Cutlass and dirk were plied;
Fettered and blind, one after one,
Plunged down the vessel's side.
The sabre smote above,
Beneath, the lean shark lay,
Waiting with wide and bloody jaw
His quick and human prey.

God of the earth! what cries
Rang upward unto thee?
Voices of agony and blood,
From ship-deck and from sea.
The last dull plunge was heard,
The last wave caught its stain,
And the unsated shark looked up

For human hearts in vain.

 . . . .

Red glowed the western waters,
The setting sun was there,
Scattering alike on wave and cloud
His fiery mesh of hair.
Amidst a group in blindness,
A solitary eye
Gazed, from the burdened slaver's deck,
Into that burning sky.

"A storm," spoke out the gazer,
"Is gathering and at hand;
Curse on 't, I'd give my other eye
For one firm rood of land."
And then he laughed, but only
His echoed laugh replied,
For the blinded and the suffering
Alone were at his side.

Night settled on the waters,
And on a stormy heaven,
While fiercely on that lone ship's track
The thunder-gust was driven.
"A sail!—thank God, a sail!"
And as the helmsman spoke,
Up through the stormy murmur
A shout of gladness broke.

Down came the stranger vessel,
Unheeding on her way,
So near that on the slaver's deck
Fell off her driven spray.
"Ho! for the love of mercy,
We're perishing and blind!"
A wail of utter agony
Came back upon the wind.

"Help us! for we are stricken
With blindness every one;
Ten days we've floated fearfully,
Unnoting star or sun.
Our ship's the slaver Leon,—
We've but a score on board;
Our slaves are all gone over,—
Help, for the love of God!"

On livid brows of agony
The broad red lightning shone;
But the roar of wind and thunder
Stifled the answering groan;
Wailed from the broken waters
A last despairing cry,
As, kindling in the stormy' light,
The stranger ship went by.

. . . .

*In the sunny Guadaloupe
A dark-hulled vessel lay,
With a crew who noted never
The nightfall or the day.
The blossom of the orange
Was white by every stream,
And tropic leaf, and flower, and bird
Were in the warns sunbeam.*

*And the sky was bright as ever,
And the moonlight slept as well,
On the palm-trees by the hillside,
And the streamlet of the dell:
And the glances of the Creole
Were still as archly deep,
And her smiles as full as ever
Of passion and of sleep.*

*But vain were bird and blossom,
The green earth and the sky,
And the smile of human faces,
To the slaver's darkened eye;
At the breaking of the morning,
At the star-lit evening time,
O'er a world of light and beauty
Fell the blackness of his crime.*

1834.

EXPOSTULATION.

Dr. Charles Follen, a German patriot, who had come to America for the freedom which was denied him in his native land, allied himself with the abolitionists, and at a convention of delegates from all the anti-slavery organizations in New England, held at Boston in May, 1834, was chairman of a committee to prepare an address to the people of New England. Toward the close of the address occurred the passage which suggested these lines. "The despotism which our fathers could not bear in their native country is expiring, and the sword of justice in her reformed hands has applied its exterminating edge to slavery. Shall the United States—the free United States, which could not bear the bonds of a king—cradle the bondage which a king is abolishing? Shall a Republic be less free than a Monarchy? Shall we, in the vigor and buoyancy of our manhood, be less energetic in righteousness than a kingdom in its age?" —Dr. Follen's Address.

"Genius of America!—Spirit of our free institutions!—where art thou? How art thou fallen, O Lucifer! son of the morning,—how art thou fallen from Heaven! Hell from beneath is moved for thee, to meet thee at thy coming! The kings of the earth cry out to thee, Aha! Aha! Art thou become like unto us?"—Speech of Samuel J. May.

OUR fellow-countrymen in chains!

Slaves, in a land of light and law!

Slaves, crouching on the very plains

Where rolled the storm of Freedom's war!

A groan from Eutaw's haunted wood,

A. wail where Camden's martyrs fell,

By every shrine of patriot blood,

From Moultrie's wall and Jasper's well!

By storied hill and hallowed grot,

By mossy wood and marshy glen,

Whence rang of old the rifle-shot,

And hurrying shout of Marion's men!

The groan of breaking hearts is there,

The falling lash, the fetter's clank!

Slaves, slaves are breathing in that air
Which old De Kalb and Sumter drank!

What, ho! our countrymen in chains!
The whip on woman's shrinking flesh!
Our soil yet reddening with the stains
Caught from her scourging, warm and fresh!
What! mothers from their children riven!
What! God's own image bought and sold!
Americans to market driven,
And bartered as the brute for gold!
Speak! shall their agony of prayer
Come thrilling to our hearts in vain?
To us whose fathers scorned to bear
The paltry menace of a chain;
To us, whose boast is loud and long
Of holy Liberty and Light;
Say, shall these writhing slaves of Wrong
Plead vainly for their plundered Right?

What! shall we send, with lavish breath,
Our sympathies across the wave,
Where Manhood, on the field of death,
Strikes for his freedom or a grave?
Shall prayers go up, and hymns be sung
For Greece, the Moslem fetter spurning,
And millions hail with pen and tongue
Our light on all her altars burning?

Shall Belgium feel, and gallant France,
By Vendome's pile and Schoenbrun's wall,
And Poland, gasping on her lance,
The impulse of our cheering call?
And shall the slave, beneath our eye,
Clank o'er our fields his hateful chain?
And toss his fettered arms on high,
And groan for Freedom's gift, in vain?

Oh, say, shall Prussia's banner be
A refuge for the stricken slave?
And shall the Russian serf go free
By Baikal's lake and Neva's wave?
And shall the wintry-bosomed Dane
Relax the iron hand of pride,
And bid his bondmen cast the chain
From fettered soul and limb aside?

Shall every flap of England's flag
Proclaim that all around are free,
From farthest Ind to each blue crag
That beetles o'er the Western Sea?
And shall we scoff at Europe's kings,
When Freedom's fire is dim with us,
And round our country's altar clings
The damning shade of Slavery's curse?

Go, let us ask of Constantine
To loose his grasp on Poland's throat;

*And beg the lord of Mahmoud's line
To spare the struggling Suliote;
Will not the scorching answer come
From turbaned Turk, and scornful Russ
"Go, loose your fettered slaves at home,
Then turn, and ask the like of us!"*

*Just God! and shall we calmly rest,
The Christian's scorn, the heathen's mirth,
Content to live the lingering jest
And by-word of a mocking Earth?
Shall our own glorious land retain
That curse which Europe scorns to bear?
Shall our own brethren drag the chain
Which not even Russia's menials wear?*

*Up, then, in Freedom's manly part,
From graybeard eld to fiery youth,
And on the nation's naked heart
Scatter the living coals of Truth!
Up! while ye slumber, deeper yet
The shadow of our fame is growing!
Up! while ye pause, our sun may set
In blood, around our altars flowing!*

*Oh! rouse ye, ere the storm comes forth,
The gathered wrath of God and man,
Like that which wasted Egypt's earth,
When hail and fire above it ran.*

Hear ye no warnings in the air?
Feel ye no earthquake underneath?
Up, up! why will ye slumber where
The sleeper only wakes in death?

Rise now for Freedom! not in strife
Like that your sterner fathers saw,
The awful waste of human life,
The glory and the guilt of war:'
But break the chain, the yoke remove,
And smite to earth Oppression's rod,
With those mild arms of Truth and Love,
Made mighty through the living God!

Down let the shrine of Moloch sink,
And leave no traces where it stood;
Nor longer let its idol drink
His daily cup of human blood;
But rear another altar there,
To Truth and Love and Mercy given,
And Freedom's gift, and Freedom's prayer,
Shall call an answer down from Heaven!

1834

HYMN.

Written for the meeting of the Anti-Slavery Society, at Chatham Street Chapel, New York, held on the 4th of the seventh month, 1834.

O THOU, whose presence went before
Our fathers in their weary way,
As with Thy chosen moved of yore
The fire by night, the cloud by day!

When from each temple of the free,
A nation's song ascends to Heaven,
Most Holy Father! unto Thee
May not our humble prayer be given?

Thy children all, though hue and form
Are varied in Thine own good will,
With Thy own holy breathings warm,
And fashioned in Thine image still.

We thank Thee, Father! hill and plain
Around us wave their fruits once more,
And clustered vine, and blossomed grain,
Are bending round each cottage door.

And peace is here; and hope and love
Are round us as a mantle thrown,
And unto Thee, supreme above,
The knee of prayer is bowed alone.

But oh, for those this day can bring,

As unto us, no joyful thrill;
For those who, under Freedom's wing,
Are bound in Slavery's fetters still:

For those to whom Thy written word
Of light and love is never given;
For those whose ears have never heard
The promise and the hope of heaven!

For broken heart, and clouded mind,
Whereon no human mercies fall;
Oh, be Thy gracious love inclined,
Who, as a Father, pitiest all!

And grant, O Father! that the time
Of Earth's deliverance may be near,
When every land and tongue and clime
The message of Thy love shall hear;

When, smitten as with fire from heaven,
The captive's chain shall sink in dust,
And to his fettered soul be given
The glorious freedom of the just,

THE YANKEE GIRL.

SHE sings by her wheel at that low cottage-door,
Which the long evening shadow is stretching before,
With a music as sweet as the music which seems
Breathed softly and faint in the ear of our dreams!

How brilliant and mirthful the light of her eye,
Like a star glancing out from the blue of the sky!
And lightly and freely her dark tresses play
O'er a brow and a bosom as lovely as they!

Who comes in his pride to that low cottage-door,
The haughty and rich to the humble and poor?
'T is the great Southern planter, the master who waves
His whip of dominion o'er hundreds of slaves.

"Nay, Ellen, for shame! Let those Yankee fools spin,
Who would pass for our slaves with a change of their skin;
Let them toil as they will at the loom or the wheel,
Too stupid for shame, and too vulgar to feel!

"But thou art too lovely and precious a gem
To be bound to their burdens and sullied by them;
For shame, Ellen, shame, cast thy bondage aside,
And away to the South, as my blessing and pride.

"Oh, come where no winter thy footsteps can wrong,
But where flowers are blossoming all the year long,
Where the shade of the palm-tree is over my home,

And the lemon and orange are white in their bloom!

"Oh, come to my home, where my servants shall all
Depart at thy bidding and come at thy call;
They shall heed thee as mistress with trembling and awe,
And each wish of thy heart shall be felt as a law."

"Oh, could ye have seen her—that pride of our girls—
Arise and cast back the dark wealth of her curls,
With a scorn in her eye which the gazer could feel,
And a glance like the sunshine that flashes on steel!

"Go back, haughty Southron! thy treasures of gold
Are dim with the blood of the hearts thou halt sold;
Thy home may be lovely, but round it I hear
The crack of the whip and the footsteps of fear!

"And the sky of thy South may be brighter than ours,
And greener thy landscapes, and fairer thy' flowers;
But dearer the blast round our mountains which raves,
Than the sweet summer zephyr which breathes over slaves!

"Full low at thy bidding thy negroes may kneel,
With the iron of bondage on spirit and heel;
Yet know that the Yankee girl sooner would be
In fetters with them, than in freedom with thee!"

1835.

THE HUNTERS OF MEN.

These lines were written when the orators of the American Colonization Society were demanding that the free blacks should be sent to Africa, and opposing Emancipation unless expatriation followed. See the report of the proceedings of the society at its annual meeting in 1834.

HAVE ye heard of our hunting, o'er mountain and glen,
Through cane-brake and forest,—the hunting of men?
The lords of our land to this hunting have gone,
As the fox-hunter follows the sound of the horn;
Hark! the cheer and the hallo! the crack of the whip,
And the yell of the hound as he fastens his grip!
All blithe are our hunters, and noble their match,
Though hundreds are caught, there are millions to catch.
So speed to their hunting, o'er mountain and glen,
Through cane-brake and forest,—the hunting of men!

Gay luck to our hunters! how nobly they ride
In the glow of their zeal, and the strength of their pride!
The priest with his cassock flung back on the wind,
Just screening the politic statesman behind;
The saint and the sinner, with cursing and prayer,
The drunk and the sober, ride merrily there.
And woman, kind woman, wife, widow, and maid,
For the good of the hunted, is lending her aid
Her foot's in the stirrup, her hand on the rein,
How blithely she rides to the hunting of men!

Oh, goodly and grand is our hunting to see,
In this "land of the brave and this home of the free."

Priest, warrior, and statesman, from Georgia to Maine,
  All mounting the saddle, all grasping the rein;
  Right merrily hunting the black man, whose sin
  Is the curl of his hair and the hue of his skin!
  Woe, now, to the hunted who turns him at bay
  Will our hunters be turned from their purpose and prey?
  Will their hearts fail within them? their nerves tremble, when
  All roughly they ride to the hunting of men?

Ho! alms for our hunters! all weary and faint,
Wax the curse of the sinner and prayer of the saint.
The horn is wound faintly, the echoes are still,
Over cane-brake and river, and forest and hill.
Haste, alms for our hunters! the hunted once more
Have turned from their flight with their backs to the shore
What right have they here in the home of the white,
Shadowed o'er by our banner of Freedom and Right?
Ho! alms for the hunters! or never again
Will they ride in their pomp to the hunting of men!

Alms, alms for our hunters! why will ye delay,
When their pride and their glory are melting away?
The parson has turned; for, on charge of his own,
Who goeth a warfare, or hunting, alone?
The politic statesman looks back with a sigh,
There is doubt in his heart, there is fear in his eye.
Oh, haste, lest that doubting and fear shall prevail,
And the head of his steed take the place of the tail.

Oh, haste, ere he leave us! for who will ride then,
  For pleasure or gain, to the hunting of men?

  1835.

STANZAS FOR THE TIMES.

The "Times" referred to were those evil times of the pro-slavery meeting in Faneuil Hall, August 21, 1835, in which a demand was made for the suppression of free speech, lest it should endanger the foundation of commercial society.

Is this the land our fathers loved,
The freedom which they toiled to win?
Is this the soil whereon they moved?
Are these the graves they slumber in?
Are we the sons by whom are borne
The mantles which the dead have worn?

And shall we crouch above these graves,
With craven soul and fettered lip?
Yoke in with marked and branded slaves,
And tremble at the driver's whip?
Bend to the earth our pliant knees,
And speak but as our masters please.

Shall outraged Nature cease to feel?
Shall Mercy's tears no longer flow?
Shall ruffian threats of cord and steel,
The dungeon's gloom, the assassin's blow,
Turn back the spirit roused to save
The Truth, our Country, and the Slave?

Of human skulls that shrine was made,
Round which the priests of Mexico
Before their loathsome idol prayed;
Is Freedom's altar fashioned so?

And must we yield to Freedom's God,
As offering meet, the negro's blood?

Shall tongues be mute, when deeds are wrought
Which well might shame extremest hell?
Shall freemen lock the indignant thought?
Shall Pity's bosom cease to swell?
Shall Honor bleed?—shall Truth succumb?
Shall pen, and press, and soul be dumb?

No; by each spot of haunted ground,
Where Freedom weeps her children's fall;
By Plymouth's rock, and Bunker's mound;
By Griswold's stained and shattered wall;
By Warren's ghost, by Langdon's shade;
By all the memories of our dead.

By their enlarging souls, which burst
The bands and fetters round them set;
By the free Pilgrim spirit nursed
Within our inmost bosoms, yet,
By all above, around, below,
Be ours the indignant answer,—No!

No; guided by our country's laws,
For truth, and right, and suffering man,
Be ours to strive in Freedom's cause,
As Christians may, as freemen can!
Still pouring on unwilling ears

That truth oppression only fears.

What! shall we guard our neighbor still,
While woman shrieks beneath his rod,
And while he tramples down at will
The image of a common God?
Shall watch and ward be round him set,
Of Northern nerve and bayonet?

And shall we know and share with him
The danger and the growing shame?
And see our Freedom's light grow dim,
Which should have filled the world with flame?
And, writhing, feel, where'er we turn,
A world's reproach around us burn?

Is 't not enough that this is borne?
And asks our haughty neighbor more?
Must fetters which his slaves have worn
Clank round the Yankee farmer's door?
Must he be told, beside his plough,
What he must speak, and when, and how?

Must he be told his freedom stands
On Slavery's dark foundations strong;
On breaking hearts and fettered hands,
On robbery, and crime, and wrong?
That all his fathers taught is vain,—
That Freedom's emblem is the chain?

Its life, its soul, from slavery drawn!
False, foul, profane! Go, teach as well
Of holy Truth from Falsehood born!
Of Heaven refreshed by airs from Hell!
Of Virtue in the arms of Vice!
Of Demons planting Paradise!

Rail on, then, brethren of the South,
Ye shall not hear the truth the less;
No seal is on the Yankee's mouth,
No fetter on the Yankee's press!
From our Green Mountains to the sea,
One voice shall thunder, We are free!

CLERICAL OPPRESSORS.

In the report of the celebrated pro-slavery meeting in Charleston, S.C., on the 4th of the ninth month, 1835, published in the Courier of that city, it is stated: "The clergy of all denominations attended in a body, lending their sanction to the proceedings, and adding by their presence to the impressive character of the scene!"

JUST God! and these are they
Who minister at thine altar, God of Right!
Men who their hands with prayer and blessing lay
On Israel's Ark of light!

What! preach, and kidnap men?
Give thanks, and rob thy own afflicted poor?
Talk of thy glorious liberty, and then
Bolt hard the captive's door?

What! servants of thy own
Merciful Son, who came to seek and save
The homeless and the outcast, fettering down
The tasked and plundered slave!

Pilate and Herod, friends!
Chief priests and rulers, as of old, combine!
Just God and holy! is that church, which lends
Strength to the spoiler, thine?

Paid hypocrites, who turn
Judgment aside, and rob the Holy Book
Of those high words of truth which search and burn
In warning and rebuke;

Feed fat, ye locusts, feed!
And, in your tasselled pulpits, thank the Lord
That, from the toiling bondman's utter need,
Ye pile your own full board.

How long, O Lord! how long
Shall such a priesthood barter truth away,
And in Thy name, for robbery and wrong
At Thy own altars pray?

Is not Thy hand stretched forth
Visibly in the heavens, to awe and smite?
Shall not the living God of all the earth,
And heaven above, do right?

Woe, then, to all who grind
Their brethren of a common Father down!
To all who plunder from the immortal mind
Its bright and glorious crown!

Woe to the priesthood! woe
To those whose hire is with the price of blood;
Perverting, darkening, changing, as they go,
The searching truths of God!

Their glory and their might
Shall perish; and their very names shall be
Vile before all the people, in the light
Of a world's liberty.

*Oh, speed the moment on
When Wrong shall cease, and Liberty and Love
And Truth and Right throughout the earth be known
As in their home above.*

1836.

A SUMMONS

Written on the adoption of Pinckney's Resolutions in the House of Representatives, and the passage of Calhoun's "Bill for excluding Papers written or printed, touching the subject of Slavery, from the U. S. Post-office," in the Senate of the United States. Mr. Pinckney's resolutions were in brief that Congress had no authority to interfere in any way with slavery in the States; that it ought not to interfere with it in the District of Columbia, and that all resolutions to that end should be laid on the table without printing. Mr. Calhoun's bill made it a penal offence for post-masters in any State, District, or Territory "knowingly to deliver, to any person whatever, any pamphlet, newspaper, handbill, or other printed paper or pictorial representation, touching the subject of slavery, where, by the laws of the said State, District, or Territory, their circulation was prohibited."

MEN of the North-land! where's the manly spirit
Of the true-hearted and the unshackled gone?
Sons of old freemen, do we but inherit
Their names alone?

Is the old Pilgrim spirit quenched within us,
Stoops the strong manhood of our souls so low,
That Mammon's lure or Party's wile can win us
To silence now?

Now, when our land to ruin's brink is verging,
In God's name, let us speak while there is time!
Now, when the padlocks for our lips are forging,
Silence is crime!

What! shall we henceforth humbly ask as favors
Rights all our own? In madness shall we barter,
For treacherous peace, the freedom Nature gave us,
God and our charter?

Here shall the statesman forge his human fetters,
Here the false jurist human rights deny,
And in the church, their proud and skilled abettors
Make truth a lie?

Torture the pages of the hallowed Bible,
To sanction crime, and robbery, and blood?
And, in Oppression's hateful service, libel
Both man and God?

Shall our New England stand erect no longer,
But stoop in chains upon her downward way,
Thicker to gather on her limbs and stronger
Day after day?

Oh no; methinks from all her wild, green mountains;
From valleys where her slumbering fathers lie;
From her blue rivers and her welling fountains,
And clear, cold sky;

From her rough coast, and isles, which hungry Ocean
Gnaws with his surges; from the fisher's skiff,
With white sail swaying to the billows' motion
Round rock and cliff;

From the free fireside of her untought farmer;
From her free laborer at his loom and wheel;
From the brown smith-shop, where, beneath the hammer,
Rings the red steel;

From each and all, if God hath not forsaken
Our land, and left us to an evil choice,
Loud as the summer thunderbolt shall waken
A People's voice.

Startling and stern! the Northern winds shall bear it
Over Potomac's to St. Mary's wave;
And buried Freedom shall awake to hear it
Within her grave.

Oh, let that voice go forth! The bondman sighing
By Santee's wave, in Mississippi's cane,
Shall feel the hope, within his bosom dying,
Revive again.
Let it go forth! The millions who are gazing
Sadly upon us from afar shall smile,
And unto God devout thanksgiving raising
Bless us the while.

Oh for your ancient freedom, pure and holy,
For the deliverance of a groaning earth,
For the wronged captive, bleeding, crushed, and lowly,
Let it go forth!

Sons of the best of fathers! will ye falter
With all they left ye perilled and at stake?
Ho! once again on Freedom's holy altar
The fire awake.

Prayer-strenthened for the trial, come together,
Put on the harness for the moral fight,
And, with the blessing of your Heavenly Father,
Maintain the right

1836.

TO THE MEMORY OF THOMAS SHIPLEY.

Thomas Shipley of Philadelphia was a lifelong Christian philanthropist, and advocate of emancipation. At his funeral thousands of colored people came to take their last look at their friend and protector. He died September 17, 1836.

GONE to thy Heavenly Father's rest!
The flowers of Eden round thee blowing,
And on thine ear the murmurs blest
Of Siloa's waters softly flowing!

Beneath that Tree of Life which gives
To all the earth its healing leaves
In the white robe of angels clad,
And wandering by that sacred river,
Whose streams of holiness make glad
The city of our God forever!

Gentlest of spirits! not for thee
Our tears are shed, our sighs are given;
Why mourn to know thou art a free
Partaker of the joys of heaven?
Finished thy work, and kept thy faith
In Christian firmness unto death;
And beautiful as sky and earth,
When autumn's sun is downward going,
The blessed memory of thy worth
Around thy place of slumber glowing!

But woe for us! who linger still
With feebler strength and hearts less lowly,

*And minds less steadfast to the will
Of Him whose every work is holy.
For not like thine, is crucified
The spirit of our human pride
And at the bondman's tale of woe,
And for the outcast and forsaken,
Not warm like thine, but cold and slow,
Our weaker sympathies awaken.*

*Darkly upon our struggling way
The storm of human hate is sweeping;
Hunted and branded, and a prey,
Our watch amidst the darkness keeping,
Oh, for that hidden strength which can
Nerve unto death the inner man
Oh, for thy spirit, tried and true,
And constant in the hour of trial,
Prepared to suffer, or to do,
In meekness and in self-denial.*

*Oh, for that spirit, meek and mild,
Derided, spurned, yet uncomplaining;
By man deserted and reviled,
Yet faithful to its trust remaining.
Still prompt and resolute to save
From scourge and chain the hunted slave;
Unwavering in the Truth's defence,
Even where the fires of Hate were burning,
The unquailing eye of innocence*

Alone upon the oppressor turning!

O loved of thousands! to thy grave,
Sorrowing of heart, thy brethren bore thee.
The poor man and the rescued slave
Wept as the broken earth closed o'er thee;
And grateful tears, like summer rain,
Quickened its dying grass again!
And there, as to some pilgrim-shrine,
Shall cone the outcast and the lowly,
Of gentle deeds and words of thine
Recalling memories sweet and holy!

Oh, for the death the righteous die!
An end, like autumn's day declining,
On human hearts, as on the sky,
With holier, tenderer beauty shining;
As to the parting soul were given
The radiance of an opening heaven!
As if that pure and blessed light,
From off the Eternal altar flowing,
Were bathing, in its upward flight,
The spirit to its worship going!

1836.

THE MORAL WARFARE.

WHEN Freedom, on her natal day,
Within her war-rocked cradle lay,
An iron race around her stood,
Baptized her infant brow in blood;
And, through the storm which round her swept,
Their constant ward and watching kept.

Then, where our quiet herds repose,
The roar of baleful battle rose,
And brethren of a common tongue
To mortal strife as tigers sprung,
And every gift on Freedom's shrine
Was man for beast, and blood for wine!

Our fathers to their graves have gone;
Their strife is past, their triumph won;
But sterner trials wait the race
Which rises in their honored place;
A moral warfare with the crime
And folly of an evil time.

So let it be. In God's own might
We gird us for the coming fight,
And, strong in Him whose cause is ours
In conflict with unholy powers,
We grasp the weapons He has given,—

The Light, and Truth, and Love of Heaven.

1836.

RITNER.

Written on reading the Message of Governor Ritner, of Pennsylvania, 1836. The fact redounds to the credit and serves to perpetuate the memory of the independent farmer and high-souled statesman, that he alone of all the Governors of the Union in 1836 met the insulting demands and menaces of the South in a manner becoming a freeman and hater of Slavery, in his message to the Legislature of Pennsylvania.

THANK God for the token! one lip is still free,

One spirit untrammelled, unbending one knee!

Like the oak of the mountain, deep-rooted and firm,

Erect, when the multitude bends to the storm;

When traitors to Freedom, and Honor, and God,

Are bowed at an Idol polluted with blood;

When the recreant North has forgotten her trust,

And the lip of her honor is low in the dust,—

Thank God, that one arm from the shackle has broken!

Thank God, that one man as a freeman has spoken!

O'er thy crags, Alleghany, a blast has been blown!

Down thy tide, Susquehanna, the murmur has gone!

To the land of the South, of the charter and chain,

Of Liberty sweetened with Slavery's pain;

Where the cant of Democracy dwells on the lips

Of the forgers of fetters, and wielders of whips!

Where "chivalric" honor means really no more

Than scourging of women, and robbing the poor!

Where the Moloch of Slavery sitteth on high,

And the words which he utters, are—Worship, or die!

Right onward, oh, speed it! Wherever the blood

Of the wronged and the guiltless is crying to God;
Wherever a slave in his fetters is pining;
Wherever the lash of the driver is twining;
Wherever from kindred, torn rudely apart,
Comes the sorrowful wail of the broken of heart;
Wherever the shackles of tyranny bind,
In silence and darkness, the God-given mind;
There, God speed it onward! its truth will be felt,
The bonds shall be loosened, the iron shall melt.

And oh, will the land where the free soul of Penn
Still lingers and breathes over mountain and glen;
Will the land where a Benezet's spirit went forth
To the peeled and the meted, and outcast of Earth;
Where the words of the Charter of Liberty first
From the soul of the sage and the patriot burst;
Where first for the wronged and the weak of their kind,
The Christian and statesman their efforts combined;
Will that land of the free and the good wear a chain?
Will the call to the rescue of Freedom be vain?

No, Ritner! her "Friends" at thy warning shall stand
Erect for the truth, like their ancestral band;
Forgetting the feuds and the strife of past time,
Counting coldness injustice, and silence a crime;
Turning back front the cavil of creeds, to unite
Once again for the poor in defence of the Right;
Breasting calmly, but firmly, the full tide of Wrong,
Overwhelmed, but not borne on its surges along;

Unappalled by the danger, the shame, and the pain,
And counting each trial for Truth as their gain!

And that bold-hearted yeomanry, honest and true,
Who, haters of fraud, give to labor its due;
Whose fathers, of old, sang in concert with thine,
On the banks of Swetara, the songs of the Rhine,—
The German-born pilgrims, who first dared to brave
The scorn of the proud in the cause of the slave;
Will the sons of such men yield the lords of the South
One brow for the brand, for the padlock one mouth?
They cater to tyrants? They rivet the chain,
Which their fathers smote off, on the negro again?

No, never! one voice, like the sound in the cloud,
When the roar of the storm waxes loud and more loud,
Wherever the foot of the freeman hath pressed
From the Delaware's marge to the Lake of the West,
On the South-going breezes shall deepen and grow
Till the land it sweeps over shall tremble below!
The voice of a people, uprisen, awake,
Pennsylvania's watchword, with Freedom at stake,
Thrilling up from each valley, flung down from each height,
"Our Country and Liberty! God for the Right!"

THE PASTORAL LETTER

The General Association of Congregational ministers in Massachusetts met at Brookfield, June 27, 1837, and issued a Pastoral Letter to the churches under its care. The immediate occasion of it was the profound sensation produced by the recent public lecture in Massachusetts by Angelina and Sarah Grimke, two noble women from South Carolina, who bore their testimony against slavery. The Letter demanded that "the perplexed and agitating subjects which are now common amongst us... should not be forced upon any church as matters for debate, at the hazard of alienation and division," and called attention to the dangers now seeming "to threaten the female character with widespread and permanent injury."

So, this is all,—the utmost reach
Of priestly power the mind to fetter!
When laymen think, when women preach,
A war of words, a "Pastoral Letter!"
Now, shame upon ye, parish Popes!
Was it thus with those, your predecessors,
Who sealed with racks, and fire, and ropes
Their loving-kindness to transgressors?

A "Pastoral Letter," grave and dull;
Alas! in hoof and horns and features,
How different is your Brookfield bull
From him who bellows from St. Peter's
Your pastoral rights and powers from harm,
Think ye, can words alone preserve them?
Your wiser fathers taught the arm
And sword of temporal power to serve them.

Oh, glorious days, when Church and State
Were wedded by your spiritual fathers!
And on submissive shoulders sat

Your Wilsons and your Cotton Mathers.
No vile "itinerant" then could mar
The beauty of your tranquil Zion,
But at his peril of the scar
Of hangman's whip and branding-iron.

Then, wholesome laws relieved the Church
Of heretic and mischief-maker,
And priest and bailiff joined in search,
By turns, of Papist, witch, and Quaker
The stocks were at each church's door,
The gallows stood on Boston Common,
A Papist's ears the pillory bore,—
The gallows-rope, a Quaker woman!

Your fathers dealt not as ye deal
With "non-professing" frantic teachers;
They bored the tongue with red-hot steel,
And flayed the backs of "female preachers."
Old Hampton, had her fields a tongue,
And Salem's streets could tell their story,
Of fainting woman dragged along,
Gashed by the whip accursed and gory!

And will ye ask me, why this taunt
Of memories sacred from the scorner?
And why with reckless hand I plant
A nettle on the graves ye honor?
Not to reproach New England's dead

This record from the past I summon,
Of manhood to the scaffold led,
And suffering and heroic woman.

No, for yourselves alone, I turn
The pages of intolerance over,
That, in their spirit, dark and stern,
Ye haply may your own discover!
For, if ye claim the "pastoral right"
To silence Freedom's voice of warning,
And from your precincts shut the light
Of Freedom's day around ye dawning;

If when an earthquake voice of power
And signs in earth and heaven are showing
That forth, in its appointed hour,
The Spirit of the Lord is going
And, with that Spirit, Freedom's light
On kindred, tongue, and people breaking,
Whose slumbering millions, at the sight,
In glory and in strength are waking!

When for the sighing of the poor,
And for the needy, God hath risen,
And chains are breaking, and a door
Is opening for the souls in prison!
If then ye would, with puny hands,
Arrest the very work of Heaven,
And bind anew the evil bands

Which God's right arm of power hath riven;

What marvel that, in many a mind,
Those darker deeds of bigot madness
Are closely with your own combined,
Yet "less in anger than in sadness"?
What marvel, if the people learn
To claim the right of free opinion?
What marvel, if at times they spurn
The ancient yoke of your dominion?

A glorious remnant linger yet,
Whose lips are wet at Freedom's fountains,
The coming of whose welcome feet
Is beautiful upon our mountains!
Men, who the gospel tidings bring
Of Liberty and Love forever,
Whose joy is an abiding spring,
Whose peace is as a gentle river!

But ye, who scorn the thrilling tale
Of Carolina's high-souled daughters,
Which echoes here the mournful wail
Of sorrow from Edisto's waters,
Close while ye may the public ear,
With malice vex, with slander wound them,
The pure and good shall throng to hear,
And tried and manly hearts surround them.

*Oh, ever may the power which led
Their way to such a fiery trial,
And strengthened womanhood to tread
The wine-press of such self-denial,
Be round them in an evil land,
With wisdom and with strength from Heaven,
With Miriam's voice, and Judith's hand,
And Deborah's song, for triumph given!*

*And what are ye who strive with God
Against the ark of His salvation,
Moved by the breath of prayer abroad,
With blessings for a dying nation?
What, but the stubble and the hay
To perish, even as flax consuming,
With all that bars His glorious way,
Before the brightness of His coming?*

*And thou, sad Angel, who so long
Hast waited for the glorious token,
That Earth from all her bonds of wrong
To liberty and light has broken,—*

*Angel of Freedom! soon to thee
The sounding trumpet shall be given,
And over Earth's full jubilee
Shall deeper joy be felt in Heaven!*

1837.

HYMN

As children of Thy gracious care,
We veil the eye, we bend the knee,
With broken words of praise and prayer,
Father and God, we come to Thee.

For Thou hast heard, O God of Right,
The sighing of the island slave;
And stretched for him the arm of might,
Not shortened that it could not save.
The laborer sits beneath his vine,
The shackled soul and hand are free;
Thanksgiving! for the work is Thine!
Praise! for the blessing is of Thee!

And oh, we feel Thy presence here,
Thy awful arm in judgment bare!
Thine eye hath seen the bondman's tear;
Thine ear hath heard the bondman's prayer.
Praise! for the pride of man is low,
The counsels of the wise are naught,
The fountains of repentance flow;
What hath our God in mercy wrought?

HYMN

Written for the celebration of the third anniversary of British emancipation at the Broadway Tabernacle, New York, first of August, 1837.

O HOLY FATHER! just and true
Are all Thy works and words and ways,
And unto Thee alone are due
Thanksgiving and eternal praise!

As children of Thy gracious care,
We veil the eye, we bend the knee,
With broken words of praise and prayer,
Father and God, we come to Thee.

For Thou hast heard, O God of Right,
The sighing of the island slave;
And stretched for him the arm of might,
Not shortened that it could not save.
The laborer sits beneath his vine,
The shackled soul and hand are free;
Thanksgiving! for the work is Thine!
Praise! for the blessing is of Thee!

And oh, we feel Thy presence here,
Thy awful arm in judgment bare!
Thine eye hath seen the bondman's tear;
Thine ear hath heard the bondman's prayer.
Praise! for the pride of man is low,
The counsels of the wise are naught,
The fountains of repentance flow;

What hath our God in mercy wrought?

Speed on Thy work, Lord God of Hosts
And when the bondman's chain is riven,
And swells from all our guilty coasts
The anthem of the free to Heaven,
Oh, not to those whom Thou hast led,
As with Thy cloud and fire before,
But unto Thee, in fear and dread,
Be praise and glory evermore.

THE FAREWELL OF A VIRGINIA SLAVE MOTHER TO HER DAUGHTERS SOLD

INTO SOUTHERN BONDAGE.

GONE, gone,—sold and gone,
To the rice-swamp dank and lone.
Where the slave-whip ceaseless swings,
Where the noisome insect stings,
Where the fever demon strews
Poison with the falling dews,
Where the sickly sunbeams glare
Through the hot and misty air;
Gone, gone,—sold and gone,
To the rice-swamp dank and lone,
From Virginia's hills and waters;
Woe is me, my stolen daughters!

Gone, gone,—sold and gone,
To the rice-swamp dank and lone.
There no mother's eye is near them,
There no mother's ear can hear them;
Never, when the torturing lash
Seams their back with many a gash,
Shall a mother's kindness bless them,
Or a mother's arms caress them.
Gone, gone,—sold and gone,
To the rice-swamp dank and lone,
From Virginia's hills and waters;
Woe is me, my stolen daughters!

Gone, gone,—sold and gone,
To the rice-swamp dank and lone.
Oh, when weary, sad, and slow,
From the fields at night they go,
Faint with toil, and racked with pain,
To their cheerless homes again,
There no brother's voice shall greet them;
There no father's welcome meet them.
Gone, gone,—sold and gone,
To the rice-swamp dank and lone,
From Virginia's hills and waters;
Woe is me, my stolen daughters!

Gone, gone,—sold and gone,
To the rice-swamp dank and lone.
From the tree whose shadow lay
On their childhood's place of play;
From the cool spring where they drank;
Rock, and hill, and rivulet bank;
From the solemn house of prayer,
And the holy counsels there;
Gone, gone,—sold and gone,
To the rice-swamp dank and lone,
From Virginia's hills and waters;
Woe is me, my stolen daughters!

Gone, gone,—sold and gone,
To the rice-swamp dank and lone;
Toiling through the weary day,

And at night the spoiler's prey.
Oh, that they had earlier died,
Sleeping calmly, side by side,
Where the tyrant's power is o'er,
And the fetter galls no more
Gone, gone,—sold and gone,
To the rice-swamp dank and lone,
From Virginia's hills and waters;
Woe is me, my stolen daughters!

Gone, gone,—sold and gone,
To the rice-swamp dank and lone.
By the holy love He beareth;
By the bruised reed He spareth;
Oh, may He, to whom alone
All their cruel wrongs are known,
Still their hope and refuge prove,
With a more than mother's love.
Gone, gone,—sold and gone,
To the rice-swamp dank and lone,
From Virginia's hills and waters;
Woe is me, my stolen daughters!

1838.

PENNSYLVANIA HALL.

Read at the dedication of Pennsylvania Hall, Philadelphia, May 15, 1838. The building was erected by an association of gentlemen, irrespective of sect or party, "that the citizens of Philadelphia should possess a room wherein the principles of Liberty, and Equality of Civil Rights, could be freely discussed, and the evils of slavery fearlessly portrayed." On the evening of the 17th it was burned by a mob, destroying the office of the Pennsylvania Freeman, of which I was editor, and with it my books and papers.

NOT with the splendors of the days of old,
The spoil of nations, and barbaric gold;
No weapons wrested from the fields of blood,
Where dark and stern the unyielding Roman stood,
And the proud eagles of his cohorts saw
A world, war-wasted, crouching to his law;

Nor blazoned car, nor banners floating gay,
Like those which swept along the Appian Way,
When, to the welcome of imperial Rome,
The victor warrior came in triumph home,
And trumpet peal, and shoutings wild and high,
Stirred the blue quiet of the Italian sky;
But calm and grateful, prayerful and sincere,
As Christian freemen only, gathering here,
We dedicate our fair and lofty Hall,
Pillar and arch, entablature and wall,
As Virtue's shrine, as Liberty's abode,
Sacred to Freedom, and to Freedom's God
Far statelier Halls, 'neath brighter skies than these,
Stood darkly mirrored in the AEgean seas,
Pillar and shrine, and life-like statues seen,
Graceful and pure, the marble shafts between;

Where glorious Athens from her rocky hill
Saw Art and Beauty subject to her will;
And the chaste temple, and the classic grove,
The hall of sages, and the bowers of love,
Arch, fane, and column, graced the shores, and gave
Their shadows to the blue Saronic wave;
And statelier rose, on Tiber's winding side,
The Pantheon's dome, the Coliseum's pride,
The Capitol, whose arches backward flung
The deep, clear cadence of the Roman tongue,
Whence stern decrees, like words of fate, went forth
To the awed nations of a conquered earth,
Where the proud Caesars in their glory came,
And Brutus lightened from his lips of flame!
Yet in the porches of Athena's halls,
And in the shadow of her stately walls,
Lurked the sad bondman, and his tears of woe
Wet the cold marble with unheeded flow;
And fetters clanked beneath the silver dome
Of the proud Pantheon of imperious Rome.
Oh, not for him, the chained and stricken slave,
By Tiber's shore, or blue Ægina's wave,
In the thronged forum, or the sages' seat,
The bold lip pleaded, and the warm heart beat;
No soul of sorrow melted at his pain,
No tear of pity rusted on his chain!

But this fair Hall to Truth and Freedom given,
Pledged to the Right before all Earth and Heaven,

A free arena for the strife of mind,
To caste, or sect, or color unconfined,
Shall thrill with echoes such as ne'er of old
From Roman hall or Grecian temple rolled;
Thoughts shall find utterance such as never yet
The Propylea or the Forum met.
Beneath its roof no gladiator's strife
Shall win applauses with the waste of life;
No lordly lictor urge the barbarous game,
No wanton Lais glory in her shame.
But here the tear of sympathy shall flow,
As the ear listens to the tale of woe;
Here in stern judgment of the oppressor's wrong
Shall strong rebukings thrill on Freedom's tongue,
No partial justice hold th' unequal scale,
No pride of caste a brother's rights assail,
No tyrant's mandates echo from this wall,
Holy to Freedom and the Rights of All!
But a fair field, where mind may close with mind,
Free as the sunshine and the chainless wind;
Where the high trust is fixed on Truth alone,
And bonds and fetters from the soul are thrown;
Where wealth, and rank, and worldly pomp, and might,
Yield to the presence of the True and Right.

And fitting is it that this Hall should stand
Where Pennsylvania's Founder led his band,
From thy blue waters, Delaware!—to press
The virgin verdure of the wilderness.

Here, where all Europe with amazement saw
The soul's high freedom trammelled by no law;
Here, where the fierce and warlike forest-men
Gathered, in peace, around the home of Penn,
Awed by the weapons Love alone had given
Drawn from the holy armory of Heaven;
Where Nature's voice against the bondman's wrong
First found an earnest and indignant tongue;
Where Lay's bold message to the proud was borne;
And Keith's rebuke, and Franklin's manly scorn!
Fitting it is that here, where Freedom first
From her fair feet shook off the Old World's dust,
Spread her white pinions to our Western blast,
And her free tresses to our sunshine cast,
One Hall should rise redeemed from Slavery's ban,
One Temple sacred to the Rights of Man!

Oh! if the spirits of the parted come,
Visiting angels, to their olden home
If the dead fathers of the land look forth
From their fair dwellings, to the things of earth,
Is it a dream, that with their eyes of love,
They gaze now on us from the bowers above?
Lay's ardent soul, and Benezet the mild,
Steadfast in faith, yet gentle as a child,
Meek-hearted Woolman, and that brother-band,
The sorrowing exiles from their "Father land,"
Leaving their homes in Krieshiem's bowers of vine,
And the blue beauty of their glorious Rhine,

To seek amidst our solemn depths of wood
Freedom from man, and holy peace with God;
Who first of all their testimonial gave
Against the oppressor, for the outcast slave,
Is it a dream that such as these look down,
And with their blessing our rejoicings crown?
Let us rejoice, that while the pulpit's door
Is barred against the pleaders for the poor;
While the Church, wrangling upon points of faith,
Forgets her bondmen suffering unto death;
While crafty Traffic and the lust of Gain
Unite to forge Oppression's triple chain,
One door is open, and one Temple free,
As a resting-place for hunted Liberty!
Where men may speak, unshackled and unawed,
High words of Truth, for Freedom and for God.
And when that truth its perfect work hath done,
And rich with blessings o'er our land hath gone;
When not a slave beneath his yoke shall pine,
From broad Potomac to the far Sabine
When unto angel lips at last is given
The silver trump of Jubilee in Heaven;
And from Virginia's plains, Kentucky's shades,
And through the dim Floridian everglades,
Rises, to meet that angel-trumpet's sound,
The voice of millions from their chains unbound;
Then, though this Hall be crumbling in decay,
Its strong walls blending with the common clay,
Yet, round the ruins of its strength shall stand

The best and noblest of a ransomed land—
Pilgrims, like these who throng around the shrine
Of Mecca, or of holy Palestine!
A prouder glory shall that ruin own
Than that which lingers round the Parthenon.
Here shall the child of after years be taught
The works of Freedom which his fathers wrought;
Told of the trials of the present hour,
Our weary strife with prejudice and power;
How the high errand quickened woman's soul,
And touched her lip as with a living coal;
How Freedom's martyrs kept their lofty faith
True and unwavering, unto bonds and death;
The pencil's art shall sketch the ruined Hall,
The Muses' garland crown its aged wall,
And History's pen for after times record
Its consecration unto Freedom's God!

THE NEW YEAR.

Addressed to the Patrons of the Pennsylvania Freeman.

THE wave is breaking on the shore,
The echo fading from the chime
Again the shadow moveth o'er
The dial-plate of time!

O seer-seen Angel! waiting now
With weary feet on sea and shore,
Impatient for the last dread vow
That time shall be no more!

Once more across thy sleepless eye
The semblance of a smile has passed:
The year departing leaves more nigh
Time's fearfullest and last.

Oh, in that dying year hath been
The sum of all since time began;
The birth and death, the joy and pain,
Of Nature and of Man.

Spring, with her change of sun and shower,
And streams released from Winter's chain,
And bursting bud, and opening flower,
And greenly growing grain;

And Summer's shade, and sunshine warm,
And rainbows o'er her hill-tops bowed,

And voices in her rising storm;
God speaking from His cloud!

And Autumn's fruits and clustering sheaves,
And soft, warm days of golden light,
The glory of her forest leaves,
And harvest-moon at night;

And Winter with her leafless grove,
And prisoned stream, and drifting snow,
The brilliance of her heaven above
And of her earth below;

And man, in whom an angel's mind
With earth's low instincts finds abode,
The highest of the links which bind
Brute nature to her God;

His infant eye bath seen the light,
His childhood's merriest laughter rung,
And active sports to manlier might
The nerves of boyhood strung!

And quiet love, and passion's fires,
Have soothed or burned in manhood's breast,
And lofty aims and low desires
By turns disturbed his rest.

The wailing of the newly-born

Has mingled with the funeral knell;
And o'er the dying's ear has gone
The merry marriage-bell.

And Wealth has filled his halls with mirth,
While Want, in many a humble shed,
Toiled, shivering by her cheerless hearth,
The live-long night for bread.

And worse than all, the human slave,
The sport of lust, and pride, and scorn!
Plucked off the crown his Maker gave,
His regal manhood gone!
Oh, still, my country! o'er thy plains,
Blackened with slavery's blight and ban,
That human chattel drags his chains,
An uncreated man!

And still, where'er to sun and breeze,
My country, is thy flag unrolled,
With scorn, the gazing stranger sees
A stain on every fold.

Oh, tear the gorgeous emblem down!
It gathers scorn from every eye,
And despots smile and good men frown
Whene'er it passes by.

Shame! shame! its starry splendors glow

Above the slaver's loathsome jail;
Its folds are ruffling even now
His crimson flag of sale.

Still round our country's proudest hall
The trade in human flesh is driven,
And at each careless hammer-fall
A human heart is riven.

And this, too, sanctioned by the men
Vested with power to shield the right,
And throw each vile and robber den
Wide open to the light.
Yet, shame upon them! there they sit,
Men of the North, subdued and still;
Meek, pliant poltroons, only fit
To work a master's will.

Sold, bargained off for Southern votes,
A passive herd of Northern mules,
Just braying through their purchased throats
Whate'er their owner rules.

And he, (2) the basest of the base,
The vilest of the vile, whose name,
Embalmed in infinite disgrace,
Is deathless in its shame!

A tool, to bolt the people's door

Against the people clamoring there,
An ass, to trample on their floor
A people's right of prayer!

Nailed to his self-made gibbet fast,
Self-pilloried to the public view,
A mark for every passing blast
Of scorn to whistle through;

There let him hang, and hear the boast
Of Southrons o'er their pliant tool,—
A new Stylites on his post,
"Sacred to ridicule!"
Look we at home! our noble hall,
To Freedom's holy purpose given,
Now rears its black and ruined wall,
Beneath the wintry heaven,

Telling the story of its doom,
The fiendish mob, the prostrate law,
The fiery jet through midnight's gloom,
Our gazing thousands saw.

Look to our State! the poor man's right
Torn from him: and the sons of those
Whose blood in Freedom's sternest fight
Sprinkled the Jersey snows,

Outlawed within the land of Penn,

That Slavery's guilty fears might cease,
And those whom God created men
Toil on as brutes in peace.

Yet o'er the blackness of the storm
A bow of promise bends on high,
And gleams of sunshine, soft and warm,
Break through our clouded sky.

East, West, and North, the shout is heard,
Of freemen rising for the right
Each valley hath its rallying word,
Each hill its signal light.
O'er Massachusetts' rocks of gray,
The strengthening light of freedom shines,
Rhode Island's Narragansett Bay,
And Vermont's snow-hung pines!

From Hudson's frowning palisades
To Alleghany's laurelled crest,
O'er lakes and prairies, streams and glades,
It shines upon the West.

Speed on the light to those who dwell
In Slavery's land of woe and sin,
And through the blackness of that hell,
Let Heaven's own light break in.

So shall the Southern conscience quake

Before that light poured full and strong,
So shall the Southern heart awake
To all the bondman's wrong.

And from that rich and sunny land
The song of grateful millions rise,
Like that of Israel's ransomed band
Beneath Arabia's skies:

And all who now are bound beneath
Our banner's shade, our eagle's wing,
From Slavery's night of moral death
To light and life shall spring.
Broken the bondman's chain, and gone
The master's guilt, and hate, and fear,
And unto both alike shall dawn
A New and Happy Year.

1839.

THE RELIC.

Written on receiving a cane wrought from a fragment of the wood-work of Pennsylvania Hall which the fire had spared.

TOKEN of friendship true and tried,
From one whose fiery heart of youth
With mine has beaten, side by side,
For Liberty and Truth;
With honest pride the gift I take,
And prize it for the giver's sake.

But not alone because it tells
Of generous hand and heart sincere;
Around that gift of friendship dwells
A memory doubly dear;
Earth's noblest aim, man's holiest thought,
With that memorial frail in wrought!

Pure thoughts and sweet like flowers unfold,
And precious memories round it cling,
Even as the Prophet's rod of old
In beauty blossoming:
And buds of feeling, pure and good,
Spring from its cold unconscious wood.

Relic of Freedom's shrine! a brand
Plucked from its burning! let it be
Dear as a jewel from the hand
Of a lost friend to me!
Flower of a perished garland left,

Of life and beauty unbereft!

Oh, if the young enthusiast bears,
O'er weary waste and sea, the stone
Which crumbled from the Forum's stairs,
Or round the Parthenon;
Or olive-bough from some wild tree
Hung over old Thermopylae:

If leaflets from some hero's tomb,
Or moss-wreath torn from ruins hoary;
Or faded flowers whose sisters bloom
On fields renowned in story;
Or fragment from the Alhambra's crest,
Or the gray rock by Druids blessed;

Sad Erin's shamrock greenly growing
Where Freedom led her stalwart kern,
Or Scotia's "rough bur thistle" blowing
On Bruce's Bannockburn;
Or Runnymede's wild English rose,
Or lichen plucked from Sempach's snows!

If it be true that things like these
To heart and eye bright visions bring,
Shall not far holier memories
To this memorial cling
Which needs no mellowing mist of time
To hide the crimson stains of crime!

Wreck of a temple, unprofaned;
Of courts where Peace with Freedom trod,
Lifting on high, with hands unstained,
Thanksgiving unto God;
Where Mercy's voice of love was pleading
For human hearts in bondage bleeding;

Where, midst the sound of rushing feet
And curses on the night-air flung,
That pleading voice rose calm and sweet
From woman's earnest tongue;
And Riot turned his scowling glance,
Awed, from her tranquil countenance!

That temple now in ruin lies!
The fire-stain on its shattered wall,
And open to the changing skies
Its black and roofless hall,
It stands before a nation's sight,
A gravestone over buried Right!
But from that ruin, as of old,
The fire-scorched stones themselves are crying,
And from their ashes white and cold
Its timbers are replying!
A voice which slavery cannot kill
Speaks from the crumbling arches still!

And even this relic from thy shrine,
O holy Freedom! Hath to me

A potent power, a voice and sign
To testify of thee;
And, grasping it, methinks I feel
A deeper faith, a stronger zeal.

And not unlike that mystic rod,
Of old stretched o'er the Egyptian wave,
Which opened, in the strength of God,
A pathway for the slave,
It yet may point the bondman's way,
And turn the spoiler from his prey.

1839.

THE WORLD'S CONVENTION OF THE FRIENDS OF EMANCIPATION,

HELD IN LONDON IN 1840.

Joseph Sturge, the founder of the British and Foreign Anti-Slavery Society, proposed the calling of a world's anti-slavery convention, and the proposal was promptly seconded by the American Anti-Slavery Society. The call was addressed to "friends of the slave of every nation and of every clime."

YES, let them gather! Summon forth
The pledged philanthropy of Earth.
From every land, whose hills have heard
The bugle blast of Freedom waking;
Or shrieking of her symbol-bird
From out his cloudy eyrie breaking
Where Justice hath one worshipper,
Or truth one altar built to her;

Where'er a human eye is weeping
O'er wrongs which Earth's sad children know;
Where'er a single heart is keeping
Its prayerful watch with human woe
Thence let them come, and greet each other,
And know in each a friend and brother!

Yes, let them come! from each green vale
Where England's old baronial halls
Still bear upon their storied walls
The grim crusader's rusted mail,
Battered by Paynim spear and brand
On Malta's rock or Syria's sand!
And mouldering pennon-staves once set

Within the soil of Palestine,
By Jordan and Gennesaret;
Or, borne with England's battle line,
O'er Acre's shattered turrets stooping,
Or, midst the camp their banners drooping,
With dews from hallowed Hermon wet,
A holier summons now is given
Than that gray hermit's voice of old,
Which unto all the winds of heaven
The banners of the Cross unrolled!
Not for the long-deserted shrine;
Not for the dull unconscious sod,
Which tells not by one lingering sign
That there the hope of Israel trod;
But for that truth, for which alone
In pilgrim eyes are sanctified
The garden moss, the mountain stone,
Whereon His holy sandals pressed,—
The fountain which His lip hath blessed,—

Whate'er hath touched His garment's hem
At Bethany or Bethlehem,
Or Jordan's river-side.
For Freedom in the name of Him
Who came to raise Earth's drooping poor,
To break the chain from every limb,
The bolt from every prison door!
For these, o'er all the earth hath passed
An ever-deepening trumpet blast,

As if an angel's breath had lent
Its vigor to the instrument.

And Wales, from Snowden's mountain wall,
Shall startle at that thrilling call,
As if she heard her bards again;
And Erin's "harp on Tara's wall"
Give out its ancient strain,
Mirthful and sweet, yet sad withal,—
The melody which Erin loves,
When o'er that harp, 'mid bursts of gladness
And slogan cries and lyke-wake sadness,
The hand of her O'Connell moves!
Scotland, from lake and tarn and rill,
And mountain hold, and heathery hill,
Shall catch and echo back the note,
As if she heard upon the air
Once more her Cameronian's prayer
And song of Freedom float.
And cheering echoes shall reply
From each remote dependency,
Where Britain's mighty sway is known,
In tropic sea or frozen zone;
Where'er her sunset flag is furling,
Or morning gun-fire's smoke is curling;
From Indian Bengal's groves of palm
And rosy fields and gales of balm,
Where Eastern pomp and power are rolled
Through regal Ava's gates of gold;

*And from the lakes and ancient woods
And dim Canadian solitudes,
Whence, sternly from her rocky throne,
Queen of the North, Quebec looks down;
And from those bright and ransomed Isles
Where all unwonted Freedom smiles,
And the dark laborer still retains
The scar of slavery's broken chains!*

*From the hoar Alps, which sentinel
The gateways of the land of Tell,
Where morning's keen and earliest glance
On Jura's rocky wall is thrown,
And from the olive bowers of France
And vine groves garlanding the Rhone,—
"Friends of the Blacks," as true and tried
As those who stood by Oge's side,
And heard the Haytien's tale of wrong,
Shall gather at that summons strong;
Broglie, Passy, and he whose song
Breathed over Syria's holy sod,
And, in the paths which Jesus trod,
And murmured midst the hills which hem
Crownless and sad Jerusalem,
Hath echoes whereso'er the tone
Of Israel's prophet-lyre is known.*

*Still let them come; from Quito's walls,
And from the Orinoco's tide,*

From Lima's Inca-haunted halls,
From Santa Fe and Yucatan,—
Men who by swart Guerrero's side
Proclaimed the deathless rights of man,
Broke every bond and fetter off,
And hailed in every sable serf
A free and brother Mexican!
Chiefs who across the Andes' chain
Have followed Freedom's flowing pennon,
And seen on Junin's fearful plain,
Glare o'er the broken ranks of Spain
The fire-burst of Bolivar's cannon!
And Hayti, from her mountain land,
Shall send the sons of those who hurled
Defiance from her blazing strand,
The war-gage from her Petion's hand,
Alone against a hostile world.

Nor all unmindful, thou, the while,
Land of the dark and mystic Nile!
Thy Moslem mercy yet may shame
All tyrants of a Christian name,
When in the shade of Gizeh's pile,
Or, where, from Abyssinian hills
El Gerek's upper fountain fills,
Or where from Mountains of the Moon
El Abiad bears his watery boon,
Where'er thy lotus blossoms swim
Within their ancient hallowed waters;

Where'er is heard the Coptic hymn,
Or song of Nubia's sable daughters;
The curse of slavery and the crime,
Thy bequest from remotest time,
At thy dark Mehemet's decree
Forevermore shall pass from thee;
And chains forsake each captive's limb
Of all those tribes, whose hills around
Have echoed back the cymbal sound
And victor horn of Ibrahim.

And thou whose glory and whose crime
To earth's remotest bound and clime,
In mingled tones of awe and scorn,
The echoes of a world have borne,
My country! glorious at thy birth,
A day-star flashing brightly forth,
The herald-sign of Freedom's dawn!
Oh, who could dream that saw thee then,
And watched thy rising from afar,
That vapors from oppression's fen
Would cloud the upward tending star?
Or, that earth's tyrant powers, which heard,
Awe-struck, the shout which hailed thy dawning,
Would rise so soon, prince, peer, and king,
To mock thee with their welcoming,
Like Hades when her thrones were stirred
To greet the down-cast Star of Morning!
"Aha! and art thou fallen thus?

Art thou become as one of us?"

Land of my fathers! there will stand,
Amidst that world-assembled band,
Those owning thy maternal claim
Unweakened by thy, crime and shame;
The sad reprovers of thy wrong;
The children thou hast spurned so long.

Still with affection's fondest yearning
To their unnatural mother turning.
No traitors they! but tried and leal,
Whose own is but thy general weal,
Still blending with the patriot's zeal
The Christian's love for human kind,
To caste and climate unconfined.

A holy gathering! peaceful all
No threat of war, no savage call
For vengeance on an erring brother!
But in their stead the godlike plan
To teach the brotherhood of man
To love and reverence one another,
As sharers of a common blood,
The children of a common God
Yet, even at its lightest word,
Shall Slavery's darkest depths be stirred:
Spain, watching from her Moro's keep
Her slave-ships traversing the deep,

And Rio, in her strength and pride,
Lifting, along her mountain-side,
Her snowy battlements and towers,
Her lemon-groves and tropic bowers,
With bitter hate and sullen fear
Its freedom-giving voice shall hear;
And where my country's flag is flowing,
On breezes from Mount Vernon blowing,
Above the Nation's council halls,
Where Freedom's praise is loud and long,
While close beneath the outward walls
The driver plies his reeking thong;
The hammer of the man-thief falls,
O'er hypocritic cheek and brow
The crimson flush of shame shall glow
And all who for their native land
Are pledging life and heart and hand,
Worn watchers o'er her changing weal,
Who fog her tarnished honor feel,
Through cottage door and council-hall
Shall thunder an awakening call.
The pen along its page shall burn
With all intolerable scorn;
An eloquent rebuke shall go
On all the winds that Southward blow;
From priestly lips, now sealed and dumb,
Warning and dread appeal shall come,
Like those which Israel heard from him,

The Prophet of the Cherubim;
  Or those which sad Esaias hurled
  Against a sin-accursed world!
  Its wizard leaves the Press shall fling
  Unceasing from its iron wing,
  With characters inscribed thereon,
  As fearful in the despot's ball
  As to the pomp of Babylon
  The fire-sign on the palace wall!

  And, from her dark iniquities,
  Methinks I see my country rise
  Not challenging the nations round
  To note her tardy justice done;
  Her captives from their chains unbound;
  Her prisons opening to the sun
  But tearfully her arms extending
  Over the poor and unoffending;
  Her regal emblem now no longer

  A bird of prey, with talons reeking,
  Above the dying captive shrieking,
  But, spreading out her ample wing,
  A broad, impartial covering,
  The weaker sheltered by the stronger
  Oh, then to Faith's anointed eyes
  The promised token shall be given;
  And on a nation's sacrifice,

Atoning for the sin of years,
And wet with penitential tears,
The fire shall fall from Heaven!

1839.

MASSACHUSETTS TO VIRGINIA.

Written on reading an account of the proceedings of the citizens of Norfolk, Va., in reference to George Latimer, the alleged fugitive slave, who was seized in Boston without warrant at the request of James B. Grey, of Norfolk, claiming to be his master. The case caused great excitement North and South, and led to the presentation of a petition to Congress, signed by more than fifty thousand citizens of Massachusetts, calling for such laws and proposed amendments to the Constitution as should relieve the Commonwealth from all further participation in the crime of oppression. George Latimer himself was finally given free papers for the sum of four hundred dollars.

THE blast from Freedom's Northern hills, upon its Southern way,
Bears greeting to Virginia from Massachusetts Bay.
No word of haughty challenging, nor battle bugle's peal,
Nor steady tread of marching files, nor clang of horsemen's steel.

No trains of deep-mouthed cannon along our highways go;
Around our silent arsenals untrodden lies the snow;
And to the land-breeze of our ports, upon their errands far,
A thousand sails of commerce swell, but none are spread for war.

We hear thy threats, Virginia! thy stormy words and high,
Swell harshly on the Southern winds which melt along our sky;
Yet, not one brown, hard hand foregoes its honest labor here,
No hewer of our mountain oaks suspends his axe in fear.
Wild are the waves which lash the reefs along St. George's bank;
Cold on the shore of Labrador the fog lies white and dank;
Through storm, and wave, and blinding mist, stout are the hearts which man
The fishing-smacks of Marblehead, the sea-boats of Cape Ann.

The cold north light and wintry sun glare on their icy forms,

Bent grimly o'er their straining lines or wrestling with the storms;
Free as the winds they drive before, rough as the waves they roam,
They laugh to scorn the slaver's threat against their rocky home.

What means the Old Dominion? Hath she forgot the day
When o'er her conquered valleys swept the Briton's steel array?
How side by side, with sons of hers, the Massachusetts men
Encountered Tarleton's charge of fire, and stout Cornwallis, then?

Forgets she how the Bay State, in answer to the call
Of her old House of Burgesses, spoke out from Faneuil Hall?
When, echoing back her Henry's cry, came pulsing on each breath
Of Northern winds, the thrilling sounds of "Liberty or Death!"

What asks the Old Dominion? If now her sons have proved
False to their fathers' memory, false to the faith they loved;
If she can scoff at Freedom, and its great charter spurn,
Must we of Massachusetts from truth and duty turn?

We hunt your bondmen, flying from Slavery's hateful hell;
Our voices, at your bidding, take up the bloodhound's yell;
We gather, at your summons, above our fathers' graves,
From Freedom's holy altar-horns to tear your wretched slaves!

Thank God! not yet so vilely can Massachusetts bow;
The spirit of her early time is with her even now;
Dream not because her Pilgrim blood moves slow and calm and cool,
She thus can stoop her chainless neck, a sister's slave and tool!

All that a sister State should do, all that a free State may,
Heart, hand, and purse we proffer, as in our early day;
But that one dark loathsome burden ye must stagger with alone,
And reap the bitter harvest which ye yourselves have sown!

Hold, while ye may, your struggling slaves, and burden God's free air
With woman's shriek beneath the lash, and manhood's wild despair;
Cling closer to the "cleaving curse" that writes upon your plains
The blasting of Almighty wrath against a land of chains.

Still shame your gallant ancestry, the cavaliers of old,
By watching round the shambles where human flesh is sold;
Gloat o'er the new-born child, and count his market value, when
The maddened mother's cry of woe shall pierce the slaver's den!

Lower than plummet soundeth, sink the Virginia name;
Plant, if ye will, your fathers' graves with rankest weeds of shame;
Be, if ye will, the scandal of God's fair universe;
We wash our hands forever of your sin and shame and curse.

A voice from lips whereon the coal from Freedom's shrine hath been,
Thrilled, as but yesterday, the hearts of Berkshire's mountain men:
The echoes of that solemn voice are sadly lingering still
In all our sunny valleys, on every wind-swept hill.
And when the prowling man-thief came hunting for his prey
Beneath the very shadow of Bunker's shaft of gray,
How, through the free lips of the son, the father's warning spoke;
How, from its bonds of trade and sect, the Pilgrim city broke!

A hundred thousand right arms were lifted up on high,
A hundred thousand voices sent back their loud reply;
Through the thronged towns of Essex the startling summons rang,
And up from bench and loom and wheel her young mechanics sprang!

The voice of free, broad Middlesex, of thousands as of one,
The shaft of Bunker calling to that of Lexington;
From Norfolk's ancient villages, from Plymouth's rocky bound
To where Nantucket feels the arms of ocean close her round;

From rich and rural Worcester, where through the calm repose
Of cultured vales and fringing woods the gentle Nashua flows,
To where Wachuset's wintry blasts the mountain larches stir,
Swelled up to Heaven the thrilling cry of "God save Latimer!"

And sandy Barnstable rose up, wet with the salt sea spray;
And Bristol sent her answering shout down Narragansett Bay
Along the broad Connecticut old Hampden felt the thrill,
And the cheer of Hampshire's woodmen swept down from Holyoke Hill.

The voice of Massachusetts! Of her free sons and daughters,
Deep calling unto deep aloud, the sound of many waters!
Against the burden of that voice what tyrant power shall stand?
No fetters in the Bay State! No slave upon her land!

Look to it well, Virginians! In calmness we have borne,
In answer to our faith and trust, your insult and your scorn;
You've spurned our kindest counsels; you've hunted for our lives;
And shaken round our hearths and homes your manacles and gyves!

*We wage no war, we lift no arm, we fling no torch within
The fire-clamps of the quaking mine beneath your soil of sin;
We leave ye with your bondmen, to wrestle, while ye can,
With the strong upward tendencies and godlike soul of man!*

*But for us and for our children, the vow which we have given
For freedom and humanity is registered in heaven;
No slave-hunt in our borders,—no pirate on our strand!
No fetters in the Bay State,—no slave upon our land!*

1843.

THE CHRISTIAN SLAVE.

In a publication of L. F. Tasistro—Random Shots and Southern Breezes—is a description of a slave auction at New Orleans, at which the auctioneer recommended the woman on the stand as "A GOOD CHRISTIAN!" It was not uncommon to see advertisements of slaves for sale, in which they were described as pious or as members of the church. In one advertisement a slave was noted as "a Baptist preacher."

A CHRISTIAN! going, gone!
Who bids for God's own image? for his grace,
Which that poor victim of the market-place
Hath in her suffering won?

My God! can such things be?
Hast Thou not said that whatsoe'er is done
Unto Thy weakest and Thy humblest one
Is even done to Thee?

In that sad victim, then,
Child of Thy pitying love, I see Thee stand;
Once more the jest-word of a mocking band,
Bound, sold, and scourged again!

A Christian up for sale!
Wet with her blood your whips, o'ertask her frame,
Make her life loathsome with your wrong and shame,
Her patience shall not fail!

A heathen hand might deal
Back on your heads the gathered wrong of years:
But her low, broken prayer and nightly tears,

Ye neither heed nor feel.

Con well thy lesson o'er,
Thou prudent teacher, tell the toiling slave
No dangerous tale of Him who came to save
The outcast and the poor.

But wisely shut the ray
Of God's free Gospel from her simple heart,
And to her darkened mind alone impart
One stern command, Obey! (3)

So shalt thou deftly raise
The market price of human flesh; and while
On thee, their pampered guest, the planters smile,
Thy church shall praise.

Grave, reverend men shall tell
From Northern pulpits how thy work was blest,
While in that vile South Sodom first and best,
Thy poor disciples sell.

Oh, shame! the Moslem thrall,
Who, with his master, to the Prophet kneels,
While turning to the sacred Kebla feels
His fetters break and fall.

Cheers for the turbaned Bey
Of robber-peopled Tunis! he hath torn

The dark slave-dungeons open, and hath borne
Their inmates into day:

But our poor slave in vain
Turns to the Christian shrine his aching eyes;
Its rites will only swell his market price,
And rivet on his chain.

God of all right! how long
Shall priestly robbers at Thine altar stand,
Lifting in prayer to Thee, the bloody hand
And haughty brow of wrong?

1843

THE SENTENCE OF JOHN L. BROWN

Oh, from the fields of cane,

From the low rice-swamp, from the trader's cell;

From the black slave-ship's foul and loathsome hell,

And coffle's weary chain;

Hoarse, horrible, and strong,

Rises to Heaven that agonizing cry,

Filling the arches of the hollow sky,

How long, O God, how long?

THE SENTENCE OF JOHN L. BROWN.

John L. Brown, a young white man of South Carolina, was in 1844 sentenced to death for aiding a young slave woman, whom he loved and had married, to escape from slavery. In pronouncing the sentence Judge O'Neale addressed to the prisoner these words of appalling blasphemy:

You are to die! To die an ignominious death—the death on the gallows! This announcement is, to you, I know, most appalling. Little did you dream of it when you stepped into the bar with an air as if you thought it was a fine frolic. But the consequences of crime are just such as you are realizing. Punishment often comes when it is least expected. Let me entreat you to take the present opportunity to commence the work of reformation. Time will be furnished you to prepare for the great change just before you. Of your past life I know nothing, except what your trial furnished. That told me that the crime for which you are to suffer was the consequence of a want of attention on your part to the duties of life. The strange woman snared you. She flattered you with her word; and you became her victim. The consequence was, that, led on by a desire to serve her, you committed the offence of aid in a slave to run away and depart from her master's service; and now, for it you are to die! You are a young man, and I fear you have been dissolute; and if so, these kindred vices have contributed a full measure to your ruin. Reflect on your past life, and make the only useful devotion of the remnant of your days in preparing for death. Remember now thy Creator in the days of thy youth is the language of inspired wisdom. This comes home appropriately to you in this trying moment. You are young; quite too young to be where you are. If you had remembered your Creator in your past days, you would not now be in a felon's place, to receive a felon's judgment. Still, it is not too late to remember your Creator. He calls early, and He calls late. He stretches out the arms of a Father's love to you—to the vilest sinner—and says: "Come unto me and be saved." You can perhaps read. If so, read the Scriptures; read them without note, and without comment; and pray to God for His assistance; and you will be able to say when you pass from prison to execution, as a poor slave said under similar circumstances: "I am glad my Friday has come." If you cannot read the Scriptures, the ministers of our holy religion will be ready to aid you. They will read and explain to you until you will be able to understand; and understanding, to call upon the only One who can help you and save you—Jesus Christ, the Lamb of God, who taketh away the sin of the world. To Him I commend you. And through Him may you have that opening of the Day-Spring of mercy from on high, which shall bless you here, and crown you as a saint in an everlasting world, forever and ever. The sentence of the law is that you be taken hence to the place from whence you came last; thence to the jail of Fairfield

District; and that there you be closely and securely confined until Friday, the 26th day of April next; on which day, between the hours of ten in the forenoon and two in the afternoon, you will be taken to the place of public execution, and there be hanged by the neck till your body be dead. And may God have mercy on your soul!

No event in the history of the anti-slavery struggle so stirred the two hemispheres as did this dreadful sentence. A cry of horror was heard from Europe. In the British House of Lords, Brougham and Denman spoke of it with mingled pathos and indignation. Thirteen hundred clergymen and church officers in Great Britain addressed a memorial to the churches of South Carolina against the atrocity. Indeed, so strong was the pressure of the sentiment of abhorrence and disgust that South Carolina yielded to it, and the sentence was commuted to scourging and banishment.

> *Ho! thou who seekest late and long*
> *A License from the Holy Book*
> *For brutal lust and fiendish wrong,*
> *Man of the Pulpit, look!*
> *Lift up those cold and atheist eyes,*
> *This ripe fruit of thy teaching see;*
> *And tell us how to heaven will rise*
> *The incense of this sacrifice—*
> *This blossom of the gallows tree!*
>
> *Search out for slavery's hour of need*
> *Some fitting text of sacred writ;*
> *Give heaven the credit of a deed*
> *Which shames the nether pit.*
> *Kneel, smooth blasphemer, unto Him*
> *Whose truth is on thy lips a lie;*
> *Ask that His bright winged cherubim*
> *May bend around that scaffold grim*
> *To guard and bless and sanctify.*

O champion of the people's cause
Suspend thy loud and vain rebuke
Of foreign wrong and Old World's laws,
Man of the Senate, look!
Was this the promise of the free,
The great hope of our early time,
That slavery's poison vine should be
Upborne by Freedom's prayer-nursed tree
O'erclustered with such fruits of crime?

Send out the summons East and West,
And South and North, let all be there
Where he who pitied the oppressed
Swings out in sun and air.
Let not a Democratic hand
The grisly hangman's task refuse;
There let each loyal patriot stand,
Awaiting slavery's command,
To twist the rope and draw the noose!

But vain is irony—unmeet
Its cold rebuke for deeds which start
In fiery and indignant beat
The pulses of the heart.
Leave studied wit and guarded phrase
For those who think but do not feel;
Let men speak out in words which raise
Where'er they fall, an answering blaze
Like flints which strike the fire from steel.

Still let a mousing priesthood ply
Their garbled text and gloss of sin,
And make the lettered scroll deny
Its living soul within:
Still let the place-fed, titled knave
Plead robbery's right with purchased lips,
And tell us that our fathers gave
For Freedom's pedestal, a slave,
The frieze and moulding, chains and whips!

But ye who own that Higher Law
Whose tablets in the heart are set,
Speak out in words of power and awe
That God is living yet!
Breathe forth once more those tones sublime
Which thrilled the burdened prophet's lyre,
And in a dark and evil time
Smote down on Israel's fast of crime
And gift of blood, a rain of fire!

Oh, not for us the graceful lay
To whose soft measures lightly move
The footsteps of the faun and fay,
O'er-locked by mirth and love!
But such a stern and startling strain
As Britain's hunted bards flung down
From Snowden to the conquered plain,
Where harshly clanked the Saxon chain,
On trampled field and smoking town.

By Liberty's dishonored name,
By man's lost hope and failing trust,
By words and deeds which bow with shame
Our foreheads to the dust,
By the exulting strangers' sneer,
Borne to us from the Old World's thrones,
And by their victims' grief who hear,
In sunless mines and dungeons drear,
How Freedom's land her faith disowns!
Speak out in acts. The time for words
Has passed, and deeds suffice alone;
In vain against the clang of swords
The wailing pipe is blown!
Act, act in God's name, while ye may!
Smite from the church her leprous limb!
Throw open to the light of day
The bondman's cell, and break away
The chains the state has bound on him!

Ho! every true and living soul,
To Freedom's perilled altar bear
The Freeman's and the Christian's whole
Tongue, pen, and vote, and prayer!
One last, great battle for the right—
One short, sharp struggle to be free!
To do is to succeed—our fight
Is waged in Heaven's approving sight;
The smile of God is Victory.
1844.

TEXAS

VOICE OF NEW ENGLAND.

The five poems immediately following indicate the intense feeling of the friends of freedom in view of the annexation of Texas, with its vast territory sufficient, as was boasted, for six new slave States.

Up the hillside, down the glen,
Rouse the sleeping citizen;
Summon out the might of men!

Like a lion growling low,
Like a night-storm rising slow,
Like the tread of unseen foe;

It is coming, it is nigh!
Stand your homes and altars by;
On your own free thresholds die.

Clang the bells in all your spires;
On the gray hills of your sires
Fling to heaven your signal-fires.

From Wachuset, lone and bleak,
Unto Berkshire's tallest peak,
Let the flame-tongued heralds speak.

Oh, for God and duty stand,
Heart to heart and hand to hand,
Round the old graves of the land.

Whoso shrinks or falters now,
Whoso to the yoke would bow,
Brand the craven on his brow!

Freedom's soil hath only place
For a free and fearless race,
None for traitors false and base.
Perish party, perish clan;
Strike together while ye can,
Like the arm of one strong man.

Like that angel's voice sublime,
Heard above a world of crime,
Crying of the end of time;
With one heart and with one mouth,
Let the North unto the South
Speak the word befitting both.

"What though Issachar be strong
Ye may load his back with wrong
Overmuch and over long:

"Patience with her cup o'errun,
With her weary thread outspun,
Murmurs that her work is done.

"Make our Union-bond a chain,
Weak as tow in Freedom's strain
Link by link shall snap in twain.

"Vainly shall your sand-wrought rope
Bind the starry cluster up,
Shattered over heaven's blue cope!

"Give us bright though broken rays,
Rather than eternal haze,
Clouding o'er the full-orbed blaze.

"Take your land of sun and bloom;
Only leave to Freedom room
For her plough, and forge, and loom;

"Take your slavery-blackened vales;
Leave us but our own free gales,
Blowing on our thousand sails.

"Boldly, or with treacherous art,
Strike the blood-wrought chain apart;
Break the Union's mighty heart;

"Work the ruin, if ye will;
Pluck upon your heads an ill
Which shall grow and deepen still.

"With your bondman's right arm bare,
With his heart of black despair,
Stand alone, if stand ye dare!

"Onward with your fell design;

Dig the gulf and draw the line
Fire beneath your feet the mine!

"Deeply, when the wide abyss
Yawns between your land and this,
Shall ye feel your helplessness.

"By the hearth, and in the bed,
Shaken by a look or tread,
Ye shall own a guilty dread.

"And the curse of unpaid toil,
Downward through your generous soil
Like a fire shall burn and spoil.

"Our bleak hills shall bud and blow,
Vines our rocks shall overgrow,
Plenty in our valleys flow;—

"And when vengeance clouds your skies,
Hither shall ye turn your eyes,
As the lost on Paradise!

"We but ask our rocky strand,
Freedom's true and brother band,
Freedom's strong and honest hand;

"Valleys by the slave untrod,

And the Pilgrim's mountain sod,
  Blessed of our fathers' God!"

  1844.

TO FANEUIL HALL.

Written in 1844, on reading a call by "a Massachusetts Freeman" for a meeting in Faneuil Hall of the citizens of Massachusetts, without distinction of party, opposed to the annexation of Texas, and the aggressions of South Carolina, and in favor of decisive action against slavery.

MEN! if manhood still ye claim,
If the Northern pulse can thrill,
Roused by wrong or stung by shame,
Freely, strongly still;
Let the sounds of traffic die
Shut the mill-gate, leave the stall,
Fling the axe and hammer by;
Throng to Faneuil Hall!

Wrongs which freemen never brooked,
Dangers grim and fierce as they,
Which, like couching lions, looked
On your fathers' way;
These your instant zeal demand,
Shaking with their earthquake-call
Every rood of Pilgrim land,
Ho, to Faneuil Hall!

From your capes and sandy bars,
From your mountain-ridges cold,
Through whose pines the westering stars
Stoop their crowns of gold;
Come, and with your footsteps wake
Echoes from that holy wall;
Once again, for Freedom's sake,

Rock your fathers' hall!

Up, and tread beneath your feet
Every cord by party spun:
Let your hearts together beat
As the heart of one.
Banks and tariffs, stocks and trade,
Let them rise or let them fall:
Freedom asks your common aid,—
Up, to Faneuil Hall!

Up, and let each voice that speaks
Ring from thence to Southern plains,
Sharply as the blow which breaks
Prison-bolts and chains!
Speak as well becomes the free
Dreaded more than steel or ball,
Shall your calmest utterance be,
Heard from Faneuil Hall!

Have they wronged us? Let us then
Render back nor threats nor prayers;
Have they chained our free-born men?
Let us unchain theirs!
Up, your banner leads the van,
Blazoned, "Liberty for all!"

Finish what your sires began!
Up, to Faneuil Hall!

TO MASSACHUSETTS.

WHAT though around thee blazes
No fiery rallying sign?
From all thy own high places,
Give heaven the light of thine!
What though unthrilled, unmoving,
The statesman stand apart,
And comes no warm approving
From Mammon's crowded mart?

Still, let the land be shaken
By a summons of thine own!
By all save truth forsaken,
Stand fast with that alone!
Shrink not from strife unequal!
With the best is always hope;
And ever in the sequel
God holds the right side up!

But when, with thine uniting,
Come voices long and loud,
And far-off hills are writing
Thy fire-words on the cloud;
When from Penobscot's fountains
A deep response is heard,
And across the Western mountains
Rolls back thy rallying word;

Shall thy line of battle falter,

With its allies just in view?
Oh, by hearth and holy altar,
My fatherland, be true!
Fling abroad thy scrolls of Freedom
Speed them onward far and fast
Over hill and valley speed them,
Like the sibyl's on the blast!

Lo! the Empire State is shaking
The shackles from her hand;
With the rugged North is waking
The level sunset land!
On they come, the free battalions
East and West and North they come,
And the heart-beat of the millions
Is the beat of Freedom's drum.

"To the tyrant's plot no favor
No heed to place-fed knaves!
Bar and bolt the door forever
Against the land of slaves!"
Hear it, mother Earth, and hear it,
The heavens above us spread!
The land is roused,—its spirit
Was sleeping, but not dead!

1844.

NEW HAMPSHIRE.

GOD bless New Hampshire! from her granite peaks
Once more the voice of Stark and Langdon speaks.
The long-bound vassal of the exulting South
For very shame her self-forged chain has broken;
Torn the black seal of slavery from her mouth,
And in the clear tones of her old time spoken!
Oh, all undreamed-of, all unhoped-for changes
The tyrant's ally proves his sternest foe;
To all his biddings, from her mountain ranges,
New Hampshire thunders an indignant No!
Who is it now despairs? Oh, faint of heart,
Look upward to those Northern mountains cold,
Flouted by Freedom's victor-flag unrolled,
And gather strength to bear a manlier part
All is not lost. The angel of God's blessing
Encamps with Freedom on the field of fight;
Still to her banner, day by day, are pressing,
Unlooked-for allies, striking for the right
Courage, then, Northern hearts! Be firm, be true:
What one brave State hath done, can ye not also do?

1845.

THE PINE-TREE.

Written on hearing that the Anti-Slavery Resolves of Stephen C. Phillips had been rejected by the Whig Convention in Faneuil Hall, in 1846.

LIFT again the stately emblem on the Bay State's rusted shield,
Give to Northern winds the Pine-Tree on our banner's tattered field.
Sons of men who sat in council with their Bibles round the board,
Answering England's royal missive with a firm, "Thus saith the Lord!"
Rise again for home and freedom! set the battle in array!
What the fathers did of old time we their sons must do to-day.

Tell us not of banks and tariffs, cease your paltry pedler cries;
Shall the good State sink her honor that your gambling stocks may rise?
Would ye barter man for cotton? That your gains may sum up higher,
Must we kiss the feet of Moloch, pass our children through the fire?
Is the dollar only real? God and truth and right a dream?
Weighed against your lying ledgers must our manhood kick the beam?

O my God! for that free spirit, which of old in Boston town
Smote the Province House with terror, struck the crest of Andros down!
For another strong-voiced Adams in the city's streets to cry,
"Up for God and Massachusetts! Set your feet on Mammon's lie!
Perish banks and perish traffic, spin your cotton's latest pound,
But in Heaven's name keep your honor, keep the heart o' the Bay State sound!"
Where's the man for Massachusetts! Where's the voice to speak her free?
Where's the hand to light up bonfires from her mountains to the sea?
Beats her Pilgrim pulse no longer? Sits she dumb in her despair?
Has she none to break the silence? Has she none to do and dare?
O my God! for one right worthy to lift up her rusted shield,
And to plant again the Pine-Tree in her banner's tattered field

1840.

TO A SOUTHERN STATESMAN.

John C. Calhoun, who had strongly urged the extension of slave territory by the annexation of Texas, even if it should involve a war with England, was unwilling to promote the acquisition of Oregon, which would enlarge the Northern domain of freedom, and pleaded as an excuse the peril of foreign complications which he had defied when the interests of slavery were involved.

Is this thy voice whose treble notes of fear
Wail in the wind? And dost thou shake to hear,
Actieon-like, the bay of thine own hounds,
Spurning the leash, and leaping o'er their bounds?
Sore-baffled statesman! when thy eager hand,
With game afoot, unslipped the hungry pack,
To hunt down Freedom in her chosen land,
Hadst thou no fear, that, erelong, doubling back,
These dogs of thine might snuff on Slavery's track?
Where's now the boast, which even thy guarded tongue,
Cold, calm, and proud, in the teeth o' the Senate flung,

O'er the fulfilment of thy baleful plan,
Like Satan's triumph at the fall of man?
How stood'st thou then, thy feet on Freedom planting,
And pointing to the lurid heaven afar,
Whence all could see, through the south windows slanting,
Crimson as blood, the beams of that Lone Star!
The Fates are just; they give us but our own;
Nemesis ripens what our hands have sown.
There is an Eastern story, not unknown,
Doubtless, to thee, of one whose magic skill
Called demons up his water-jars to fill;

Deftly and silently, they did his will,
But, when the task was done, kept pouring still.
In vain with spell and charm the wizard wrought,
Faster and faster were the buckets brought,
Higher and higher rose the flood around,
Till the fiends clapped their hands above their master drowned
So, Carolinian, it may prove with thee,
For God still overrules man's schemes, and takes
Craftiness in its self-set snare, and makes
The wrath of man to praise Him. It may be,
That the roused spirits of Democracy
May leave to freer States the same wide door
Through which thy slave-cursed Texas entered in,
From out the blood and fire, the wrong and sin,
Of the stormed-city and the ghastly plain,
Beat by hot hail, and wet with bloody rain,
The myriad-handed pioneer may pour,
And the wild West with the roused North combine
And heave the engineer of evil with his mine.

1846.

AT WASHINGTON.

Suggested by a visit to the city of Washington, in the 12th month of 1845.

WITH a cold and wintry noon-light
On its roofs and steeples shed,
Shadows weaving with the sunlight
From the gray sky overhead,
Broadly, vaguely, all around me, lies the half-built
town outspread.

Through this broad street, restless ever,
Ebbs and flows a human tide,
Wave on wave a living river;
Wealth and fashion side by side;
Toiler, idler, slave and master, in the same quick
current glide.

Underneath yon dome, whose coping
Springs above them, vast and tall,
Grave men in the dust are groping
For the largess, base and small,
Which the hand of Power is scattering, crumbs
which from its table fall.

Base of heart! They vilely barter
Honor's wealth for party's place;
Step by step on Freedom's charter
Leaving footprints of disgrace;
For to-day's poor pittance turning from the great
hope of their race.

Yet, where festal lamps are throwing
Glory round the dancer's hair,
Gold-tressed, like an angel's, flowing
Backward on the sunset air;
And the low quick pulse of music beats its measure sweet and rare.

There to-night shall woman's glances,
Star-like, welcome give to them;
Fawning fools with shy advances
Seek to touch their garments' hem,
With the tongue of flattery glozing deeds which God and Truth condemn.

From this glittering lie my vision
Takes a broader, sadder range,
Full before me have arisen
Other pictures dark and strange;
From the parlor to the prison must the scene and witness change.

Hark! the heavy gate is swinging
On its hinges, harsh and slow;
One pale prison lamp is flinging
On a fearful group below
Such a light as leaves to terror whatsoe'er it does not show.

Pitying God! Is that a woman

On whose wrist the shackles clash?
Is that shriek she utters human,
Underneath the stinging lash?
Are they men whose eyes of madness from that sad
procession flash?

Still the dance goes gayly onward
What is it to Wealth and Pride
That without the stars are looking
On a scene which earth should hide?
That the slave-ship lies in waiting, rocking
on Potomac's tide!

Vainly to that mean Ambition
Which, upon a rival's fall,
Winds above its old condition,
With a reptile's slimy crawl,
Shall the pleading voice of sorrow, shall the slave
in anguish call.
Vainly to the child of Fashion,
Giving to ideal woe
Graceful luxury of compassion,
Shall the stricken mourner go;
Hateful seems the earnest sorrow, beautiful the
hollow show!

Nay, my words are all too sweeping:
In this crowded human mart,
Feeling is not dead, but sleeping;

Man's strong will and woman's heart,
In the coming strife for Freedom, yet shall bear
their generous part.

And from yonder sunny valleys,
Southward in the distance lost,
Freedom yet shall summon allies
Worthier than the North can boast,
With the Evil by their hearth-stones grappling at
severer cost.
Now, the soul alone is willing
Faint the heart and weak the knee;
And as yet no lip is thrilling
With the mighty words, "Be Free!"
Tarrieth long the land's Good Angel, but his
advent is to be!

Meanwhile, turning from the revel
To the prison-cell my sight,
For intenser hate of evil,
For a keener sense of right,
Shaking off thy dust, I thank thee, City of the
Slaves, to-night!

"To thy duty now and ever!
Dream no more of rest or stay
Give to Freedom's great endeavor
All thou art and hast to-day:"
Thus, above the city's murmur, saith a Voice, or

seems to say.

Ye with heart and vision gifted
To discern and love the right,

Whose worn faces have been lifted
To the slowly-growing light,
Where from Freedom's sunrise drifted slowly
back the murk of night
Ye who through long years of trial
Still have held your purpose fast,
While a lengthening shade the dial
from the westering sunshine cast,
And of hope each hour's denial seemed an echo of
the last!

O my brothers! O my sisters
Would to God that ye were near,
Gazing with me down the vistas
Of a sorrow strange and drear;
Would to God that ye were listeners to the Voice
I seem to hear!

With the storm above us driving,
With the false earth mined below,
Who shall marvel if thus striving
We have counted friend as foe;
Unto one another giving in the darkness blow for
blow.

Well it may be that our natures
Have grown sterner and more hard,
And the freshness of their features
Somewhat harsh and battle-scarred,
And their harmonies of feeling overtasked and
rudely jarred.

Be it so. It should not swerve us
From a purpose true and brave;
Dearer Freedom's rugged service
Than the pastime of the slave;
Better is the storm above it than the quiet of
the grave.

Let us then, uniting, bury
All our idle feuds in dust,
And to future conflicts carry
Mutual faith and common trust;
Always he who most forgiveth in his brother is
most just.

From the eternal shadow rounding
All our sun and starlight here,
Voices of our lost ones sounding
Bid us be of heart and cheer,
Through the silence, down the spaces, falling on
the inward ear.

Know we not our dead are looking

Downward with a sad surprise,
All our strife of words rebuking
With their mild and loving eyes?
Shall we grieve the holy angels? Shall we cloud
their blessed skies?

Let us draw their mantles o'er us
Which have fallen in our way;
Let us do the work before us,
Cheerly, bravely, while we may,
Ere the long night-silence cometh, and with us it is
not day!

THE BRANDED HAND.

Captain Jonathan Walker, of Harwich, Mass., was solicited by several fugitive slaves at Pensacola, Florida, to carry them in his vessel to the British West Indies. Although well aware of the great hazard of the enterprise he attempted to comply with the request, but was seized at sea by an American vessel, consigned to the authorities at Key West, and thence sent back to Pensacola, where, after a long and rigorous confinement in prison, he was tried and sentenced to be branded on his right hand with the letters "S.S." (slave-stealer) and amerced in a heavy fine.

WELCOME home again, brave seaman! with thy
thoughtful brow and gray,
And the old heroic spirit of our earlier, better day;
With that front of calm endurance, on whose
steady nerve in vain
Pressed the iron of the prison, smote the fiery
shafts of pain.

Is the tyrant's brand upon thee? Did the brutal
cravens aim
To make God's truth thy falsehood, His holiest
work thy shame?
When, all blood-quenched, from the torture the
iron was withdrawn,
How laughed their evil angel the baffled fools to
scorn!

They change to wrong the duty which God hath
written out
On the great heart of humanity, too legible for
doubt!
They, the loathsome moral lepers, blotched from

footsole up to crown,
Give to shame what God hath given unto honor
and renown!

Why, that brand is highest honor! than its traces
never yet
Upon old armorial hatchments was a prouder blazon
set;
And thy unborn generations, as they tread our
rocky strand,
Shall tell with pride the story of their father's
branded hand!

As the Templar home was welcome, bearing back-
from Syrian wars
The scars of Arab lances and of Paynim scimitars,
The pallor of the prison, and the shackle's crimson span,
So we meet thee, so we greet thee, truest friend of
God and man.

He suffered for the ransom of the dear Redeemer's grave,
Thou for His living presence in the bound and
bleeding slave;
He for a soil no longer by the feet of angels trod,
Thou for the true Shechinah, the present home of God.

For, while the jurist, sitting with the slave-whip
o'er him swung,
From the tortured truths of freedom the lie of

slavery wrung,
And the solemn priest to Moloch, on each God-deserted shrine,
Broke the bondman's heart for bread, poured the bondman's blood for wine;

While the multitude in blindness to a far-off Saviour knelt,
And spurned, the while, the temple where a present Saviour dwelt;
Thou beheld'st Him in the task-field, in the prison shadows dim,
And thy mercy to the bondman, it was mercy unto Him!

In thy lone and long night-watches, sky above and wave below,
Thou didst learn a higher wisdom than the babbling schoolmen know;
God's stars and silence taught thee, as His angels only can,
That the one sole sacred thing beneath the cope of heaven is Man!

That he who treads profanely on the scrolls of law and creed,
In the depth of God's great goodness may find mercy in his need;
But woe to him who crushes the soul with chain and rod,

And herds with lower natures the awful form of God!

Then lift that manly right-hand, bold ploughman of the wave!
Its branded palm shall prophesy, "Salvation to the Slave!"
Hold up its fire-wrought language, that whoso reads may feel
His heart swell strong within him, his sinews change to steel.

Hold it up before our sunshine, up against our Northern air;
Ho! men of Massachusetts, for the love of God, look there!
Take it henceforth for your standard, like the Bruce's heart of yore,
In the dark strife closing round ye, let that hand be seen before!

And the masters of the slave-land shall tremble at that sign,
When it points its finger Southward along the Puritan line
Can the craft of State avail them? Can a Christless church withstand,
In the van of Freedom's onset, the coming of that band?
1846.

THE FREED ISLANDS.

Written for the anniversary celebration of the first of August, at Milton, 7846.

A FEW brief years have passed away
Since Britain drove her million slaves
Beneath the tropic's fiery ray
God willed their freedom; and to-day
Life blooms above those island graves!

He spoke! across the Carib Sea,
We heard the clash of breaking chains,
And felt the heart-throb of the free,
The first, strong pulse of liberty
Which thrilled along the bondman's veins.

Though long delayed, and far, and slow,
The Briton's triumph shall be ours
Wears slavery here a prouder brow
Than that which twelve short years ago
Scowled darkly from her island bowers?

Mighty alike for good or ill
With mother-land, we fully share
The Saxon strength, the nerve of steel,
The tireless energy of will,
The power to do, the pride to dare.

What she has done can we not do?
Our hour and men are both at hand;

The blast which Freedom's angel blew
O'er her green islands, echoes through
Each valley of our forest land.

Hear it, old Europe! we have sworn
The death of slavery. When it falls,
Look to your vassals in their turn,
Your poor dumb millions, crushed and worn,
Your prisons and your palace walls!

O kingly mockers! scoffing show
What deeds in Freedom's name we do;
Yet know that every taunt ye throw
Across the waters, goads our slow
Progression towards the right and true.

Not always shall your outraged poor,
Appalled by democratic crime,
Grind as their fathers ground before;
The hour which sees our prison door
Swing wide shall be their triumph time.
On then, my brothers! every blow
Ye deal is felt the wide earth through;
Whatever here uplifts the low
Or humbles Freedom's hateful foe,
Blesses the Old World through the New.

Take heart! The promised hour draws near;
I hear the downward beat of wings,

*And Freedom's trumpet sounding clear
"Joy to the people! woe and fear
To new-world tyrants, old-world kings!"*

A LETTER.

Supposed to be written by the chairman of the "Central Clique" at Concord, N. H., to the Hon. M. N., Jr., at Washington, giving the result of the election. The following verses were published in the Boston Chronotype in 1846. They refer to the contest in New Hampshire, which resulted in the defeat of the pro-slavery Democracy, and in the election of John P. Hale to the United States Senate. Although their authorship was not acknowledged, it was strongly suspected. They furnish a specimen of the way, on the whole rather good-natured, in which the liberty-lovers of half a century ago answered the social and political outlawry and mob violence to which they were subjected.

'T is over, Moses! All is lost
I hear the bells a-ringing;
Of Pharaoh and his Red Sea host
I hear the Free-Wills singing (4)
We're routed, Moses, horse and foot,
If there be truth in figures,
With Federal Whigs in hot pursuit,
And Hale, and all the "niggers."

Alack! alas! this month or more
We've felt a sad foreboding;
Our very dreams the burden bore
Of central cliques exploding;
Before our eyes a furnace shone,
Where heads of dough were roasting,
And one we took to be your own
The traitor Hale was toasting!

Our Belknap brother (5) heard with awe
The Congo minstrels playing;
At Pittsfield Reuben Leavitt (6) saw
The ghost of Storrs a-praying;

And Calroll's woods were sad to see,
With black-winged crows a-darting;
And Black Snout looked on Ossipee,
New-glossed with Day and Martin.

We thought the "Old Man of the Notch"
His face seemed changing wholly—
His lips seemed thick; his nose seemed flat;
His misty hair looked woolly;
And Coos teamsters, shrieking, fled
From the metamorphosed figure.
"Look there!" they said, "the Old Stone Head
Himself is turning nigger!"

The schoolhouse, out of Canaan hauled
Seemed turning on its track again,
And like a great swamp-turtle crawled
To Canaan village back again,
Shook off the mud and settled flat
Upon its underpinning;
A nigger on its ridge-pole sat,
From ear to ear a-grinning.

Gray H———d heard o' nights the sound
Of rail-cars onward faring;
Right over Democratic ground
The iron horse came tearing.
A flag waved o'er that spectral train,
As high as Pittsfield steeple;

Its emblem was a broken chain;
Its motto: "To the people!"

I dreamed that Charley took his bed,
With Hale for his physician;
His daily dose an old "unread
And unreferred" petition. (8)
There Hayes and Tuck as nurses sat,
As near as near could be, man;
They leeched him with the "Democrat;"
They blistered with the "Freeman."

Ah! grisly portents! What avail
Your terrors of forewarning?
We wake to find the nightmare Hale
Astride our breasts at morning!
From Portsmouth lights to Indian stream
Our foes their throats are trying;
The very factory-spindles seem
To mock us while they're flying.

The hills have bonfires; in our streets
Flags flout us in our faces;
The newsboys, peddling off their sheets,
Are hoarse with our disgraces.
In vain we turn, for gibing wit
And shoutings follow after,
As if old Kearsarge had split
His granite sides with laughter.

What boots it that we pelted out
The anti-slavery women, (9)
And bravely strewed their hall about
With tattered lace and trimming?
Was it for such a sad reverse
Our mobs became peacemakers,
And kept their tar and wooden horse
For Englishmen and Quakers?

For this did shifty Atherton
Make gag rules for the Great House?
Wiped we for this our feet upon
Petitions in our State House?
Plied we for this our axe of doom,
No stubborn traitor sparing,
Who scoffed at our opinion loom,
And took to homespun wearing?

Ah, Moses! hard it is to scan
These crooked providences,
Deducing from the wisest plan
The saddest consequences!
Strange that, in trampling as was meet
The nigger-men's petition,
We sprang a mine beneath our feet
Which opened up perdition.

How goodly, Moses, was the game
In which we've long been actors,

Supplying freedom with the name
And slavery with the practice
Our smooth words fed the people's mouth,
Their ears our party rattle;
We kept them headed to the South,
As drovers do their cattle.

But now our game of politics
The world at large is learning;
And men grown gray in all our tricks
State's evidence are turning.
Votes and preambles subtly spun
They cram with meanings louder,
And load the Democratic gun
With abolition powder.
The ides of June! Woe worth the day
When, turning all things over,
The traitor Hale shall make his hay
From Democratic clover!
Who then shall take him in the law,
Who punish crime so flagrant?
Whose hand shall serve, whose pen shall draw,
A writ against that "vagrant"?

Alas! no hope is left us here,
And one can only pine for
The envied place of overseer
Of slaves in Carolina!
Pray, Moses, give Calhoun the wink,

And see what pay he's giving!
We've practised long enough, we think,
To know the art of driving.

And for the faithful rank and file,
Who know their proper stations,
Perhaps it may be worth their while
To try the rice plantations.
Let Hale exult, let Wilson scoff,
To see us southward scamper;
The slaves, we know, are "better off
Than laborers in New Hampshire!"

LINES FROM A LETTER TO A YOUNG CLERICAL FRIEND.

A STRENGTH Thy service cannot tire,
A faith which doubt can never dim,
A heart of love, a lip of fire,
O Freedom's God! be Thou to him!

Speak through him words of power and fear,
As through Thy prophet bards of old,
And let a scornful people hear
Once more Thy Sinai-thunders rolled.

For lying lips Thy blessing seek,
And hands of blood are raised to Thee,
And On Thy children, crushed and weak,
The oppressor plants his kneeling knee.

Let then, O God! Thy servant dare
Thy truth in all its power to tell,
Unmask the priestly thieves, and tear
The Bible from the grasp of hell!

From hollow rite and narrow span
Of law and sect by Thee released,
Oh, teach him that the Christian man
Is holier than the Jewish priest.

Chase back the shadows, gray and old,
Of the dead ages, from his way,

And let his hopeful eyes behold
The dawn of Thy millennial day;

That day when fettered limb and mind
Shall know the truth which maketh free,
And he alone who loves his kind
Shall, childlike, claim the love of Thee!

DANIEL NEALL.

Dr. Neall, a worthy disciple of that venerated philanthropist, Warner Mifflin, whom the Girondist statesman, Jean Pierre Brissot, pronounced "an angel of mercy, the best man he ever knew," was one of the noble band of Pennsylvania abolitionists, whose bravery was equalled only by their gentleness and tenderness. He presided at the great anti-slavery meeting in Pennsylvania Hall, May 17, 1838, when the Hall was surrounded by a furious mob. I was standing near him while the glass of the windows broken by missiles showered over him, and a deputation from the rioters forced its way to the platform, and demanded that the meeting should be closed at once. Dr. Neall drew up his tall form to its utmost height. "I am here," he said, "the president of this meeting, and I will be torn in pieces before I leave my place at your dictation. Go back to those who sent you. I shall do my duty." Some years after, while visiting his relatives in his native State of Delaware, he was dragged from the house of his friends by a mob of slave-holders and brutally maltreated. He bore it like a martyr of the old times; and when released, told his persecutors that he forgave them, for it was not they but Slavery which had done the wrong. If they should ever be in Philadelphia and needed hospitality or aid, let them call on him.

I.

FRIEND of the Slave, and yet the friend of all;

Lover of peace, yet ever foremost when

The need of battling Freedom called for men

To plant the banner on the outer wall;

Gentle and kindly, ever at distress

Melted to more than woman's tenderness,

Yet firm and steadfast, at his duty's post

Fronting the violence of a maddened host,

Like some gray rock from which the waves are tossed!

Knowing his deeds of love, men questioned not

The faith of one whose walk and word were right;

Who tranquilly in Life's great task-field wrought,

And, side by side with evil, scarcely caught
A stain upon his pilgrim garb of white
Prompt to redress another's wrong, his own
Leaving to Time and Truth and Penitence alone.

II.
Such was our friend. Formed on the good old plan,
A true and brave and downright honest man
He blew no trumpet in the market-place,
Nor in the church with hypocritic face
Supplied with cant the lack of Christian grace;
Loathing pretence, he did with cheerful will
What others talked of while their hands were still;
And, while "Lord, Lord!" the pious tyrants cried,
Who, in the poor, their Master crucified,
His daily prayer, far better understood
In acts than words, was simply doing good.
So calm, so constant was his rectitude,
That by his loss alone we know its worth,
And feel how true a man has walked with us on earth.

6th, 6th month, 1846.

SONG OF SLAVES IN THE DESERT.

"Sebah, Oasis of Fezzan, 10th March, 1846.—This evening the female slaves were unusually excited in singing, and I had the curiosity to ask my negro servant, Said, what they were singing about. As many of them were natives of his own country, he had no difficulty in translating the Mandara or Bornou language. I had often asked the Moors to translate their songs for me, but got no satisfactory account from them. Said at first said, 'Oh, they sing of Rubee' (God). 'What do you mean?' I replied, impatiently. 'Oh, don't you know?' he continued, 'they asked God to give them their Atka?' (certificate of freedom). I inquired, 'Is that all?' Said: 'No; they say, "Where are we going? The world is large. O God! Where are we going? O God!"' I inquired, 'What else?' Said: 'They remember their country, Bornou, and say, "Bornou was a pleasant country, full of all good things; but this is a bad country, and we are miserable!"' 'Do they say anything else?' Said: 'No; they repeat these words over and over again, and add, "O God! give us our Atka, and let us return again to our dear home."'

"I am not surprised I got little satisfaction when I asked the Moors about the songs of their slaves. Who will say that the above words are not a very appropriate song? What could have been more congenially adapted to their then woful condition? It is not to be wondered at that these poor bondwomen cheer up their hearts, in their long, lonely, and painful wanderings over the desert, with words and sentiments like these; but I have often observed that their fatigue and sufferings were too great for them to strike up this melancholy dirge, and many days their plaintive strains never broke over the silence of the desert."— Richardson's Journal in Africa.

WHERE are we going? where are we going,

Where are we going, Rubee?

Lord of peoples, lord of lands,

Look across these shining sands,

Through the furnace of the noon,

Through the white light of the moon.

Strong the Ghiblee wind is blowing,

Strange and large the world is growing!

Speak and tell us where we are going,

Where are we going, Rubee?

Bornou land was rich and good,
Wells of water, fields of food,
Dourra fields, and bloom of bean,
And the palm-tree cool and green
Bornou land we see no longer,
Here we thirst and here we hunger,
Here the Moor-man smites in anger
Where are we going, Rubee?

When we went from Bornou land,
We were like the leaves and sand,
We were many, we are few;
Life has one, and death has two
Whitened bones our path are showing,
Thou All-seeing, thou All-knowing
Hear us, tell us, where are we going,
Where are we going, Rubee?

Moons of marches from our eyes
Bornou land behind us lies;
Stranger round us day by day
Bends the desert circle gray;
Wild the waves of sand are flowing,
Hot the winds above them blowing,—
Lord of all things! where are we going?
Where are we going, Rubee?
We are weak, but Thou art strong;
Short our lives, but Thine is long;
We are blind, but Thou hast eyes;

We are fools, but Thou art wise!
Thou, our morrow's pathway knowing
Through the strange world round us growing,
Hear us, tell us where are we going,
Where are we going, Rubee?

1847.

TO DELAWARE.

Written during the discussion in the Legislature of that State, in the winter of 1846-47, of a bill for the abolition of slavery.

THRICE welcome to thy sisters of the East,
To the strong tillers of a rugged home,
With spray-wet locks to Northern winds released,
And hardy feet o'erswept by ocean's foam;
And to the young nymphs of the golden West,
Whose harvest mantles, fringed with prairie bloom,
Trail in the sunset,—O redeemed and blest,
To the warm welcome of thy sisters come!
Broad Pennsylvania, down her sail-white bay
Shall give thee joy, and Jersey from her plains,
And the great lakes, where echo, free alway,
Moaned never shoreward with the clank of chains,
Shall weave new sun-bows in their tossing spray,
And all their waves keep grateful holiday.
And, smiling on thee through her mountain rains,
Vermont shall bless thee; and the granite peaks,
And vast Katahdin o'er his woods, shall wear
Their snow-crowns brighter in the cold, keen air;
And Massachusetts, with her rugged cheeks
O'errun with grateful tears, shall turn to thee,
When, at thy bidding, the electric wire
Shall tremble northward with its words of fire;
Glory and praise to God! another State is free!

1847.

YORKTOWN.

Dr. Thacher, surgeon in Scammel's regiment, in his description of the siege of Yorktown, says: "The labor on the Virginia plantations is performed altogether by a species of the human race cruelly wrested from their native country, and doomed to perpetual bondage, while their masters are manfully contending for freedom and the natural rights of man. Such is the inconsistency of human nature." Eighteen hundred slaves were found at Yorktown, after its surrender, and restored to their masters. Well was it said by Dr. Barnes, in his late work on Slavery: "No slave was any nearer his freedom after the surrender of Yorktown than when Patrick Henry first taught the notes of liberty to echo among the hills and vales of Virginia."

FROM Yorktown's ruins, ranked and still,
Two lines stretch far o'er vale and hill
Who curbs his steed at head of one?
Hark! the low murmur: Washington!
Who bends his keen, approving glance,
Where down the gorgeous line of France
Shine knightly star and plume of snow?
Thou too art victor, Rochambeau!
The earth which bears this calm array
Shook with the war-charge yesterday,

Ploughed deep with hurrying hoof and wheel,
Shot-sown and bladed thick with steel;
October's clear and noonday sun
Paled in the breath-smoke of the gun,
And down night's double blackness fell,
Like a dropped star, the blazing shell.

Now all is hushed: the gleaming lines
Stand moveless as the neighboring pines;
While through them, sullen, grim, and slow,

The conquered hosts of England go
O'Hara's brow belies his dress,
Gay Tarleton's troop rides bannerless:
Shout, from thy fired and wasted homes,
Thy scourge, Virginia, captive comes!

Nor thou alone; with one glad voice
Let all thy sister States rejoice;
Let Freedom, in whatever clime
She waits with sleepless eye her time,
Shouting from cave and mountain wood
Make glad her desert solitude,
While they who hunt her quail with fear;
The New World's chain lies broken here!

But who are they, who, cowering, wait
Within the shattered fortress gate?
Dark tillers of Virginia's soil,
Classed with the battle's common spoil,
With household stuffs, and fowl, and swine,
With Indian weed and planters' wine,
With stolen beeves, and foraged corn,—
Are they not men, Virginian born?

Oh, veil your faces, young and brave!
Sleep, Scammel, in thy soldier grave
Sons of the Northland, ye who set
Stout hearts against the bayonet,
And pressed with steady footfall near

The moated battery's blazing tier,
Turn your scarred faces from the sight,
Let shame do homage to the right!

Lo! fourscore years have passed; and where
The Gallic bugles stirred the air,
And, through breached batteries, side by side,
To victory stormed the hosts allied,
And brave foes grounded, pale with pain,
The arms they might not lift again,
As abject as in that old day
The slave still toils his life away.

Oh, fields still green and fresh in story,
Old days of pride, old names of glory,
Old marvels of the tongue and pen,
Old thoughts which stirred the hearts of men,
Ye spared the wrong; and over all
Behold the avenging shadow fall!
Your world-wide honor stained with shame,—
Your freedom's self a hollow name!

Where's now the flag of that old war?
Where flows its stripe? Where burns its star?
Bear witness, Palo Alto's day,
Dark Vale of Palms, red Monterey,
Where Mexic Freedom, young and weak,
Fleshes the Northern eagle's beak;
Symbol of terror and despair,

Of chains and slaves, go seek it there!

Laugh, Prussia, midst thy iron ranks
Laugh, Russia, from thy Neva's banks!
Brave sport to see the fledgling born
Of Freedom by its parent torn!
Safe now is Speilberg's dungeon cell,
Safe drear Siberia's frozen hell
With Slavery's flag o'er both unrolled,
What of the New World fears the Old?

1847.

RANDOLPH OF ROANOKE.

O MOTHER EARTH! upon thy lap
Thy weary ones receiving,
And o'er them, silent as a dream,
Thy grassy mantle weaving,
Fold softly in thy long embrace
That heart so worn and broken,
And cool its pulse of fire beneath
Thy shadows old and oaken.

Shut out from him the bitter word
And serpent hiss of scorning;
Nor let the storms of yesterday
Disturb his quiet morning.
Breathe over him forgetfulness
Of all save deeds of kindness,
And, save to smiles of grateful eyes,
Press down his lids in blindness.

There, where with living ear and eye
He heard Potomac's flowing,
And, through his tall ancestral trees,
Saw autumn's sunset glowing,
He sleeps, still looking to the west,
Beneath the dark wood shadow,
As if he still would see the sun
Sink down on wave and meadow.

Bard, Sage, and Tribune! in himself

All moods of mind contrasting,—
The tenderest wail of human woe,
The scorn like lightning blasting;
The pathos which from rival eyes
Unwilling tears could summon,
The stinging taunt, the fiery burst
Of hatred scarcely human!

Mirth, sparkling like a diamond shower,
From lips of life-long sadness;
Clear picturings of majestic thought
Upon a ground of madness;
And over all Romance and Song
A classic beauty throwing,
And laurelled Clio at his side
Her storied pages showing.
All parties feared him: each in turn
Beheld its schemes disjointed,
As right or left his fatal glance
And spectral finger pointed.
Sworn foe of Cant, he smote it down
With trenchant wit unsparing,
And, mocking, rent with ruthless hand
The robe Pretence was wearing.

Too honest or too proud to feign
A love he never cherished,
Beyond Virginia's border line
His patriotism perished.

While others hailed in distant skies
Our eagle's dusky pinion,
He only saw the mountain bird
Stoop o'er his Old Dominion!

Still through each change of fortune strange,
Racked nerve, and brain all burning,
His loving faith in Mother-land
Knew never shade of turning;
By Britain's lakes, by Neva's tide,
Whatever sky was o'er him,
He heard her rivers' rushing sound,
Her blue peaks rose before him.

He held his slaves, yet made withal
No false and vain pretences,
Nor paid a lying priest to seek
For Scriptural defences.
His harshest words of proud rebuke,
His bitterest taunt and scorning,
Fell fire-like on the Northern brow
That bent to him in fawning.

He held his slaves; yet kept the while
His reverence for the Human;
In the dark vassals of his will
He saw but Man and Woman!
No hunter of God's outraged poor
His Roanoke valley entered;

No trader in the souls of men
Across his threshold ventured.
And when the old and wearied man
Lay down for his last sleeping,
And at his side, a slave no more,
His brother-man stood weeping,
His latest thought, his latest breath,
To Freedom's duty giving,
With failing tongue and trembling hand
The dying blest the living.

Oh, never bore his ancient State
A truer son or braver
None trampling with a calmer scorn
On foreign hate or favor.
He knew her faults, yet never stooped
His proud and manly feeling
To poor excuses of the wrong
Or meanness of concealing.

But none beheld with clearer eye
The plague-spot o'er her spreading,
None heard more sure the steps of Doom
Along her future treading.
For her as for himself he spake,
When, his gaunt frame upbracing,
He traced with dying hand "Remorse!"
And perished in the tracing.

As from the grave where Henry sleeps,
From Vernon's weeping willow,
And from the grassy pall which hides
The Sage of Monticello,
So from the leaf-strewn burial-stone
Of Randolph's lowly dwelling,
Virginia! o'er thy land of slaves
A warning voice is swelling!

And hark! from thy deserted fields
Are sadder warnings spoken,
From quenched hearths, where thy exiled sons
Their household gods have broken.
The curse is on thee,—wolves for men,
And briers for corn-sheaves giving
Oh, more than all thy dead renown
Were now one hero living

1847.

THE LOST STATESMAN.

Written on hearing of the death of Silas Wright of New York.

As they who, tossing midst the storm at night,
While turning shoreward, where a beacon shone,
Meet the walled blackness of the heaven alone,
So, on the turbulent waves of party tossed,
In gloom and tempest, men have seen thy light
Quenched in the darkness. At thy hour of noon,
While life was pleasant to thy undimmed sight,
And, day by day, within thy spirit grew
A holier hope than young Ambition knew,
As through thy rural quiet, not in vain,
Pierced the sharp thrill of Freedom's cry of pain,
Man of the millions, thou art lost too soon
Portents at which the bravest stand aghast,—
The birth-throes of a Future, strange and vast,
Alarm the land; yet thou, so wise and strong,
Suddenly summoned to the burial bed,
Lapped in its slumbers deep and ever long,
Hear'st not the tumult surging overhead.
Who now shall rally Freedom's scattering host?
Who wear the mantle of the leader lost?
Who stay the march of slavery? He whose voice
Hath called thee from thy task-field shall not lack
Yet bolder champions, to beat bravely back
The wrong which, through his poor ones, reaches Him:
Yet firmer hands shall Freedom's torchlights trim,
And wave them high across the abysmal black,

Till bound, dumb millions there shall see them and rejoice.
10th mo., 1847.

THE SLAVES OF MARTINIQUE.

Suggested by a daguerreotype taken from a small French engraving of two negro figures, sent to the writer by Oliver Johnson.

BEAMS of noon, like burning lances, through the tree-tops flash and glisten,
As she stands before her lover, with raised face to look and listen.

Dark, but comely, like the maiden in the ancient Jewish song
Scarcely has the toil of task-fields done her graceful beauty wrong.

He, the strong one and the manly, with the vassal's garb and hue,
Holding still his spirit's birthright, to his higher nature true;

Hiding deep the strengthening purpose of a freeman in his heart,
As the gregree holds his Fetich from the white man's gaze apart.

Ever foremost of his comrades, when the driver's morning horn
Calls away to stifling mill-house, to the fields of cane and corn.

Fall the keen and burning lashes never on his back

or limb;
Scarce with look or word of censure, turns the driver unto him.

Yet, his brow is always thoughtful, and his eye is hard and stern;
Slavery's last and humblest lesson he has never deigned to learn.

And, at evening, when his comrades dance before their master's door,
Folding arms and knitting forehead, stands he silent evermore.

God be praised for every instinct which rebels against a lot
Where the brute survives the human, and man's upright form is not!

As the serpent-like bejuco winds his spiral fold on fold
Round the tall and stately ceiba, till it withers in his hold;

Slow decays the forest monarch, closer girds the fell embrace,
Till the tree is seen no longer, and the vine is in its place;

So a base and bestial nature round the vassal's manhood twines,
And the spirit wastes beneath it, like the ceiba choked with vines.

God is Love, saith the Evangel; and our world of woe and sin
Is made light and happy only when a Love is shining in.

Ye whose lives are free as sunshine, finding, wheresoe'er ye roam,
Smiles of welcome, looks of kindness, making all the world like home;

In the veins of whose affections kindred blood is but a part.,
Of one kindly current throbbing from the universal heart;

Can ye know the deeper meaning of a love in Slavery nursed,
Last flower of a lost Eden, blooming in that Soil accursed?

Love of Home, and Love of Woman!—dear to all, but doubly dear
To the heart whose pulses elsewhere measure only hate and fear.

All around the desert circles, underneath a brazen sky,
Only one green spot remaining where the dew is never dry!

From the horror of that desert, from its atmosphere of hell,
Turns the fainting spirit thither, as the diver seeks his bell.

'T is the fervid tropic noontime; faint and low the sea-waves beat;
Hazy rise the inland mountains through the glimmer of the heat,—

Where, through mingled leaves and blossoms, arrowy sunbeams flash and glisten,
Speaks her lover to the slave-girl, and she lifts her head to listen:—
"We shall live as slaves no longer! Freedom's hour is close at hand!
Rocks her bark upon the waters, rests the boat upon the strand!

"I have seen the Haytien Captain; I have seen his swarthy crew,
Haters of the pallid faces, to their race and color true.

"They have sworn to wait our coming till the night has passed its noon,
And the gray and darkening waters roll above the sunken moon!"
Oh, the blessed hope of freedom! how with joy and glad surprise,
For an instant throbs her bosom, for an instant beam her eyes!

But she looks across the valley, where her mother's hut is seen,
Through the snowy bloom of coffee, and the lemon-leaves so green.

And she answers, sad and earnest: "It were wrong for thee to stay;
God hath heard thy prayer for freedom, and his finger points the way.

"Well I know with what endurance, for the sake of me and mine,
Thou hast borne too long a burden never meant for souls like thine.

"Go; and at the hour of midnight, when our last farewell is o'er,
Kneeling on our place of parting, I will bless thee from the shore.

*"But for me, my mother, lying on her sick-bed
all the day,
Lifts her weary head to watch me, coming through
the twilight gray.
"Should I leave her sick and helpless, even freedom,
shared with thee,
Would be sadder far than bondage, lonely toil, and
stripes to me.*

*"For my heart would die within me, and my brain
would soon be wild;
I should hear my mother calling through the twilight
for her child!"*

*Blazing upward from the ocean, shines the sun of
morning-time,
Through the coffee-trees in blossom, and green
hedges of the lime.*

*Side by side, amidst the slave-gang, toil the lover
and the maid;
Wherefore looks he o'er the waters, leaning forward
on his spade?*

*Sadly looks he, deeply sighs he: 't is the Haytien's
sail he sees,
Like a white cloud of the mountains, driven seaward
by the breeze.*

But his arm a light hand presses, and he hears a low voice call
Hate of Slavery, hope of Freedom, Love is mightier than all.
1848.

THE CURSE OF THE CHARTER-BREAKERS.

The rights and liberties affirmed by Magna Charta were deemed of such importance, in the thirteenth century, that the Bishops, twice a year, with tapers burning, and in their pontifical robes, pronounced, in the presence of the king and the representatives of the estates of England, the greater excommunication against the infringer of that instrument. The imposing ceremony took place in the great Hall of Westminster. A copy of the curse, as pronounced in 1253, declares that, "by the authority of Almighty God, and the blessed Apostles and Martyrs, and all the saints in heaven, all those who violate the English liberties, and secretly or openly, by deed, word, or counsel, do make statutes, or observe then being made, against said liberties, are accursed and sequestered from the company of heaven and the sacraments of the Holy Church."

William Penn, in his admirable political pamphlet, England's Present Interest Considered, alluding to the curse of the Charter- breakers, says: "I am no Roman Catholic, and little value their other curses; yet I declare I would not for the world incur this curse, as every man deservedly doth, who offers violence to the fundamental freedom thereby repeated and confirmed."

IN Westminster's royal halls,
Robed in their pontificals,
England's ancient prelates stood
For the people's right and good.
Closed around the waiting crowd,
Dark and still, like winter's cloud;
King and council, lord and knight,
Squire and yeoman, stood in sight;
Stood to hear the priest rehearse,
In God's name, the Church's curse,
By the tapers round them lit,
Slowly, sternly uttering it.

"Right of voice in framing laws,
Right of peers to try each cause;
Peasant homestead, mean and small,

Sacred as the monarch's hall,—

"Whoso lays his hand on these,
England's ancient liberties;
Whoso breaks, by word or deed,
England's vow at Runnymede;

"Be he Prince or belted knight,
Whatsoe'er his rank or might,
If the highest, then the worst,
Let him live and die accursed.

"Thou, who to Thy Church hast given
Keys alike, of hell and heaven,
Make our word and witness sure,
Let the curse we speak endure!"

Silent, while that curse was said,
Every bare and listening head
Bowed in reverent awe, and then
All the people said, Amen!

Seven times the bells have tolled,
For the centuries gray and old,
Since that stoled and mitred band
Cursed the tyrants of their land.
Since the priesthood, like a tower,
Stood between the poor and power;
And the wronged and trodden down

Blessed the abbot's shaven crown.

Gone, thank God, their wizard spell,
Lost, their keys of heaven and hell;
Yet I sigh for men as bold
As those bearded priests of old.

Now, too oft the priesthood wait
At the threshold of the state;
Waiting for the beck and nod
Of its power as law and God.

Fraud exults, while solemn words
Sanctify his stolen hoards;
Slavery laughs, while ghostly lips
Bless his manacles and whips.

Not on them the poor rely,
Not to them looks liberty,
Who with fawning falsehood cower
To the wrong, when clothed with power.

Oh, to see them meanly cling,
Round the master, round the king,
Sported with, and sold and bought,—
Pitifuller sight is not!

Tell me not that this must be
God's true priest is always free;

Free, the needed truth to speak,
Right the wronged, and raise the weak.

Not to fawn on wealth and state,
Leaving Lazarus at the gate;
Not to peddle creeds like wares;
Not to mutter hireling prayers;

Nor to paint the new life's bliss
On the sable ground of this;
Golden streets for idle knave,
Sabbath rest for weary slave!
Not for words and works like these,
Priest of God, thy mission is;
But to make earth's desert glad,
In its Eden greenness clad;

And to level manhood bring
Lord and peasant, serf and king;
And the Christ of God to find
In the humblest of thy kind!

Thine to work as well as pray,
Clearing thorny wrongs away;
Plucking up the weeds of sin,
Letting heaven's warm sunshine in;

Watching on the hills of Faith;
Listening what the spirit saith,

Of the dim-seen light afar,
Growing like a nearing star.

God's interpreter art thou,
To the waiting ones below;
'Twixt them and its light midway
Heralding the better day;

Catching gleams of temple spires,
Hearing notes of angel choirs,
Where, as yet unseen of them,
Comes the New Jerusalem!

Like the seer of Patmos gazing,
On the glory downward blazing;
Till upon Earth's grateful sod
Rests the City of our God!

1848.

PAEAN.

This poem indicates the exultation of the anti-slavery party in view of the revolt of the friends of Martin Van Buren in New York, from the Democratic Presidential nomination in 1848.

Now, joy and thanks forevermore!
The dreary night has wellnigh passed,
The slumbers of the North are o'er,
The Giant stands erect at last!

More than we hoped in that dark time
When, faint with watching, few and worn,
We saw no welcome day-star climb
The cold gray pathway of the morn!

O weary hours! O night of years!
What storms our darkling pathway swept,
Where, beating back our thronging fears,
By Faith alone our march we kept.

How jeered the scoffing crowd behind,
How mocked before the tyrant train,
As, one by one, the true and kind
Fell fainting in our path of pain!

They died, their brave hearts breaking slow,
But, self-forgetful to the last,
In words of cheer and bugle blow
Their breath upon the darkness passed.

A mighty host, on either hand,
Stood waiting for the dawn of day
To crush like reeds our feeble band;
The morn has come, and where are they?

Troop after troop their line forsakes;
With peace-white banners waving free,
And from our own the glad shout breaks,
Of Freedom and Fraternity!

Like mist before the growing light,
The hostile cohorts melt away;
Our frowning foemen of the night
Are brothers at the dawn of day.

As unto these repentant ones
We open wide our toil-worn ranks,
Along our line a murmur runs
Of song, and praise, and grateful thanks.

Sound for the onset! Blast on blast!
Till Slavery's minions cower and quail;
One charge of fire shall drive them fast
Like chaff before our Northern gale!

O prisoners in your house of pain,
Dumb, toiling millions, bound and sold,
Look! stretched o'er Southern vale and plain,
The Lord's delivering hand behold!

Above the tyrant's pride of power,
His iron gates and guarded wall,
The bolts which shattered Shinar's tower
Hang, smoking, for a fiercer fall.
Awake! awake! my Fatherland!
It is thy Northern light that shines;
This stirring march of Freedom's band
The storm-song of thy mountain pines.

Wake, dwellers where the day expires!
And hear, in winds that sweep your lakes
And fan your prairies' roaring fires,
The signal-call that Freedom makes!

1848.

THE CRISIS.

Written on learning the terms of the treaty with Mexico.

ACROSS the Stony Mountains, o'er the desert's
drouth and sand,
The circles of our empire touch the western ocean's
strand;
From slumberous Timpanogos, to Gila, wild and
free,
Flowing down from Nuevo-Leon to California's sea;
And from the mountains of the east, to Santa
Rosa's shore,
The eagles of Mexitli shall beat the air no more.

O Vale of Rio Bravo! Let thy simple children
weep;
Close watch about their holy fire let maids of
Pecos keep;
Let Taos send her cry across Sierra Madre's pines,
And Santa Barbara toll her bells amidst her corn
and vines;
For lo! the pale land-seekers come, with eager eyes
of gain,
Wide scattering, like the bison herds on broad
Salada's plain.

Let Sacramento's herdsmen heed what sound the
winds bring down
Of footsteps on the crisping snow, from cold
Nevada's crown!

Full hot and fast the Saxon rides, with rein of travel slack,
And, bending o'er his saddle, leaves the sunrise at his back;
By many a lonely river, and gorge of fir and pine,
On many a wintry hill-top, his nightly camp-fires shine.

O countrymen and brothers! that land of lake and plain,
Of salt wastes alternating with valleys fat with grain;
Of mountains white with winter, looking downward, cold, serene,
On their feet with spring-vines tangled and lapped in softest green;
Swift through whose black volcanic gates, o'er many a sunny vale,
Wind-like the Arapahoe sweeps the bison's dusty trail!

Great spaces yet untravelled, great lakes whose mystic shores
The Saxon rifle never heard, nor dip of Saxon oars;
Great herds that wander all unwatched, wild steeds that none have tamed,
Strange fish in unknown streams, and birds the Saxon never named;

*Deep mines, dark mountain crucibles, where Nature's
chemic powers
Work out the Great Designer's will; all these ye
say are ours!*

*Forever ours! for good or ill, on us the burden
lies;
God's balance, watched by angels, is hung across
the skies.
Shall Justice, Truth, and Freedom turn the poised
and trembling scale?
Or shall the Evil triumph, and robber Wrong prevail?
Shall the broad land o'er which our flag in starry
splendor waves,
Forego through us its freedom, and bear the tread
of slaves?
The day is breaking in the East of which the
prophets told,
And brightens up the sky of Time the Christian
Age of Gold;
Old Might to Right is yielding, battle blade to
clerkly pen,
Earth's monarchs are her peoples, and her serfs
stand up as men;*

*The isles rejoice together, in a day are nations
born,
And the slave walks free in Tunis, and by Stamboul's
Golden Horn!*

Is this, O countrymen of mine! a day for us to sow
The soil of new-gained empire with slavery's seeds of woe?
To feed with our fresh life-blood the Old World's cast-off crime,
Dropped, like some monstrous early birth, from the tired lap of Time?
To run anew the evil race the old lost nations ran,
And die like them of unbelief of God, and wrong of man?

Great Heaven! Is this our mission? End in this the prayers and tears,
The toil, the strife, the watchings of our younger, better years?
Still as the Old World rolls in light, shall ours in shadow turn,
A beamless Chaos, cursed of God, through outer darkness borne?
Where the far nations looked for light, a blackness in the air?
Where for words of hope they listened, the long wail of despair?

The Crisis presses on us; face to face with us it stands,
With solemn lips of question, like the Sphinx in Egypt's sands!
This day we fashion Destiny, our web of Fate we

spin;
This day for all hereafter choose we holiness or sin;
Even now from starry Gerizim, or Ebal's cloudy crown,
We call the dews of blessing or the bolts of cursing down!

By all for which the martyrs bore their agony and shame;
By all the warning words of truth with which the prophets came;
By the Future which awaits us; by all the hopes which cast
Their faint and trembling beams across the blackness of the Past;
And by the blessed thought of Him who for Earth's freedom died,
O my people! O my brothers! let us choose the righteous side.

So shall the Northern pioneer go joyful on his way;
To wed Penobseot's waters to San Francisco's bay;
To make the rugged places smooth, and sow the vales with grain;
And bear, with Liberty and Law, the Bible in his train
The mighty West shall bless the East, and sea shall

answer sea,
And mountain unto mountain call, Praise God, for we are free

1845.

LINES ON THE PORTRAIT OF A CELEBRATED PUBLISHER.

A pleasant print to peddle out
In lands of rice and cotton;
The model of that face in dough
Would make the artist's fortune.
For Fame to thee has come unsought,
While others vainly woo her,
In proof how mean a thing can make
A great man of its doer.
To whom shall men thyself compare,
Since common models fail 'em,
Save classic goose of ancient Rome,
Or sacred ass of Balaam?
The gabble of that wakeful goose
Saved Rome from sack of Brennus;
The braying of the prophet's ass
Betrayed the angel's menace!

So when Guy Fawkes, in petticoats,
And azure-tinted hose oil,
Was twisting from thy love-lorn sheets
The slow-match of explosion—
An earthquake blast that would have tossed
The Union as a feather,
Thy instinct saved a perilled land
And perilled purse together.

Just think of Carolina's sage

Sent whirling like a Dervis,
Of Quattlebum in middle air
Performing strange drill-service!
Doomed like Assyria's lord of old,
Who fell before the Jewess,
Or sad Abimelech, to sigh,
"Alas! a woman slew us!"

Thou saw'st beneath a fair disguise
The danger darkly lurking,
And maiden bodice dreaded more
Than warrior's steel-wrought jerkin.
How keen to scent the hidden plot!
How prompt wert thou to balk it,
With patriot zeal and pedler thrift,
For country and for pocket!

Thy likeness here is doubtless well,
But higher honor's due it;
On auction-block and negro-jail
Admiring eyes should view it.
Or, hung aloft, it well might grace
The nation's senate-chamber—
A greedy Northern bottle-fly
Preserved in Slavery's amber!

1850.

DERNE.

The storming of the city of Derne, in 1805, by General Eaton, at the head of nine Americans, forty Greeks, and a motley array of Turks and Arabs, was one of those feats of hardihood and daring which have in all ages attracted the admiration of the multitude. The higher and holier heroism of Christian self-denial and sacrifice, in the humble walks of private duty, is seldom so well appreciated.

NIGHT on the city of the Moor!
On mosque and tomb, and white-walled shore,
On sea-waves, to whose ceaseless knock
The narrow harbor-gates unlock,
On corsair's galley, carack tall,
And plundered Christian caraval!
The sounds of Moslem life are still;
No mule-bell tinkles down the hill;
Stretched in the broad court of the khan,
The dusty Bornou caravan
Lies heaped in slumber, beast and man;
The Sheik is dreaming in his tent,
His noisy Arab tongue o'erspent;
The kiosk's glimmering lights are gone,
The merchant with his wares withdrawn;
Rough pillowed on some pirate breast,
The dancing-girl has sunk to rest;
And, save where measured footsteps fall
Along the Bashaw's guarded wall,
Or where, like some bad dream, the Jew
Creeps stealthily his quarter through,
Or counts with fear his golden heaps,
The City of the Corsair sleeps.

But where yon prison long and low
Stands black against the pale star-glow,
Chafed by the ceaseless wash of waves,
There watch and pine the Christian slaves;
Rough-bearded men, whose far-off wives
Wear out with grief their lonely lives;
And youth, still flashing from his eyes
The clear blue of New England skies,
A treasured lock of whose soft hair
Now wakes some sorrowing mother's prayer;
Or, worn upon some maiden breast,
Stirs with the loving heart's unrest.

A bitter cup each life must drain,
The groaning earth is cursed with pain,
And, like the scroll the angel bore
The shuddering Hebrew seer before,
O'erwrit alike, without, within,
With all the woes which follow sin;
But, bitterest of the ills beneath
Whose load man totters down to death,
Is that which plucks the regal crown
Of Freedom from his forehead down,
And snatches from his powerless hand
The sceptred sign of self-command,
Effacing with the chain and rod
The image and the seal of God;
Till from his nature, day by day,
The manly virtues fall away,

And leave him naked, blind and mute,
The godlike merging in the brute!

Why mourn the quiet ones who die
Beneath affection's tender eye,
Unto their household and their kin
Like ripened corn-sheaves gathered in?
O weeper, from that tranquil sod,
That holy harvest-home of God,
Turn to the quick and suffering, shed
Thy tears upon the living dead
Thank God above thy dear ones' graves,
They sleep with Him, they are not slaves.

What dark mass, down the mountain-sides
Swift-pouring, like a stream divides?
A long, loose, straggling caravan,
Camel and horse and armed man.
The moon's low crescent, glimmering o'er
Its grave of waters to the shore,
Lights tip that mountain cavalcade,
And gleams from gun and spear and blade
Near and more near! now o'er them falls
The shadow of the city walls.
Hark to the sentry's challenge, drowned
In the fierce trumpet's charging sound!
The rush of men, the musket's peal,
The short, sharp clang of meeting steel!

*Vain, Moslem, vain thy lifeblood poured
So freely on thy foeman's sword!
Not to the swift nor to the strong
The battles of the right belong;
For he who strikes for Freedom wears
The armor of the captive's prayers,
And Nature proffers to his cause
The strength of her eternal laws;
While he whose arm essays to bind
And herd with common brutes his kind
Strives evermore at fearful odds
With Nature and the jealous gods,
And dares the dread recoil which late
Or soon their right shall vindicate.*

*'T is done, the horned crescent falls
The star-flag flouts the broken walls
Joy to the captive husband! joy
To thy sick heart, O brown-locked boy!
In sullen wrath the conquered Moor
Wide open flings your dungeon-door,
And leaves ye free from cell and chain,
The owners of yourselves again.
Dark as his allies desert-born,
Soiled with the battle's stain, and worn
With the long marches of his band
Through hottest wastes of rock and sand,
Scorched by the sun and furnace-breath
Of the red desert's wind of death,*

With welcome words and grasping hands,
The victor and deliverer stands!

The tale is one of distant skies;
The dust of half a century lies
Upon it; yet its hero's name
Still lingers on the lips of Fame.
Men speak the praise of him who gave
Deliverance to the Moorman's slave,
Yet dare to brand with shame and crime
The heroes of our land and time,—
The self-forgetful ones, who stake
Home, name, and life for Freedom's sake.
God mend his heart who cannot feel
The impulse of a holy zeal,
And sees not, with his sordid eyes,
The beauty of self-sacrifice
Though in the sacred place he stands,
Uplifting consecrated hands,
Unworthy are his lips to tell
Of Jesus' martyr-miracle,
Or name aright that dread embrace
Of suffering for a fallen race!

1850.

A SABBATH SCENE.

This poem finds its justification in the readiness with which, even in the North, clergymen urged the prompt execution of the Fugitive Slave Law as a Christian duty, and defended the system of slavery as a Bible institution.

SCARCE had the solemn Sabbath-bell
Ceased quivering in the steeple,
Scarce had the parson to his desk
Walked stately through his people,
When down the summer-shaded street
A wasted female figure,
With dusky brow and naked feet,

Came rushing wild and eager.
She saw the white spire through the trees,
She heard the sweet hymn swelling
O pitying Christ! a refuge give
That poor one in Thy dwelling!

Like a scared fawn before the hounds,
Right up the aisle she glided,
While close behind her, whip in hand,
A lank-haired hunter strided.

She raised a keen and bitter cry,
To Heaven and Earth appealing;
Were manhood's generous pulses dead?
Had woman's heart no feeling?

A score of stout hands rose between

The hunter and the flying:
Age clenched his staff, and maiden eyes
Flashed tearful, yet defying.

"Who dares profane this house and day?"
Cried out the angry pastor.
"Why, bless your soul, the wench's a slave,
And I'm her lord and master!

"I've law and gospel on my side,
And who shall dare refuse me?"
Down came the parson, bowing low,
"My good sir, pray excuse me!

"Of course I know your right divine
To own and work and whip her;
Quick, deacon, throw that Polyglott
Before the wench, and trip her!"

Plump dropped the holy tome, and o'er
Its sacred pages stumbling,
Bound hand and foot, a slave once more,
The hapless wretch lay trembling.

I saw the parson tie the knots,
The while his flock addressing,
The Scriptural claims of slavery
With text on text impressing.

"Although," said he, "on Sabbath day
All secular occupations
Are deadly sins, we must fulfil
Our moral obligations:

"And this commends itself as one
To every conscience tender;
As Paul sent back Onesimus,
My Christian friends, we send her!"

Shriek rose on shriek,—the Sabbath air
Her wild cries tore asunder;
I listened, with hushed breath, to hear
God answering with his thunder!

All still! the very altar's cloth
Had smothered down her shrieking,
And, dumb, she turned from face to face,
For human pity seeking!

I saw her dragged along the aisle,
Her shackles harshly clanking;
I heard the parson, over all,
The Lord devoutly thanking!

My brain took fire: "Is this," I cried,
"The end of prayer and preaching?
Then down with pulpit, down with priest,
And give us Nature's teaching!

"Foul shame and scorn be on ye all
Who turn the good to evil,
And steal the Bible, from the Lord,
To give it to the Devil!

"Than garbled text or parchment law
I own a statute higher;
And God is true, though every book
And every man's a liar!"

Just then I felt the deacon's hand
In wrath my coattail seize on;
I heard the priest cry, "Infidel!"
The lawyer mutter, "Treason!"

I started up,—where now were church,
Slave, master, priest, and people?
I only heard the supper-bell,
Instead of clanging steeple.

But, on the open window's sill,
O'er which the white blooms drifted,
The pages of a good old Book
The wind of summer lifted,

And flower and vine, like angel wings
Around the Holy Mother,
Waved softly there, as if God's truth
And Mercy kissed each other.

And freely from the cherry-bough
Above the casement swinging,
With golden bosom to the sun,
The oriole was singing.

As bird and flower made plain of old
The lesson of the Teacher,
So now I heard the written Word
Interpreted by Nature.

For to my ear methought the breeze
Bore Freedom's blessed word on;
Thus saith the Lord: Break every yoke,
Undo the heavy burden

1850.

IN THE EVIL DAYS.

This and the four following poems have special reference to that darkest hour in the aggression of slavery which preceded the dawn of a better day, when the conscience of the people was roused to action.

THE evil days have come, the poor
Are made a prey;
Bar up the hospitable door,
Put out the fire-lights, point no more
The wanderer's way.

For Pity now is crime; the chain
Which binds our States
Is melted at her hearth in twain,
Is rusted by her tears' soft rain
Close up her gates.

Our Union, like a glacier stirred
By voice below,
Or bell of kine, or wing of bird,
A beggar's crust, a kindly word
May overthrow!

Poor, whispering tremblers! yet we boast
Our blood and name;
Bursting its century-bolted frost,
Each gray cairn on the Northman's coast
Cries out for shame!

Oh for the open firmament,

*The prairie free,
The desert hillside, cavern-rent,
The Pawnee's lodge, the Arab's tent,
The Bushman's tree!*

*Than web of Persian loom most rare,
Or soft divan,
Better the rough rock, bleak and bare,
Or hollow tree, which man may share
With suffering man.*

*I hear a voice: "Thus saith the Law,
Let Love be dumb;
Clasping her liberal hands in awe,
Let sweet-lipped Charity withdraw
From hearth and home."*

*I hear another voice: "The poor
Are thine to feed;
Turn not the outcast from thy door,
Nor give to bonds and wrong once more
Whom God hath freed."
Dear Lord! between that law and Thee
No choice remains;
Yet not untrue to man's decree,
Though spurning its rewards, is he
Who bears its pains.*

Not mine Sedition's trumpet-blast

And threatening word;
I read the lesson of the Past,
That firm endurance wins at last
More than the sword.

O clear-eyed Faith, and Patience thou
So calm and strong!
Lend strength to weakness, teach us how
The sleepless eyes of God look through
This night of wrong.

1850.

MOLOCH IN STATE STREET.

In a foot-note of the Report of the Senate of Massachusetts on the case of the arrest and return to bondage of the fugitive slave Thomas Sims it is stated that—"It would have been impossible for the U. S. marshal thus successfully to have resisted the law of the State, without the assistance of the municipal authorities of Boston, and the countenance and support of a numerous, wealthy, and powerful body of citizens. It was in evidence that 1500 of the most wealthy and respectable citizens-merchants, bankers, and others— volunteered their services to aid the marshal on this occasion. . . . No watch was kept upon the doings of the marshal, and while the State officers slept, after the moon had gone down, in the darkest hour before daybreak, the accused was taken out of our jurisdiction by the armed police of the city of Boston."

THE moon has set: while yet the dawn
Breaks cold and gray,
Between the midnight and the morn
Bear off your prey!

On, swift and still! the conscious street
Is panged and stirred;
Tread light! that fall of serried feet
The dead have heard!

The first drawn blood of Freedom's veins
Gushed where ye tread;
Lo! through the dusk the martyr-stains
Blush darkly red!

Beneath the slowly waning stars
And whitening day,
What stern and awful presence bars
That sacred way?

What faces frown upon ye, dark
With shame and pain?
Come these from Plymouth's Pilgrim bark?
Is that young Vane?

Who, dimly beckoning, speed ye on
With mocking cheer?
Lo! spectral Andros, Hutchinson,
And Gage are here!

For ready mart or favoring blast
Through Moloch's fire,
Flesh of his flesh, unsparing, passed
The Tyrian sire.

Ye make that ancient sacrifice
Of Mail to Gain,
Your traffic thrives, where Freedom dies,
Beneath the chain.

Ye sow to-day; your harvest, scorn
And hate, is near;
How think ye freemen, mountain-born,
The tale will hear?

Thank God! our mother State can yet
Her fame retrieve;
To you and to your children let
The scandal cleave.

Chain Hall and Pulpit, Court and Press,
Make gods of gold;
Let honor, truth, and manliness
Like wares be sold.

Your hoards are great, your walls are strong,
But God is just;
The gilded chambers built by wrong
Invite the rust.

What! know ye not the gains of Crime
Are dust and dross;
Its ventures on the waves of time
Foredoomed to loss!

And still the Pilgrim State remains
What she hath been;
Her inland hills, her seaward plains,
Still nurture men!

Nor wholly lost the fallen mart;
Her olden blood
Through many a free and generous heart
Still pours its flood.

That brave old blood, quick-flowing yet,
Shall know no check,
Till a free people's foot is set
On Slavery's neck.

Even now, the peal of bell and gun,
And hills aflame,
Tell of the first great triumph won
In Freedom's name. (10)

The long night dies: the welcome gray
Of dawn we see;
Speed up the heavens thy perfect day,
God of the free!

1851.

OFFICIAL PIETY.

Suggested by reading a state paper, wherein the higher law is invoked to sustain the lower one.

A Pious magistrate! sound his praise throughout
The wondering churches. Who shall henceforth doubt
That the long-wished millennium draweth nigh?
Sin in high places has become devout,
Tithes mint, goes painful-faced, and prays its lie
Straight up to Heaven, and calls it piety!
The pirate, watching from his bloody deck
The weltering galleon, heavy with the gold
Of Acapulco, holding death in check
While prayers are said, brows crossed, and beads are told;
The robber, kneeling where the wayside cross
On dark Abruzzo tells of life's dread loss
From his own carbine, glancing still abroad
For some new victim, offering thanks to God!
Rome, listening at her altars to the cry
Of midnight Murder, while her hounds of hell
Scour France, from baptized cannon and holy bell
And thousand-throated priesthood, loud and high,
Pealing Te Deums to the shuddering sky,
"Thanks to the Lord, who giveth victory!"
What prove these, but that crime was ne'er so black
As ghostly cheer and pious thanks to lack?
Satan is modest. At Heaven's door he lays
His evil offspring, and, in Scriptural phrase
And saintly posture, gives to God the praise
And honor of the monstrous progeny.

What marvel, then, in our own time to see
His old devices, smoothly acted o'er,—
Official piety, locking fast the door
Of Hope against three million soups of men,—
Brothers, God's children, Christ's redeemed,—and then,
With uprolled eyeballs and on bended knee,
Whining a prayer for help to hide the key!

1853.

THE RENDITION.

On the 2d of June, 1854, Anthony Burns, a fugitive slave from Virginia, after being under arrest for ten days in the Boston Court House, was remanded to slavery under the Fugitive Slave Act, and taken down State Street to a steamer chartered by the United States Government, under guard of United States troops and artillery, Massachusetts militia and Boston police. Public excitement ran high, a futile attempt to rescue Burns having been made during his confinement, and the streets were crowded with tens of thousands of people, of whom many came from other towns and cities of the State to witness the humiliating spectacle.

I HEARD the train's shrill whistle call,
I saw an earnest look beseech,
And rather by that look than speech
My neighbor told me all.

And, as I thought of Liberty
Marched handcuffed down that sworded street,
The solid earth beneath my feet
Reeled fluid as the sea.

I felt a sense of bitter loss,—
Shame, tearless grief, and stifling wrath,
And loathing fear, as if my path
A serpent stretched across.

All love of home, all pride of place,
All generous confidence and trust,
Sank smothering in that deep disgust
And anguish of disgrace.

Down on my native hills of June,

And home's green quiet, hiding all,
Fell sudden darkness like the fall
Of midnight upon noon.

And Law, an unloosed maniac, strong,
Blood-drunken, through the blackness trod,
Hoarse-shouting in the ear of God
The blasphemy of wrong.

"O Mother, from thy memories proud,
Thy old renown, dear Commonwealth,
Lend this dead air a breeze of health,
And smite with stars this cloud.

"Mother of Freedom, wise and brave,
Rise awful in thy strength," I said;
Ah me! I spake but to the dead;
I stood upon her grave!

6th mo., 1854.

ARISEN AT LAST.

On the passage of the bill to protect the rights and liberties of the people of the State against the Fugitive Slave Act.

I SAID I stood upon thy grave,
My Mother State, when last the moon
Of blossoms clomb the skies of June.

And, scattering ashes on my head,
I wore, undreaming of relief,
The sackcloth of thy shame and grief.

Again that moon of blossoms shines
On leaf and flower and folded wing,
And thou hast risen with the spring!

Once more thy strong maternal arms
Are round about thy children flung,—
A lioness that guards her young!

No threat is on thy closed lips,
But in thine eye a power to smite
The mad wolf backward from its light.

Southward the baffled robber's track
Henceforth runs only; hereaway,
The fell lycanthrope finds no prey.

Henceforth, within thy sacred gates,
His first low howl shall downward draw

The thunder of thy righteous law.

Not mindless of thy trade and gain,
But, acting on the wiser plan,
Thou'rt grown conservative of man.

So shalt thou clothe with life the hope,
Dream-painted on the sightless eyes
Of him who sang of Paradise,—

The vision of a Christian man,
In virtue, as in stature great
Embodied in a Christian State.

And thou, amidst thy sisterhood
Forbearing long, yet standing fast,
Shalt win their grateful thanks at last;

When North and South shall strive no more,
And all their feuds and fears be lost
In Freedom's holy Pentecost.

6th mo., 1855.

THE HASCHISH.

OF all that Orient lands can vaunt
Of marvels with our own competing,
The strangest is the Haschish plant,
And what will follow on its eating.

What pictures to the taster rise,
Of Dervish or of Almeh dances!
Of Eblis, or of Paradise,
Set all aglow with Houri glances!

The poppy visions of Cathay,
The heavy beer-trance of the Suabian;
The wizard lights and demon play
Of nights Walpurgis and Arabian!

The Mollah and the Christian dog
Change place in mad metempsychosis;
The Muezzin climbs the synagogue,
The Rabbi shakes his beard at Moses!

The Arab by his desert well
Sits choosing from some Caliph's daughters,
And hears his single camel's bell
Sound welcome to his regal quarters.

The Koran's reader makes complaint
Of Shitan dancing on and off it;
The robber offers alms, the saint

Drinks Tokay and blasphemes the Prophet.

Such scenes that Eastern plant awakes;
But we have one ordained to beat it,
The Haschish of the West, which makes
Or fools or knaves of all who eat it.

The preacher eats, and straight appears
His Bible in a new translation;
Its angels negro overseers,
And Heaven itself a snug plantation!

The man of peace, about whose dreams
The sweet millennial angels cluster,
Tastes the mad weed, and plots and schemes,
A raving Cuban filibuster!

The noisiest Democrat, with ease,
It turns to Slavery's parish beadle;
The shrewdest statesman eats and sees
Due southward point the polar needle.

The Judge partakes, and sits erelong
Upon his bench a railing blackguard;
Decides off-hand that right is wrong,
And reads the ten commandments backward.

O potent plant! so rare a taste
Has never Turk or Gentoo gotten;

*The hempen Haschish of the East
Is powerless to our Western Cotton!*

1854.

FOR RIGHTEOUSNESS' SAKE.

Inscribed to friends under arrest for treason against the slave power.

THE age is dull and mean. Men creep,
Not walk; with blood too pale and tame
To pay the debt they owe to shame;
Buy cheap, sell dear; eat, drink, and sleep
Down-pillowed, deaf to moaning want;
Pay tithes for soul-insurance; keep
Six days to Mammon, one to Cant.

In such a time, give thanks to God,
That somewhat of the holy rage
With which the prophets in their age
On all its decent seemings trod,
Has set your feet upon the lie,
That man and ox and soul and clod
Are market stock to sell and buy!

The hot words from your lips, my own,
To caution trained, might not repeat;
But if some tares among the wheat
Of generous thought and deed were sown,
No common wrong provoked your zeal;
The silken gauntlet that is thrown
In such a quarrel rings like steel.

The brave old strife the fathers saw
For Freedom calls for men again
Like those who battled not in vain

For England's Charter, Alfred's law;
And right of speech and trial just
Wage in your name their ancient war
With venal courts and perjured trust.

God's ways seem dark, but, soon or late,
They touch the shining hills of day;
The evil cannot brook delay,
The good can well afford to wait.
Give ermined knaves their hour of crime;
Ye have the future grand and great,
The safe appeal of Truth to Time!

1855.

THE KANSAS EMIGRANTS.

This poem and the three following were called out by the popular movement of Free State men to occupy the territory of Kansas, and by the use of the great democratic weapon—an over-powering majority—to settle the conflict on that ground between Freedom and Slavery. The opponents of the movement used another kind of weapon.

WE cross the prairie as of old
The pilgrims crossed the sea,
To make the West, as they the East,
The homestead of the free!

We go to rear a wall of men
On Freedom's southern line,
And plant beside the cotton-tree
The rugged Northern pine!

We're flowing from our native hills
As our free rivers flow;
The blessing of our Mother-land
Is on us as we go.

We go to plant her common schools,
On distant prairie swells,
And give the Sabbaths of the wild
The music of her bells.

Upbearing, like the Ark of old,
The Bible in our van,
We go to test the truth of God
Against the fraud of man.

No pause, nor rest, save where the streams
That feed the Kansas run,
Save where our Pilgrim gonfalon
Shall flout the setting sun.

We'll tread the prairie as of old
Our fathers sailed the sea,
And make the West, as they the East,
The homestead of the free!

1854.

LETTER FROM A MISSIONARY OF THE METHODIST EPISCOPAL CHURCH SOUTH,

IN KANSAS, TO A DISTINGUISHED POLITICIAN.

DOUGLAS MISSION, August, 1854,

LAST week—the Lord be praised for all His mercies
To His unworthy servant!—I arrived
Safe at the Mission, via Westport; where
I tarried over night, to aid in forming
A Vigilance Committee, to send back,
In shirts of tar, and feather-doublets quilted
With forty stripes save one, all Yankee comers,
Uncircumcised and Gentile, aliens from
The Commonwealth of Israel, who despise
The prize of the high calling of the saints,
Who plant amidst this heathen wilderness
Pure gospel institutions, sanctified
By patriarchal use. The meeting opened
With prayer, as was most fitting. Half an hour,
Or thereaway, I groaned, and strove, and wrestled,
As Jacob did at Penuel, till the power
Fell on the people, and they cried 'Amen!'
"Glory to God!" and stamped and clapped their hands;
And the rough river boatmen wiped their eyes;
"Go it, old hoss!" they cried, and cursed the niggers—
Fulfilling thus the word of prophecy,
"Cursed be Cannan." After prayer, the meeting
Chose a committee—good and pious men—
A Presbyterian Elder, Baptist deacon,
A local preacher, three or four class-leaders,

Anxious inquirers, and renewed backsliders,
A score in all—to watch the river ferry,
(As they of old did watch the fords of Jordan,)
And cut off all whose Yankee tongues refuse
The Shibboleth of the Nebraska bill.
And then, in answer to repeated calls,
I gave a brief account of what I saw
In Washington; and truly many hearts
Rejoiced to know the President, and you
And all the Cabinet regularly hear
The gospel message of a Sunday morning,
Drinking with thirsty souls of the sincere
Milk of the Word. Glory! Amen, and Selah!

Here, at the Mission, all things have gone well
The brother who, throughout my absence, acted
As overseer, assures me that the crops
Never were better. I have lost one negro,
A first-rate hand, but obstinate and sullen.
He ran away some time last spring, and hid
In the river timber. There my Indian converts
Found him, and treed and shot him. For the rest,
The heathens round about begin to feel
The influence of our pious ministrations
And works of love; and some of them already
Have purchased negroes, and are settling down
As sober Christians! Bless the Lord for this!
I know it will rejoice you. You, I hear,
Are on the eve of visiting Chicago,

To fight with the wild beasts of Ephesus,
Long John, and Dutch Free-Soilers. May your arm
Be clothed with strength, and on your tongue be found
The sweet oil of persuasion. So desires
Your brother and co-laborer. Amen!

P.S. All's lost. Even while I write these lines,
The Yankee abolitionists are coming
Upon us like a flood—grim, stalwart men,
Each face set like a flint of Plymouth Rock
Against our institutions—staking out
Their farm lots on the wooded Wakarusa,
Or squatting by the mellow-bottomed Kansas;
The pioneers of mightier multitudes,
The small rain-patter, ere the thunder shower
Drowns the dry prairies. Hope from man is not.
Oh, for a quiet berth at Washington,
Snug naval chaplaincy, or clerkship, where
These rumors of free labor and free soil
Might never meet me more. Better to be
Door-keeper in the White House, than to dwell
Amidst these Yankee tents, that, whitening, show
On the green prairie like a fleet becalmed.
Methinks I hear a voice come up the river
From those far bayous, where the alligators
Mount guard around the camping filibusters
"Shake off the dust of Kansas. Turn to Cuba—
(That golden orange just about to fall,
O'er-ripe, into the Democratic lap;)

Keep pace with Providence, or, as we say,
Manifest destiny. Go forth and follow
The message of our gospel, thither borne
Upon the point of Quitman's bowie-knife,
And the persuasive lips of Colt's revolvers.
There may'st thou, underneath thy vine and figtree,
Watch thy increase of sugar cane and negroes,
Calm as a patriarch in his eastern tent!"
Amen: So mote it be. So prays your friend.

BURIAL OF BARBER.

Thomas Barber was shot December 6, 1855, near Lawrence, Kansas.

BEAR him, comrades, to his grave;
Never over one more brave
Shall the prairie grasses weep,
In the ages yet to come,
When the millions in our room,
What we sow in tears, shall reap.

Bear him up the icy hill,
With the Kansas, frozen still
As his noble heart, below,
And the land he came to till
With a freeman's thews and will,
And his poor hut roofed with snow.

One more look of that dead face,
Of his murder's ghastly trace!
One more kiss, O widowed one
Lay your left hands on his brow,
Lift your right hands up, and vow
That his work shall yet be done.

Patience, friends! The eye of God
Every path by Murder trod
Watches, lidless, day and night;
And the dead man in his shroud,
And his widow weeping loud,
And our hearts, are in His sight.

Every deadly threat that swells
With the roar of gambling hells,
Every brutal jest and jeer,
Every wicked thought and plan
Of the cruel heart of man,
Though but whispered, He can hear!

We in suffering, they in crime,
Wait the just award of time,
Wait the vengeance that is due;
Not in vain a heart shall break,
Not a tear for Freedom's sake
Fall unheeded: God is true.

While the flag with stars bedecked
Threatens where it should protect,
And the Law shakes Hands with Crime,
What is left us but to wait,
Match our patience to our fate,
And abide the better time?

Patience, friends! The human heart
Everywhere shall take our part,
Everywhere for us shall pray;
On our side are nature's laws,
And God's life is in the cause
That we suffer for to-day.

Well to suffer is divine;
Pass the watchword down the line,
Pass the countersign: "Endure."
Not to him who rashly dares,
But to him who nobly bears,
Is the victor's garland sure.

Frozen earth to frozen breast,
Lay our slain one down to rest;
Lay him down in hope and faith,
And above the broken sod,
Once again, to Freedom's God,
Pledge ourselves for life or death,

That the State whose walls we lay,
In our blood and tears, to-day,
Shall be free from bonds of shame,
And our goodly land untrod
By the feet of Slavery, shod
With cursing as with flame!

Plant the Buckeye on his grave,
For the hunter of the slave
In its shadow cannot rest;
And let martyr mound and tree
Be our pledge and guaranty
Of the freedom of the West!

1856.

TO PENNSYLVANIA.

O STATE prayer-founded! never hung
Such choice upon a people's tongue,
Such power to bless or ban,
As that which makes thy whisper Fate,
For which on thee the centuries wait,
And destinies of man!

Across thy Alleghanian chain,
With groanings from a land in pain,
The west-wind finds its way:
Wild-wailing from Missouri's flood
The crying of thy children's blood
Is in thy ears to-day!

And unto thee in Freedom's hour
Of sorest need God gives the power
To ruin or to save;
To wound or heal, to blight or bless
With fertile field or wilderness,
A free home or a grave!

Then let thy virtue match the crime,
Rise to a level with the time;
And, if a son of thine
Betray or tempt thee, Brutus-like
For Fatherland and Freedom strike
As Justice gives the sign.

Wake, sleeper, from thy dream of ease,
The great occasion's forelock seize;
And let the north-wind strong,
And golden leaves of autumn, be
Thy coronal of Victory
And thy triumphal song.

10th me., 1856.

LE MARAIS DU CYGNE.

The massacre of unarmed and unoffending men, in Southern Kansas, in May, 1858, took place near the Marais du Cygne of the French voyageurs.

A BLUSH as of roses
Where rose never grew!
Great drops on the bunch-grass,
But not of the dew!
A taint in the sweet air
For wild bees to shun!
A stain that shall never
Bleach out in the sun.

Back, steed of the prairies
Sweet song-bird, fly back!
Wheel hither, bald vulture!
Gray wolf, call thy pack!
The foul human vultures
Have feasted and fled;
The wolves of the Border
Have crept from the dead.

From the hearths of their cabins,
The fields of their corn,
Unwarned and unweaponed,
The victims were torn,—
By the whirlwind of murder
Swooped up and swept on
To the low, reedy fen-lands,
The Marsh of the Swan.

*With a vain plea for mercy
No stout knee was crooked;
In the mouths of the rifles
Right manly they looked.
How paled the May sunshine,
O Marais du Cygne!
On death for the strong life,
On red grass for green!*

*In the homes of their rearing,
Yet warm with their lives,
Ye wait the dead only,
Poor children and wives!
Put out the red forge-fire,
The smith shall not come;
Unyoke the brown oxen,
The ploughman lies dumb.*

*Wind slow from the Swan's Marsh,
O dreary death-train,
With pressed lips as bloodless
As lips of the slain!
Kiss down the young eyelids,
Smooth down the gray hairs;
Let tears quench the curses
That burn through your prayers.*

*Strong man of the prairies,
Mourn bitter and wild!*

Wail, desolate woman!
Weep, fatherless child!
But the grain of God springs up
From ashes beneath,
And the crown of his harvest
Is life out of death.

Not in vain on the dial
The shade moves along,
To point the great contrasts
Of right and of wrong:
Free homes and free altars,
Free prairie and flood,—
The reeds of the Swan's Marsh,
Whose bloom is of blood!

On the lintels of Kansas
That blood shall not dry;
Henceforth the Bad Angel
Shall harmless go by;
Henceforth to the sunset,
Unchecked on her way,
Shall Liberty follow
The march of the day.

THE PASS OF THE SIERRA.

ALL night above their rocky bed
They saw the stars march slow;
The wild Sierra overhead,
The desert's death below.

The Indian from his lodge of bark,
The gray bear from his den,
Beyond their camp-fire's wall of dark,
Glared on the mountain men.

Still upward turned, with anxious strain,
Their leader's sleepless eye,
Where splinters of the mountain chain
Stood black against the sky.

The night waned slow: at last, a glow,
A gleam of sudden fire,
Shot up behind the walls of snow,
And tipped each icy spire.

"Up, men!" he cried, "yon rocky cone,
To-day, please God, we'll pass,
And look from Winter's frozen throne
On Summer's flowers and grass!"

They set their faces to the blast,
They trod the eternal snow,
And faint, worn, bleeding, hailed at last

The promised land below.

Behind, they saw the snow-cloud tossed
By many an icy horn;
Before, warm valleys, wood-embossed,
And green with vines and corn.

They left the Winter at their backs
To flap his baffled wing,
And downward, with the cataracts,
Leaped to the lap of Spring.

Strong leader of that mountain band,
Another task remains,
To break from Slavery's desert land
A path to Freedom's plains.

The winds are wild, the way is drear,
Yet, flashing through the night,
Lo! icy ridge and rocky spear
Blaze out in morning light!

Rise up, Fremont! and go before;
The hour must have its Man;
Put on the hunting-shirt once more,
And lead in Freedom's van!
8th mo., 1856.

A SONG FOR THE TIME.

Written in the summer of 1856, during the political campaign of the Free Soil party under the candidacy of John C. Fremont.

Up, laggards of Freedom!—our free flag is cast
To the blaze of the sun and the wings of the blast;
Will ye turn from a struggle so bravely begun,
From a foe that is breaking, a field that's half won?

Whoso loves not his kind, and who fears not the Lord,
Let him join that foe's service, accursed and abhorred
Let him do his base will, as the slave only can,—
Let him put on the bloodhound, and put off the Man!

Let him go where the cold blood that creeps in his veins
Shall stiffen the slave-whip, and rust on his chains;
Where the black slave shall laugh in his bonds, to behold
The White Slave beside him, self-fettered and sold!

But ye, who still boast of hearts beating and warm,
Rise, from lake shore and ocean's, like waves in a storm,
Come, throng round our banner in Liberty's name,
Like winds from your mountains, like prairies aflame!

Our foe, hidden long in his ambush of night,
Now, forced from his covert, stands black in the light.
Oh, the cruel to Man, and the hateful to God,
Smite him down to the earth, that is cursed where he trod!

For deeper than thunder of summer's loud shower,

On the dome of the sky God is striking the hour!
Shall we falter before what we've prayed for so long,
When the Wrong is so weak, and the Right is so strong?

Come forth all together! come old and come young,
Freedom's vote in each hand, and her song on each tongue;
Truth naked is stronger than Falsehood in mail;
The Wrong cannot prosper, the Right cannot fail.

Like leaves of the summer once numbered the foe,
But the hoar-frost is falling, the northern winds blow;
Like leaves of November erelong shall they fall,
For earth wearies of them, and God's over all!

WHAT OF THE DAY?

Written during the stirring weeks when the great political battle for Freedom under Fremont's leadership was permitting strong hope of success,—a hope overshadowed and solemnized by a sense of the magnitude of the barbaric evil, and a forecast of the unscrupulous and desperate use of all its powers in the last and decisive struggle.

A SOUND of tumult troubles all the air,
Like the low thunders of a sultry sky
Far-rolling ere the downright lightnings glare;
The hills blaze red with warnings; foes draw nigh,
Treading the dark with challenge and reply.
Behold the burden of the prophet's vision;
The gathering hosts,—the Valley of Decision,
Dusk with the wings of eagles wheeling o'er.
Day of the Lord, of darkness and not light!
It breaks in thunder and the whirlwind's roar
Even so, Father! Let Thy will be done;
Turn and o'erturn, end what Thou hast begun
In judgment or in mercy: as for me,
If but the least and frailest, let me be
Evermore numbered with the truly free
Who find Thy service perfect liberty!
I fain would thank Thee that my mortal life
Has reached the hour (albeit through care and pain)
When Good and Evil, as for final strife,
Close dim and vast on Armageddon's plain;
And Michael and his angels once again
Drive howling back the Spirits of the Night.
Oh for the faith to read the signs aright
And, from the angle of Thy perfect sight,

See Truth's white banner floating on before;
And the Good Cause, despite of venal friends,
And base expedients, move to noble ends;
See Peace with Freedom make to Time amends,
And, through its cloud of dust, the threshing-floor,
Flailed by the thunder, heaped with chaffless grain.

1856.

A SONG, INSCRIBED TO THE FREMONT CLUBS.

Written after the election in 1586, which showed the immense gains of the Free Soil party, and insured its success in 1860.

BENEATH thy skies, November!
Thy skies of cloud and rain,
Around our blazing camp-fires
We close our ranks again.
Then sound again the bugles,
Call the muster-roll anew;
If months have well-nigh won the field,
What may not four years do?

For God be praised! New England
Takes once more her ancient place;
Again the Pilgrim's banner
Leads the vanguard of the race.
Then sound again the bugles, etc.

Along the lordly Hudson,
A shout of triumph breaks;
The Empire State is speaking,
From the ocean to the lakes.
Then sound again the bugles, etc.

The Northern hills are blazing,
The Northern skies are bright;
And the fair young West is turning
Her forehead to the light!

Then sound again the bugles, etc.

Push every outpost nearer,
Press hard the hostile towers!
Another Balaklava,
And the Malakoff is ours!
Then sound again the bugles,
Call the muster-roll anew;
If months have well-nigh won the field,
What may not four years do?

THE PANORAMA.

"A! fredome is a nobill thing!
Fredome mayse man to haif liking.
Fredome all solace to man giffis;
He levys at ese that frely levys
A nobil hart may haif nane ese
Na ellvs nocht that may him plese
Gyff Fredome failythe."
ARCHDEACON BARBOUR.

THROUGH the long hall the shuttered windows shed
A dubious light on every upturned head;
On locks like those of Absalom the fair,
On the bald apex ringed with scanty hair,
On blank indifference and on curious stare;
On the pale Showman reading from his stage
The hieroglyphics of that facial page;
Half sad, half scornful, listening to the bruit
Of restless cane-tap and impatient foot,
And the shrill call, across the general din,
"Roll up your curtain! Let the show begin!"

At length a murmur like the winds that break
Into green waves the prairie's grassy lake,
Deepened and swelled to music clear and loud,
And, as the west-wind lifts a summer cloud,
The curtain rose, disclosing wide and far
A green land stretching to the evening star,
Fair rivers, skirted by primeval trees
And flowers hummed over by the desert bees,

*Marked by tall bluffs whose slopes of greenness show
Fantastic outcrops of the rock below;
The slow result of patient Nature's pains,
And plastic fingering of her sun and rains;
Arch, tower, and gate, grotesquely windowed hall,
And long escarpment of half-crumbled wall,
Huger than those which, from steep hills of vine,
Stare through their loopholes on the travelled Rhine;
Suggesting vaguely to the gazer's mind
A fancy, idle as the prairie wind,
Of the land's dwellers in an age unguessed;
The unsung Jotuns of the mystic West.*

*Beyond, the prairie's sea-like swells surpass
The Tartar's marvels of his Land of Grass,
Vast as the sky against whose sunset shores
Wave after wave the billowy greenness pours;
And, onward still, like islands in that main
Loom the rough peaks of many a mountain chain,
Whence east and west a thousand waters run
From winter lingering under summer's sun.
And, still beyond, long lines of foam and sand
Tell where Pacific rolls his waves a-land,
From many a wide-lapped port and land-locked bay,
Opening with thunderous pomp the world's highway
To Indian isles of spice, and marts of far Cathay.*

*"Such," said the Showman, as the curtain fell,
"Is the new Canaan of our Israel;*

The land of promise to the swarming North,
Which, hive-like, sends its annual surplus forth,
To the poor Southron on his worn-out soil,
Scathed by the curses of unnatural toil;
To Europe's exiles seeking home and rest,
And the lank nomads of the wandering West,
Who, asking neither, in their love of change
And the free bison's amplitude of range,
Rear the log-hut, for present shelter meant,
Not future comfort, like an Arab's tent."

Then spake a shrewd on-looker, "Sir," said he,
"I like your picture, but I fain would see
A sketch of what your promised land will be
When, with electric nerve, and fiery-brained,
With Nature's forces to its chariot chained,
The future grasping, by the past obeyed,
The twentieth century rounds a new decade."

Then said the Showman, sadly: "He who grieves
Over the scattering of the sibyl's leaves
Unwisely mourns. Suffice it, that we know
What needs must ripen from the seed we sow;
That present time is but the mould wherein
We cast the shapes of holiness and sin.
A painful watcher of the passing hour,
Its lust of gold, its strife for place and power;
Its lack of manhood, honor, reverence, truth,
Wise-thoughted age, and generous-hearted youth;

Nor yet unmindful of each better sign,
The low, far lights, which on th' horizon shine,
Like those which sometimes tremble on the rim
Of clouded skies when day is closing dim,
Flashing athwart the purple spears of rain
The hope of sunshine on the hills again
I need no prophet's word, nor shapes that pass
Like clouding shadows o'er a magic glass;
For now, as ever, passionless and cold,
Doth the dread angel of the future hold
Evil and good before us, with no voice
Or warning look to guide us in our choice;
With spectral hands outreaching through the gloom
The shadowy contrasts of the coming doom.
Transferred from these, it now remains to give
The sun and shade of Fate's alternative."

Then, with a burst of music, touching all
The keys of thrifty life,—the mill-stream's fall,
The engine's pant along its quivering rails,
The anvil's ring, the measured beat of flails,
The sweep of scythes, the reaper's whistled tune,
Answering the summons of the bells of noon,
The woodman's hail along the river shores,
The steamboat's signal, and the dip of oars
Slowly the curtain rose from off a land
Fair as God's garden. Broad on either hand
The golden wheat-fields glimmered in the sun,
And the tall maize its yellow tassels spun.

Smooth highways set with hedge-rows living green,
With steepled towns through shaded vistas seen,
The school-house murmuring with its hive-like swarm,
The brook-bank whitening in the grist-mill's storm,
The painted farm-house shining through the leaves
Of fruited orchards bending at its eaves,
Where live again, around the Western hearth,
The homely old-time virtues of the North;
Where the blithe housewife rises with the day,
And well-paid labor counts his task a play.
And, grateful tokens of a Bible free,
And the free Gospel of Humanity,
Of diverse-sects and differing names the shrines,
One in their faith, whate'er their outward signs,
Like varying strophes of the same sweet hymn
From many a prairie's swell and river's brim,
A thousand church-spires sanctify the air
Of the calm Sabbath, with their sign of prayer.

Like sudden nightfall over bloom and green
The curtain dropped: and, momently, between
The clank of fetter and the crack of thong,
Half sob, half laughter, music swept along;
A strange refrain, whose idle words and low,
Like drunken mourners, kept the time of woe;
As if the revellers at a masquerade
Heard in the distance funeral marches played.
Such music, dashing all his smiles with tears,
The thoughtful voyager on Ponchartrain hears,

Where, through the noonday dusk of wooded shores
The negro boatman, singing to his oars,
With a wild pathos borrowed of his wrong
Redeems the jargon of his senseless song.
"Look," said the Showman, sternly, as he rolled
His curtain upward. "Fate's reverse behold!"

A village straggling in loose disarray
Of vulgar newness, premature decay;
A tavern, crazy with its whiskey brawls,
With "Slaves at Auction!" garnishing its walls;
Without, surrounded by a motley crowd,
The shrewd-eyed salesman, garrulous and loud,
A squire or colonel in his pride of place,
Known at free fights, the caucus, and the race,
Prompt to proclaim his honor without blot,
And silence doubters with a ten-pace shot,
Mingling the negro-driving bully's rant
With pious phrase and democratic cant,
Yet never scrupling, with a filthy jest,
To sell the infant from its mother's breast,
Break through all ties of wedlock, home, and kin,
Yield shrinking girlhood up to graybeard sin;
Sell all the virtues with his human stock,
The Christian graces on his auction-block,
And coolly count on shrewdest bargains driven
In hearts regenerate, and in souls forgiven!

Look once again! The moving canvas shows

A slave plantation's slovenly repose,
Where, in rude cabins rotting midst their weeds,
The human chattel eats, and sleeps, and breeds;
And, held a brute, in practice, as in law,
Becomes in fact the thing he's taken for.
There, early summoned to the hemp and corn,
The nursing mother leaves her child new-born;
There haggard sickness, weak and deathly faint,
Crawls to his task, and fears to make complaint;
And sad-eyed Rachels, childless in decay,
Weep for their lost ones sold and torn away!
Of ampler size the master's dwelling stands,
In shabby keeping with his half-tilled lands;
The gates unhinged, the yard with weeds unclean,
The cracked veranda with a tipsy lean.
Without, loose-scattered like a wreck adrift,
Signs of misrule and tokens of unthrift;
Within, profusion to discomfort joined,
The listless body and the vacant mind;
The fear, the hate, the theft and falsehood, born
In menial hearts of toil, and stripes, and scorn
There, all the vices, which, like birds obscene,
Batten on slavery loathsome and unclean,
From the foul kitchen to the parlor rise,
Pollute the nursery where the child-heir lies,
Taint infant lips beyond all after cure,
With the fell poison of a breast impure;
Touch boyhood's passions with the breath of flame,
From girlhood's instincts steal the blush of shame.

So swells, from low to high, from weak to strong,
The tragic chorus of the baleful wrong;
Guilty or guiltless, all within its range
Feel the blind justice of its sure revenge.

Still scenes like these the moving chart reveals.
Up the long western steppes the blighting steals;
Down the Pacific slope the evil Fate
Glides like a shadow to the Golden Gate
From sea to sea the drear eclipse is thrown,
From sea to sea the Mauvaises Terres have grown,
A belt of curses on the New World's zone!

The curtain fell. All drew a freer breath,
As men are wont to do when mournful death
Is covered from their sight. The Showman stood
With drooping brow in sorrow's attitude
One moment, then with sudden gesture shook
His loose hair back, and with the air and look
Of one who felt, beyond the narrow stage
And listening group, the presence of the age,
And heard the footsteps of the things to be,
Poured out his soul in earnest words and free.

"O friends!" he said, "in this poor trick of paint
You see the semblance, incomplete and faint,
Of the two-fronted Future, which, to-day,
Stands dim and silent, waiting in your way.
To-day, your servant, subject to your will;

To-morrow, master, or for good or ill.
If the dark face of Slavery on you turns,
If the mad curse its paper barrier spurns,
If the world granary of the West is made
The last foul market of the slaver's trade,
Why rail at fate? The mischief is your own.
Why hate your neighbor? Blame yourselves alone!

"Men of the North! The South you charge with wrong
Is weak and poor, while you are rich and strong.
If questions,—idle and absurd as those
The old-time monks and Paduan doctors chose,—
Mere ghosts of questions, tariffs, and dead banks,
And scarecrow pontiffs, never broke your ranks,
Your thews united could, at once, roll back
The jostled nation to its primal track.
Nay, were you simply steadfast, manly, just,
True to the faith your fathers left in trust,
If stainless honor outweighed in your scale
A codfish quintal or a factory bale,
Full many a noble heart, (and such remain
In all the South, like Lot in Siddim's plain,
Who watch and wait, and from the wrong's control
Keep white and pure their chastity of soul,)
Now sick to loathing of your weak complaints,
Your tricks as sinners, and your prayers as saints,
Would half-way meet the frankness of your tone,
And feel their pulses beating with your own.

*"The North! the South! no geographic line
Can fix the boundary or the point define,
Since each with each so closely interblends,
Where Slavery rises, and where Freedom ends.
Beneath your rocks the roots, far-reaching, hide
Of the fell Upas on the Southern side;
The tree whose branches in your northwinds wave
Dropped its young blossoms on Mount Vernon's grave;
The nursling growth of Monticello's crest
Is now the glory of the free Northwest;
To the wise maxims of her olden school
Virginia listened from thy lips, Rantoul;
Seward's words of power, and Sumner's fresh renown,
Flow from the pen that Jefferson laid down!
And when, at length, her years of madness o'er,
Like the crowned grazer on Euphrates' shore,
From her long lapse to savagery, her mouth
Bitter with baneful herbage, turns the South,
Resumes her old attire, and seeks to smooth
Her unkempt tresses at the glass of truth,
Her early faith shall find a tongue again,
New Wythes and Pinckneys swell that old refrain,
Her sons with yours renew the ancient pact,
The myth of Union prove at last a fact!
Then, if one murmur mars the wide content,
Some Northern lip will drawl the last dissent,
Some Union-saving patriot of your own
Lament to find his occupation gone.*

"Grant that the North's insulted, scorned, betrayed,
O'erreached in bargains with her neighbor made,
When selfish thrift and party held the scales
For peddling dicker, not for honest sales,—
Whom shall we strike? Who most deserves our blame?
The braggart Southron, open in his aim,
And bold as wicked, crashing straight through all
That bars his purpose, like a cannon-ball?
Or the mean traitor, breathing northern air,
With nasal speech and puritanic hair,
Whose cant the loss of principle survives,
As the mud-turtle e'en its head outlives;
Who, caught, chin-buried in some foul offence,
Puts on a look of injured innocence,
And consecrates his baseness to the cause
Of constitution, union, and the laws?

"Praise to the place-man who can hold aloof
His still unpurchased manhood, office-proof;
Who on his round of duty walks erect,
And leaves it only rich in self-respect;
As More maintained his virtue's lofty port
In the Eighth Henry's base and bloody court.
But, if exceptions here and there are found,
Who tread thus safely on enchanted ground,
The normal type, the fitting symbol still
Of those who fatten at the public mill,
Is the chained dog beside his master's door,
Or Circe's victim, feeding on all four!

"Give me the heroes who, at tuck of drum,
Salute thy staff, immortal Quattlebum!
Or they who, doubly armed with vote and gun,
Following thy lead, illustrious Atchison,
Their drunken franchise shift from scene to scene,
As tile-beard Jourdan did his guillotine!
Rather than him who, born beneath our skies,
To Slavery's hand its supplest tool supplies;
The party felon whose unblushing face
Looks from the pillory of his bribe of place,
And coolly makes a merit of disgrace,
Points to the footmarks of indignant scorn,
Shows the deep scars of satire's tossing horn;
And passes to his credit side the sum
Of all that makes a scoundrel's martyrdom!

"Bane of the North, its canker and its moth!
These modern Esaus, bartering rights for broth!
Taxing our justice, with their double claim,
As fools for pity, and as knaves for blame;
Who, urged by party, sect, or trade, within
The fell embrace of Slavery's sphere of sin,
Part at the outset with their moral sense,
The watchful angel set for Truth's defence;
Confound all contrasts, good and ill; reverse
The poles of life, its blessing and its curse;
And lose thenceforth from their perverted sight
The eternal difference 'twixt the wrong and right;
To them the Law is but the iron span

That girds the ankles of imbruted man;
To them the Gospel has no higher aim
Than simple sanction of the master's claim,
Dragged in the slime of Slavery's loathsome trail,
Like Chalier's Bible at his ass's tail!

"Such are the men who, with instinctive dread,
Whenever Freedom lifts her drooping head,
Make prophet-tripods of their office-stools,
And scare the nurseries and the village schools
With dire presage of ruin grim and great,
A broken Union and a foundered State!
Such are the patriots, self-bound to the stake
Of office, martyrs for their country's sake
Who fill themselves the hungry jaws of Fate;
And by their loss of manhood save the State.
In the wide gulf themselves like Cortius throw,
And test the virtues of cohesive dough;
As tropic monkeys, linking heads and tails,
Bridge o'er some torrent of Ecuador's vales!

"Such are the men who in your churches rave
To swearing-point, at mention of the slave!
When some poor parson, haply unawares,
Stammers of freedom in his timid prayers;
Who, if some foot-sore negro through the town
Steals northward, volunteer to hunt him down.
Or, if some neighbor, flying from disease,
Courts the mild balsam of the Southern breeze,

With hue and cry pursue him on his track,
And write Free-soiler on the poor man's back.
Such are the men who leave the pedler's cart,
While faring South, to learn the driver's art,
Or, in white neckcloth, soothe with pious aim
The graceful sorrows of some languid dame,
Who, from the wreck of her bereavement, saves
The double charm of widowhood and slaves
Pliant and apt, they lose no chance to show
To what base depths apostasy can go;
Outdo the natives in their readiness
To roast a negro, or to mob a press;
Poise a tarred schoolmate on the lyncher's rail,
Or make a bonfire of their birthplace mail!

"So some poor wretch, whose lips no longer bear
The sacred burden of his mother's prayer,
By fear impelled, or lust of gold enticed,
Turns to the Crescent from the Cross of Christ,
And, over-acting in superfluous zeal,
Crawls prostrate where the faithful only kneel,
Out-howls the Dervish, hugs his rags to court
The squalid Santon's sanctity of dirt;
And, when beneath the city gateway's span
Files slow and long the Meccan caravan,
And through its midst, pursued by Islam's prayers,
The prophet's Word some favored camel bears,
The marked apostate has his place assigned
The Koran-bearer's sacred rump behind,

With brush and pitcher following, grave and mute,
In meek attendance on the holy brute!

"Men of the North! beneath your very eyes,
By hearth and home, your real danger lies.
Still day by day some hold of freedom falls
Through home-bred traitors fed within its walls.
Men whom yourselves with vote and purse sustain,
At posts of honor, influence, and gain;
The right of Slavery to your sons to teach,
And 'South-side' Gospels in your pulpits preach,
Transfix the Law to ancient freedom dear
On the sharp point of her subverted spear,
And imitate upon her cushion plump
The mad Missourian lynching from his stump;
Or, in your name, upon the Senate's floor
Yield up to Slavery all it asks, and more;
And, ere your dull eyes open to the cheat,
Sell your old homestead underneath your feet
While such as these your loftiest outlooks hold,
While truth and conscience with your wares are sold,
While grave-browed merchants band themselves to aid
An annual man-hunt for their Southern trade,
What moral power within your grasp remains
To stay the mischief on Nebraska's plains?
High as the tides of generous impulse flow,
As far rolls back the selfish undertow;
And all your brave resolves, though aimed as true
As the horse-pistol Balmawhapple drew,

To Slavery's bastions lend as slight a shock
As the poor trooper's shot to Stirling rock!

"Yet, while the need of Freedom's cause demands
The earnest efforts of your hearts and hands,
Urged by all motives that can prompt the heart
To prayer and toil and manhood's manliest part;
Though to the soul's deep tocsin Nature joins
The warning whisper of her Orphic pines,
The north-wind's anger, and the south-wind's sigh,
The midnight sword-dance of the northern sky,
And, to the ear that bends above the sod
Of the green grave-mounds in the Fields of God,
In low, deep murmurs of rebuke or cheer,
The land's dead fathers speak their hope or fear,
Yet let not Passion wrest from Reason's hand
The guiding rein and symbol of command.
Blame not the caution proffering to your zeal
A well-meant drag upon its hurrying wheel;
Nor chide the man whose honest doubt extends
To the means only, not the righteous ends;
Nor fail to weigh the scruples and the fears
Of milder natures and serener years.
In the long strife with evil which began
With the first lapse of new-created man,
Wisely and well has Providence assigned
To each his part,—some forward, some behind;
And they, too, serve who temper and restrain

The o'erwarm heart that sets on fire the brain.
True to yourselves, feed Freedom's altar-flame
With what you have; let others do the same.

"Spare timid doubters; set like flint your face
Against the self-sold knaves of gain and place
Pity the weak; but with unsparing hand
Cast out the traitors who infest the land;
From bar, press, pulpit, cast them everywhere,
By dint of fasting, if you fail by prayer.
And in their place bring men of antique mould,
Like the grave fathers of your Age of Gold;
Statesmen like those who sought the primal fount
Of righteous law, the Sermon on the Mount;
Lawyers who prize, like Quincy, (to our day
Still spared, Heaven bless him!) honor more than pay,
And Christian jurists, starry-pure, like Jay;
Preachers like Woolman, or like them who bore
The faith of Wesley to our Western shore,
And held no convert genuine till he broke
Alike his servants' and the Devil's yoke;
And priests like him who Newport's market trod,
And o'er its slave-ships shook the bolts of God!
So shall your power, with a wise prudence used,
Strong but forbearing, firm but not abused,
In kindly keeping with the good of all,
The nobler maxims of the past recall,
Her natural home-born right to Freedom give,

And leave her foe his robber-right,—to live.

Live, as the snake does in his noisome fen!
Live, as the wolf does in his bone-strewn den!
Live, clothed with cursing like a robe of flame,
The focal point of million-fingered shame!
Live, till the Southron, who, with all his faults,
Has manly instincts, in his pride revolts,
Dashes from off him, midst the glad world's cheers,
The hideous nightmare of his dream of years,
And lifts, self-prompted, with his own right hand,
The vile encumbrance from his glorious land!

"So, wheresoe'er our destiny sends forth
Its widening circles to the South or North,
Where'er our banner flaunts beneath the stars
Its mimic splendors and its cloudlike bars,
There shall Free Labor's hardy children stand
The equal sovereigns of a slaveless land.
And when at last the hunted bison tires,
And dies o'ertaken by the squatter's fires;
And westward, wave on wave, the living flood
Breaks on the snow-line of majestic Hood;
And lonely Shasta listening hears the tread
Of Europe's fair-haired children, Hesper-led;
And, gazing downward through his boar-locks, sees
The tawny Asian climb his giant knees,
The Eastern sea shall hush his waves to hear
Pacific's surf-beat answer Freedom's cheer,

And one long rolling fire of triumph run
Between the sunrise and the sunset gun!"

. . . .

My task is done. The Showman and his show,
Themselves but shadows, into shadows go;
And, if no song of idlesse I have sung,
Nor tints of beauty on the canvas flung;
If the harsh numbers grate on tender ears,
And the rough picture overwrought appears,
With deeper coloring, with a sterner blast,
Before my soul a voice and vision passed,
Such as might Milton's jarring trump require,
Or glooms of Dante fringed with lurid fire.
Oh, not of choice, for themes of public wrong
I leave the green and pleasant paths of song,
The mild, sweet words which soften and adorn,
For sharp rebuke and bitter laugh of scorn.
More dear to me some song of private worth,
Some homely idyl of my native North,
Some summer pastoral of her inland vales,
Or, grim and weird, her winter fireside tales
Haunted by ghosts of unreturning sails,
Lost barks at parting hung from stem to helm
With prayers of love like dreams on Virgil's elm.
Nor private grief nor malice holds my pen;
I owe but kindness to my fellow-men;
And, South or North, wherever hearts of prayer

Their woes and weakness to our Father bear,
Wherever fruits of Christian love are found
In holy lives, to me is holy ground.
But the time passes. It were vain to crave
A late indulgence. What I had I gave.
Forget the poet, but his warning heed,
And shame his poor word with your nobler deed.

1856.

ON A PRAYER-BOOK,

WITH ITS FRONTISPIECE, ARY SCHEFFER'S "CHRISTUS CONSOLATOR," AMERICANIZED BY THE OMISSION OF THE BLACK MAN.

It is hardly to be credited, yet is true, that in the anxiety of the Northern merchant to conciliate his Southern customer, a publisher was found ready thus to mutilate Scheffer's picture. He intended his edition for use in the Southern States undoubtedly, but copies fell into the hands of those who believed literally in a gospel which was to preach liberty to the captive.

O ARY SCHEFFER! when beneath thine eye,

Touched with the light that cometh from above,

Grew the sweet picture of the dear Lord's love,

No dream hadst thou that Christian hands would tear

Therefrom the token of His equal care,

And make thy symbol of His truth a lie

The poor, dumb slave whose shackles fall away

In His compassionate gaze, grubbed smoothly out,

To mar no more the exercise devout

Of sleek oppression kneeling down to pray

Where the great oriel stains the Sabbath day!

Let whoso can before such praying-books

Kneel on his velvet cushion; I, for one,

Would sooner bow, a Parsee, to the sun,

Or tend a prayer-wheel in Thibetar brooks,

Or beat a drum on Yedo's temple-floor.

No falser idol man has bowed before,

In Indian groves or islands of the sea,

Than that which through the quaint-carved Gothic door

Looks forth,—a Church without humanity!

Patron of pride, and prejudice, and wrong,—

The rich man's charm and fetich of the strong,

The Eternal Fulness meted, clipped, and shorn,
The seamless robe of equal mercy torn,
The dear Christ hidden from His kindred flesh,
And, in His poor ones, crucified afresh!
Better the simple Lama scattering wide,
Where sweeps the storm Alechan's steppes along,
His paper horses for the lost to ride,
And wearying Buddha with his prayers to make
The figures living for the traveller's sake,
Than he who hopes with cheap praise to beguile
The ear of God, dishonoring man the while;
Who dreams the pearl gate's hinges, rusty grown,
Are moved by flattery's oil of tongue alone;
That in the scale Eternal Justice bears
The generous deed weighs less than selfish prayers,
And words intoned with graceful unction move
The Eternal Goodness more than lives of truth and love.
Alas, the Church! The reverend head of Jay,
Enhaloed with its saintly silvered hair,
Adorns no more the places of her prayer;
And brave young Tyng, too early called away,
Troubles the Haman of her courts no more
Like the just Hebrew at the Assyrian's door;
And her sweet ritual, beautiful but dead
As the dry husk from which the grain is shed,
And holy hymns from which the life devout
Of saints and martyrs has wellnigh gone out,
Like candles dying in exhausted air,
For Sabbath use in measured grists are ground;

And, ever while the spiritual mill goes round,
Between the upper and the nether stones,
Unseen, unheard, the wretched bondman groans,
And urges his vain plea, prayer-smothered, anthem-drowned!

O heart of mine, keep patience! Looking forth,
As from the Mount of Vision, I behold,
Pure, just, and free, the Church of Christ on earth;
The martyr's dream, the golden age foretold!
And found, at last, the mystic Graal I see,
Brimmed with His blessing, pass from lip to lip
In sacred pledge of human fellowship;
And over all the songs of angels hear;
Songs of the love that casteth out all fear;
Songs of the Gospel of Humanity!
Lo! in the midst, with the same look He wore,
Healing and blessing on Genesaret's shore,
Folding together, with the all-tender might
Of His great love, the dark bands and the white,
Stands the Consoler, soothing every pain,
Making all burdens light, and breaking every chain.

1859.

THE SUMMONS.

MY ear is full of summer sounds,
Of summer sights my languid eye;
Beyond the dusty village bounds
I loiter in my daily rounds,
And in the noon-time shadows lie.

I hear the wild bee wind his horn,
The bird swings on the ripened wheat,
The long green lances of the corn
Are tilting in the winds of morn,
The locust shrills his song of heat.

Another sound my spirit hears,
A deeper sound that drowns them all;
A voice of pleading choked with tears,
The call of human hopes and fears,
The Macedonian cry to Paul!

The storm-bell rings, the trumpet blows;
I know the word and countersign;
Wherever Freedom's vanguard goes,
Where stand or fall her friends or foes,
I know the place that should be mine.

Shamed be the hands that idly fold,
And lips that woo the reed's accord,
When laggard Time the hour has tolled
For true with false and new with old
To fight the battles of the Lord!

O brothers! blest by partial Fate
With power to match the will and deed,
To him your summons comes too late
Who sinks beneath his armor's weight,
And has no answer but God-speed!
1860.

TO WILLIAM H. SEWARD.

On the 12th of January, 1861, Mr. Seward delivered in the Senate chamber a speech on The State of the Union, in which he urged the paramount duty of preserving the Union, and went as far as it was possible to go, without surrender of principles, in concessions to the Southern party, concluding his argument with these words: "Having submitted my own opinions on this great crisis, it remains only to say, that I shall cheerfully lend to the government my best support in whatever prudent yet energetic efforts it shall make to preserve the public peace, and to maintain and preserve the Union; advising, only, that it practise, as far as possible, the utmost moderation, forbearance, and conciliation.

"This Union has not yet accomplished what good for mankind was manifestly designed by Him who appoints the seasons and prescribes the duties of states and empires. No; if it were cast down by faction to-day, it would rise again and re-appear in all its majestic proportions to-morrow. It is the only government that can stand here. Woe! woe! to the man that madly lifts his hand against it. It shall continue and endure; and men, in after times, shall declare that this generation, which saved the Union from such sudden and unlooked-for dangers, surpassed in magnanimity even that one which laid its foundations in the eternal principles of liberty, justice, and humanity."

STATESMAN, I thank thee! and, if yet dissent

Mingles, reluctant, with my large content,

I cannot censure what was nobly meant.

But, while constrained to hold even Union less

Than Liberty and Truth and Righteousness,

I thank thee in the sweet and holy name

Of peace, for wise calm words that put to shame

Passion and party. Courage may be shown

Not in defiance of the wrong alone;

He may be bravest who, unweaponed, bears

The olive branch, and, strong in justice, spares

The rash wrong-doer, giving widest scope,

To Christian charity and generous hope.

If, without damage to the sacred cause

*Of Freedom and the safeguard of its laws—
If, without yielding that for which alone
We prize the Union, thou canst save it now
From a baptism of blood, upon thy brow
A wreath whose flowers no earthly soil have known;
Woven of the beatitudes, shall rest,
And the peacemaker be forever blest!*

1861.

IN WAR TIME.

TO SAMUEL E. SEWALL AND HARRIET W. SEWAll, OF MELROSE.

These lines to my old friends stood as dedication in the volume which contained a collection of pieces under the general title of In War Time. The group belonging distinctly under that title I have retained here; the other pieces in the volume are distributed among the appropriate divisions.

OLOR ISCANUS queries: "Why should we

Vex at the land's ridiculous miserie?"

So on his Usk banks, in the blood-red dawn

Of England's civil strife, did careless Vaughan

Bemock his times. O friends of many years!

Though faith and trust are stronger than our fears,

And the signs promise peace with liberty,

Not thus we trifle with our country's tears

And sweat of agony. The future's gain

Is certain as God's truth; but, meanwhile, pain

Is bitter and tears are salt: our voices take

A sober tone; our very household songs

Are heavy with a nation's griefs and wrongs;

And innocent mirth is chastened for the sake

Of the brave hearts that nevermore shall beat,

The eyes that smile no more, the unreturning

feet!

1863

THY WILL BE DONE.

WE see not, know not; all our way
Is night,—with Thee alone is day
From out the torrent's troubled drift,
Above the storm our prayers we lift,
Thy will be done!

The flesh may fail, the heart may faint,
But who are we to make complaint,
Or dare to plead, in times like these,
The weakness of our love of ease?
Thy will be done!

We take with solemn thankfulness
Our burden up, nor ask it less,
And count it joy that even we
May suffer, serve, or wait for Thee,
Whose will be done!

Though dim as yet in tint and line,
We trace Thy picture's wise design,
And thank Thee that our age supplies
Its dark relief of sacrifice.
Thy will be done!

And if, in our unworthiness,
Thy sacrificial wine we press;
If from Thy ordeal's heated bars
Our feet are seamed with crimson scars,

Thy will be done!

If, for the age to come, this hour
Of trial hath vicarious power,
And, blest by Thee, our present pain,
Be Liberty's eternal gain,
Thy will be done!

Strike, Thou the Master, we Thy keys,
The anthem of the destinies!
The minor of Thy loftier strain,
Our hearts shall breathe the old refrain,
Thy will be done!
1861.

A WORD FOR THE HOUR.

THE firmament breaks up. In black eclipse
Light after light goes out. One evil star,
Luridly glaring through the smoke of war,
As in the dream of the Apocalypse,
Drags others down. Let us not weakly weep
Nor rashly threaten. Give us grace to keep
Our faith and patience; wherefore should we leap
On one hand into fratricidal fight,
Or, on the other, yield eternal right,
Frame lies of law, and good and ill confound?
What fear we? Safe on freedom's vantage-ground
Our feet are planted: let us there remain
In unrevengeful calm, no means untried
Which truth can sanction, no just claim denied,
The sad spectators of a suicide!
They break the links of Union: shall we light
The fires of hell to weld anew the chain
On that red anvil where each blow is pain?
Draw we not even now a freer breath,
As from our shoulders falls a load of death
Loathsome as that the Tuscan's victim bore
When keen with life to a dead horror bound?
Why take we up the accursed thing again?
Pity, forgive, but urge them back no more
Who, drunk with passion, flaunt disunion's rag
With its vile reptile-blazon. Let us press
The golden cluster on our brave old flag
In closer union, and, if numbering less,

Brighter shall shine the stars which still remain.

16th First mo., 1861.

"EIN FESTE BURG IST UNSER GOTT."

LUTHER'S HYMN.

WE wait beneath the furnace-blast
The pangs of transformation;
Not painlessly doth God recast
And mould anew the nation.
Hot burns the fire
Where wrongs expire;
Nor spares the hand
That from the land
Uproots the ancient evil.

The hand-breadth cloud the sages feared
Its bloody rain is dropping;
The poison plant the fathers spared
All else is overtopping.
East, West, South, North,
It curses the earth;
All justice dies,
And fraud and lies
Live only in its shadow.

What gives the wheat-field blades of steel?
What points the rebel cannon?
What sets the roaring rabble's heel
On the old star-spangled pennon?
What breaks the oath
Of the men o' the South?
What whets the knife

For the Union's life?—
Hark to the answer: Slavery!

Then waste no blows on lesser foes
In strife unworthy freemen.
God lifts to-day the veil, and shows
The features of the demon
O North and South,
Its victims both,
Can ye not cry,
"Let slavery die!"
And union find in freedom?

What though the cast-out spirit tear
The nation in his going?
We who have shared the guilt must share
The pang of his o'erthrowing!
Whate'er the loss,
Whate'er the cross,
Shall they complain
Of present pain
Who trust in God's hereafter?

For who that leans on His right arm
Was ever yet forsaken?
What righteous cause can suffer harm
If He its part has taken?
Though wild and loud,
And dark the cloud,

Behind its folds
His hand upholds
The calm sky of to-morrow!

Above the maddening cry for blood,
Above the wild war-drumming,
Let Freedom's voice be heard, with good
The evil overcoming.
Give prayer and purse
To stay the Curse
Whose wrong we share,
Whose shame we bear,
Whose end shall gladden Heaven!

In vain the bells of war shall ring
Of triumphs and revenges,
While still is spared the evil thing
That severs and estranges.
But blest the ear
That yet shall hear
The jubilant bell
That rings the knell
Of Slavery forever!

Then let the selfish lip be dumb,
And hushed the breath of sighing;
Before the joy of peace must come
The pains of purifying.
God give us grace

Each in his place
To bear his lot,
And, murmuring not,
Endure and wait and labor!

1861.

TO JOHN C. FREMONT.

On the 31st of August, 1861, General Fremont, then in charge of the Western Department, issued a proclamation which contained a clause, famous as the first announcement of emancipation: "The property," it declared, "real and personal, of all persons in the State of Missouri, who shall take up arms against the United States, or who shall be directly proven to have taken active part with their enemies in the field, is declared to be confiscated to the public use; and their slaves, if any they have, are hereby declared free men." Mr. Lincoln regarded the proclamation as premature and countermanded it, after vainly endeavoring to persuade Fremont of his own motion to revoke it.

THY error, Fremont, simply was to act
A brave man's part, without the statesman's tact,
And, taking counsel but of common sense,
To strike at cause as well as consequence.
Oh, never yet since Roland wound his horn
At Roncesvalles, has a blast been blown
Far-heard, wide-echoed, startling as thine own,
Heard from the van of freedom's hope forlorn
It had been safer, doubtless, for the time,
To flatter treason, and avoid offence
To that Dark Power whose underlying crime
Heaves upward its perpetual turbulence.
But if thine be the fate of all who break
The ground for truth's seed, or forerun their years
Till lost in distance, or with stout hearts make
A lane for freedom through the level spears,
Still take thou courage! God has spoken through thee,
Irrevocable, the mighty words, Be free!
The land shakes with them, and the slave's dull ear
Turns from the rice-swamp stealthily to hear.
Who would recall them now must first arrest

The winds that blow down from the free Northwest,
Ruffling the Gulf; or like a scroll roll back
The Mississippi to its upper springs.
Such words fulfil their prophecy, and lack
But the full time to harden into things.

1861.

THE WATCHERS.

BESIDE a stricken field I stood;
On the torn turf, on grass and wood,
Hung heavily the dew of blood.

Still in their fresh mounds lay the slain,
But all the air was quick with pain
And gusty sighs and tearful rain.

Two angels, each with drooping head
And folded wings and noiseless tread,
Watched by that valley of the dead.

The one, with forehead saintly bland
And lips of blessing, not command,
Leaned, weeping, on her olive wand.

The other's brows were scarred and knit,
His restless eyes were watch-fires lit,
His hands for battle-gauntlets fit.
"How long!"—I knew the voice of Peace,—
"Is there no respite? no release?
When shall the hopeless quarrel cease?

"O Lord, how long!! One human soul
Is more than any parchment scroll,
Or any flag thy winds unroll.

"What price was Ellsworth's, young and brave?

*How weigh the gift that Lyon gave,
Or count the cost of Winthrop's grave?*

*"O brother! if thine eye can see,
Tell how and when the end shall be,
What hope remains for thee and me."*

*Then Freedom sternly said: "I shun
No strife nor pang beneath the sun,
When human rights are staked and won.*

*"I knelt with Ziska's hunted flock,
I watched in Toussaint's cell of rock,
I walked with Sidney to the block.*

*"The moor of Marston felt my tread,
Through Jersey snows the march I led,
My voice Magenta's charges sped.*

*"But now, through weary day and night,
I watch a vague and aimless fight
For leave to strike one blow aright.*

*"On either side my foe they own
One guards through love his ghastly throne,
And one through fear to reverence grown.*

*"Why wait we longer, mocked, betrayed,
By open foes, or those afraid*

To speed thy coming through my aid?

"Why watch to see who win or fall?
I shake the dust against them all,
I leave them to their senseless brawl."

"Nay," Peace implored: "yet longer wait;
The doom is near, the stake is great
God knoweth if it be too late.

"Still wait and watch; the way prepare
Where I with folded wings of prayer
May follow, weaponless and bare."

"Too late!" the stern, sad voice replied,
"Too late!" its mournful echo sighed,
In low lament the answer died.

A rustling as of wings in flight,
An upward gleam of lessening white,
So passed the vision, sound and sight.

But round me, like a silver bell
Rung down the listening sky to tell
Of holy help, a sweet voice fell.

"Still hope and trust," it sang; "the rod
Must fall, the wine-press must be trod,

But all is possible with God!"

1862.

TO ENGLISHMEN.

Written when, in the stress of our terrible war, the English ruling class, with few exceptions, were either coldly indifferent or hostile to the party of freedom. Their attitude was illustrated by caricatures of America, among which was one of a slaveholder and cowhide, with the motto, "Haven't I a right to wallop my nigger?"

You flung your taunt across the wave
We bore it as became us,
Well knowing that the fettered slave
Left friendly lips no option save
To pity or to blame us.

You scoffed our plea. "Mere lack of will,
Not lack of power," you told us
We showed our free-state records; still
You mocked, confounding good and ill,
Slave-haters and slaveholders.

We struck at Slavery; to the verge
Of power and means we checked it;
Lo!—presto, change! its claims you urge,
Send greetings to it o'er the surge,
And comfort and protect it.

But yesterday you scarce could shake,
In slave-abhorring rigor,
Our Northern palms for conscience' sake
To-day you clasp the hands that ache
With "walloping the nigger!"

O Englishmen!—in hope and creed,

In blood and tongue our brothers!
We too are heirs of Runnymede;
And Shakespeare's fame and Cromwell's deed
Are not alone our mother's.

"Thicker than water," in one rill
Through centuries of story
Our Saxon blood has flowed, and still
We share with you its good and ill,
The shadow and the glory.

Joint heirs and kinfolk, leagues of wave
Nor length of years can part us
Your right is ours to shrine and grave,
The common freehold of the brave,
The gift of saints and martyrs.
Our very sins and follies teach
Our kindred frail and human
We carp at faults with bitter speech,
The while, for one unshared by each,
We have a score in common.

We bowed the heart, if not the knee,
To England's Queen, God bless her
We praised you when your slaves went free
We seek to unchain ours. Will ye
Join hands with the oppressor?

And is it Christian England cheers

The bruiser, not the bruised?
And must she run, despite the tears
And prayers of eighteen hundred years,
Amuck in Slavery's crusade?

Oh, black disgrace! Oh, shame and loss
Too deep for tongue to phrase on
Tear from your flag its holy cross,
And in your van of battle toss
The pirate's skull-bone blazon!

1862.

MITHRIDATES AT CHIOS.

It is recorded that the Chians, when subjugated by Mithridates of Cappadocia, were delivered up to their own slaves, to be carried away captive to Colchis. Athenxus considers this a just punishment for their wickedness in first introducing the slave-trade into Greece. From this ancient villany of the Chians the proverb arose, "The Chian hath bought himself a master."

KNOW'ST thou, O slave-cursed land
How, when the Chian's cup of guilt
Was full to overflow, there came
God's justice in the sword of flame
That, red with slaughter to its hilt,
Blazed in the Cappadocian victor's hand?

The heavens are still and far;
But, not unheard of awful Jove,
The sighing of the island slave
Was answered, when the AEgean wave
The keels of Mithridates clove,
And the vines shrivelled in the breath of war.

"Robbers of Chios! hark,"
The victor cried, "to Heaven's decree!
Pluck your last cluster from the vine,
Drain your last cup of Chian wine;
Slaves of your slaves, your doom shall be,
In Colchian mines by Phasis rolling dark."

Then rose the long lament
From the hoar sea-god's dusky caves
The priestess rent her hair and cried,

"Woe! woe! The gods are sleepless-eyed!"
And, chained and scourged, the slaves of slaves,
The lords of Chios into exile went.

"The gods at last pay well,"
So Hellas sang her taunting song,
"The fisher in his net is caught,
The Chian hath his master bought;"
And isle from isle, with laughter long,
Took up and sped the mocking parable.

Once more the slow, dumb years
Bring their avenging cycle round,
And, more than Hellas taught of old,
Our wiser lesson shall be told,
Of slaves uprising, freedom-crowned,
To break, not wield, the scourge wet with their blood and tears.

1868.

AT PORT ROYAL.

In November, 1861, a Union force under Commodore Dupont and General Sherman captured Port Royal, and from this point as a basis of operations, the neighboring islands between Charleston and Savannah were taken possession of. The early occupation of this district, where the negro population was greatly in excess of the white, gave an opportunity which was at once seized upon, of practically emancipating the slaves and of beginning that work of civilization which was accepted as the grave responsibility of those who had labored for freedom.

THE tent-lights glimmer on the land,
The ship-lights on the sea;
The night-wind smooths with drifting sand
Our track on lone Tybee.

At last our grating keels outslide,
Our good boats forward swing;
And while we ride the land-locked tide,
Our negroes row and sing.

For dear the bondman holds his gifts
Of music and of song
The gold that kindly Nature sifts
Among his sands of wrong:

The power to make his toiling days
And poor home-comforts please;
The quaint relief of mirth that plays
With sorrow's minor keys.

Another glow than sunset's fire
Has filled the west with light,

Where field and garner, barn and byre,
Are blazing through the night.

The land is wild with fear and hate,
The rout runs mad and fast;
From hand to hand, from gate to gate
The flaming brand is passed.

The lurid glow falls strong across
Dark faces broad with smiles
Not theirs the terror, hate, and loss
That fire yon blazing piles.

With oar-strokes timing to their song,
They weave in simple lays
The pathos of remembered wrong,
The hope of better days,—

The triumph-note that Miriam sung,
The joy of uncaged birds
Softening with Afric's mellow tongue
Their broken Saxon words.

SONG OF THE NEGRO BOATMEN.

Oh, praise an' tanks! De Lord he come
To set de people free;
An' massa tink it day ob doom,
An' we ob jubilee.
De Lord dat heap de Red Sea waves
He jus' as 'trong as den;
He say de word: we las' night slaves;
To-day, de Lord's freemen.
De yam will grow, de cotton blow,
We'll hab de rice an' corn;
Oh nebber you fear, if nebber you hear
De driver blow his horn!

Ole massa on he trabbels gone;
He leaf de land behind
De Lord's breff blow him furder on,
Like corn-shuck in de wind.
We own de hoe, we own de plough,
We own de hands dat hold;
We sell de pig, we sell de cow,
But nebber chile be sold.
De yam will grow, de cotton blow,
We'll hab de rice an' corn;
Oh nebber you fear, if nebber you hear
De driver blow his horn!

We pray de Lord: he gib us signs
Dat some day we be free;
De norf-wind tell it to de pines,

De wild-duck to de sea;
We tink it when de church-bell ring,
We dream it in de dream;
De rice-bird mean it when he sing,
De eagle when be scream.
De yam will grow, de cotton blow,
We'll hab de rice an' corn
Oh nebber you fear, if nebber you hear
De driver blow his horn!

We know de promise nebber fail,
An' nebber lie de word;
So like de 'postles in de jail,
We waited for de Lord
An' now he open ebery door,
An' trow away de key;
He tink we lub him so before,
We hub him better free.
De yam will grow, de cotton blow,
He'll gib de rice an' corn;
Oh nebber you fear, if nebber you hear
De driver blow his horn!

So sing our dusky gondoliers;
And with a secret pain,
And smiles that seem akin to tears,
We hear the wild refrain.

We dare not share the negro's trust,

Nor yet his hope deny;
We only know that God is just,
And every wrong shall die.

Rude seems the song; each swarthy face,
Flame-lighted, ruder still
We start to think that hapless race
Must shape our good or ill;

That laws of changeless justice bind
Oppressor with oppressed;
And, close as sin and suffering joined,
We march to Fate abreast.
Sing on, poor hearts! your chant shall be
Our sign of blight or bloom,
The Vala-song of Liberty,
Or death-rune of our doom!

1862.

ASTRAEA AT THE CAPITOL.

ABOLITION OF SLAVERY IN THE DISTRICT OF COLUMBIA, 1862.

WHEN first I saw our banner wave
Above the nation's council-hall,
I heard beneath its marble wall
The clanking fetters of the slave!

In the foul market-place I stood,
And saw the Christian mother sold,
And childhood with its locks of gold,
Blue-eyed and fair with Saxon blood.

I shut my eyes, I held my breath,
And, smothering down the wrath and shame
That set my Northern blood aflame,
Stood silent,—where to speak was death.

Beside me gloomed the prison-cell
Where wasted one in slow decline
For uttering simple words of mine,
And loving freedom all too well.

The flag that floated from the dome
Flapped menace in the morning air;
I stood a perilled stranger where
The human broker made his home.

For crime was virtue: Gown and Sword

And Law their threefold sanction gave,
And to the quarry of the slave
Went hawking with our symbol-bird.

On the oppressor's side was power;
And yet I knew that every wrong,
However old, however strong,
But waited God's avenging hour.

I knew that truth would crush the lie,
Somehow, some time, the end would be;
Yet scarcely dared I hope to see
The triumph with my mortal eye.

But now I see it! In the sun
A free flag floats from yonder dome,
And at the nation's hearth and home
The justice long delayed is done.

Not as we hoped, in calm of prayer,
The message of deliverance comes,
But heralded by roll of drums
On waves of battle-troubled air!

Midst sounds that madden and appall,
The song that Bethlehem's shepherds knew!
The harp of David melting through
The demon-agonies of Saul!

Not as we hoped; but what are we?
Above our broken dreams and plans
God lays, with wiser hand than man's,
The corner-stones of liberty.

I cavil not with Him: the voice
That freedom's blessed gospel tells
Is sweet to me as silver bells,
Rejoicing! yea, I will rejoice!

Dear friends still toiling in the sun;
Ye dearer ones who, gone before,
Are watching from the eternal shore
The slow work by your hands begun,

Rejoice with me! The chastening rod
Blossoms with love; the furnace heat
Grows cool beneath His blessed feet
Whose form is as the Son of God!

Rejoice! Our Marah's bitter springs
Are sweetened; on our ground of grief
Rise day by day in strong relief
The prophecies of better things.

Rejoice in hope! The day and night
Are one with God, and one with them
Who see by faith the cloudy hem

Of Judgment fringed with Mercy's light.

1862.

THE BATTLE AUTUMN OF 1862.

THE *flags of war like storm-birds fly*,
The charging trumpets blow;
Yet rolls no thunder in the sky,
No earthquake strives below.

And, calm and patient, Nature keeps
Her ancient promise well,
Though o'er her bloom and greenness sweeps
The battle's breath of hell.

And still she walks in golden hours
Through harvest-happy farms,
And still she wears her fruits and flowers
Like jewels on her arms.

What mean the gladness of the plain,
This joy of eve and morn,
The mirth that shakes the beard of grain
And yellow locks of corn?

Ah! eyes may well be full of tears,
And hearts with hate are hot;
But even-paced come round the years,
And Nature changes not.

She meets with smiles our bitter grief,
With songs our groans of pain;
She mocks with tint of flower and leaf

The war-field's crimson stain.

Still, in the cannon's pause, we hear
Her sweet thanksgiving-psalm;
Too near to God for doubt or fear,
She shares the eternal calm.

She knows the seed lies safe below
The fires that blast and burn;
For all the tears of blood we sow
She waits the rich return.

She sees with clearer eye than ours
The good of suffering born,—
The hearts that blossom like her flowers,
And ripen like her corn.

Oh, give to us, in times like these,
The vision of her eyes;
And make her fields and fruited trees
Our golden prophecies

Oh, give to us her finer ear
Above this stormy din,
We too would hear the bells of cheer
Ring peace and freedom in.

1862.

HYMN,

SUNG AT CHRISTMAS BY THE SCHOLARS OF ST. HELENA'S ISLAND, S. C.

OH, none in all the world before
Were ever glad as we!
We're free on Carolina's shore,
We're all at home and free.

Thou Friend and Helper of the poor,
Who suffered for our sake,
To open every prison door,
And every yoke to break!

Bend low Thy pitying face and mild,
And help us sing and pray;
The hand that blessed the little child,
Upon our foreheads lay.

We hear no more the driver's horn,
No more the whip we fear,
This holy day that saw Thee born
Was never half so dear.

The very oaks are greener clad,
The waters brighter smile;
Oh, never shone a day so glad
On sweet St. Helen's Isle.

We praise Thee in our songs to-day,

To Thee in prayer we call,
Make swift the feet and straight the way
Of freedom unto all.

Come once again, O blessed Lord!
Come walking on the sea!
And let the mainlands hear the word
That sets the islands free!

1863.

THE PROCLAMATION.

President Lincoln's proclamation of emancipation was issued January 1, 1863.

SAINT PATRICK, slave to Milcho of the herds
Of Ballymena, wakened with these words
"Arise, and flee
Out from the land of bondage, and be free!"

Glad as a soul in pain, who hears from heaven
The angels singing of his sins forgiven,
And, wondering, sees
His prison opening to their golden keys,

He rose a man who laid him down a slave,
Shook from his locks the ashes of the grave,
And outward trod
Into the glorious liberty of God.

He cast the symbols of his shame away;
And, passing where the sleeping Milcho lay,
Though back and limb
Smarted with wrong, he prayed, "God pardon him!"

So went he forth; but in God's time he came
To light on Uilline's hills a holy flame;
And, dying, gave
The land a saint that lost him as a slave.

O dark, sad millions, patiently and dumb
Waiting for God, your hour at last has come,
And freedom's song
Breaks the long silence of your night of wrong!
Arise and flee! shake off the vile restraint
Of ages; but, like Ballymena's saint,
The oppressor spare,
Heap only on his head the coals of prayer.

Go forth, like him! like him return again,
To bless the land whereon in bitter pain
Ye toiled at first,
And heal with freedom what your slavery cursed.

1863.

ANNIVERSARY POEM.

Read before the Alumni of the Friends' Yearly Meeting School, at the Annual Meeting at Newport, R. I., 15th 6th mo., 1863.

ONCE more, dear friends, you meet beneath
A clouded sky
Not yet the sword has found its sheath,
And on the sweet spring airs the breath
Of war floats by.

Yet trouble springs not from the ground,
Nor pain from chance;
The Eternal order circles round,
And wave and storm find mete and bound
In Providence.

Full long our feet the flowery ways
Of peace have trod,
Content with creed and garb and phrase:
A harder path in earlier days
Led up to God.

Too cheaply truths, once purchased dear,
Are made our own;
Too long the world has smiled to hear
Our boast of full corn in the ear
By others sown;

To see us stir the martyr fires
Of long ago,

*And wrap our satisfied desires
In the singed mantles that our sires
Have dropped below.*

*But now the cross our worthies bore
On us is laid;
Profession's quiet sleep is o'er,
And in the scale of truth once more
Our faith is weighed.*

*The cry of innocent blood at last
Is calling down
An answer in the whirlwind-blast,
The thunder and the shadow cast
From Heaven's dark frown.*

*The land is red with judgments. Who
Stands guiltless forth?
Have we been faithful as we knew,
To God and to our brother true,
To Heaven and Earth.*

*How faint, through din of merchandise
And count of gain,
Have seemed to us the captive's cries!
How far away the tears and sighs
Of souls in pain!*

This day the fearful reckoning comes

To each and all;
We hear amidst our peaceful homes
The summons of the conscript drums,
The bugle's call.

Our path is plain; the war-net draws
Round us in vain,
While, faithful to the Higher Cause,
We keep our fealty to the laws
Through patient pain.

The levelled gun, the battle-brand,
We may not take
But, calmly loyal, we can stand
And suffer with our suffering land
For conscience' sake.
Why ask for ease where all is pain?
Shall we alone
Be left to add our gain to gain,
When over Armageddon's plain
The trump is blown?

To suffer well is well to serve;
Safe in our Lord
The rigid lines of law shall curve
To spare us; from our heads shall swerve
Its smiting sword.

And light is mingled with the gloom,

And joy with grief;
Divinest compensations come,
Through thorns of judgment mercies bloom
In sweet relief.

Thanks for our privilege to bless,
By word and deed,
The widow in her keen distress,
The childless and the fatherless,
The hearts that bleed!

For fields of duty, opening wide,
Where all our powers
Are tasked the eager steps to guide
Of millions on a path untried
The slave is ours!
Ours by traditions dear and old,
Which make the race
Our wards to cherish and uphold,
And cast their freedom in the mould
Of Christian grace.

And we may tread the sick-bed floors
Where strong men pine,
And, down the groaning corridors,
Pour freely from our liberal stores
The oil and wine.

Who murmurs that in these dark days

His lot is cast?
God's hand within the shadow lays
The stones whereon His gates of praise
Shall rise at last.

Turn and o'erturn, O outstretched Hand
Nor stint, nor stay;
The years have never dropped their sand
On mortal issue vast and grand
As ours to-day.

Already, on the sable ground
Of man's despair
Is Freedom's glorious picture found,
With all its dusky hands unbound
Upraised in prayer.
Oh, small shall seem all sacrifice
And pain and loss,
When God shall wipe the weeping eyes,
For suffering give the victor's prize,
The crown for cross.

BARBARA FRIETCHIE.

This poem was written in strict conformity to the account of the incident as I had it from respectable and trustworthy sources. It has since been the subject of a good deal of conflicting testimony, and the story was probably incorrect in some of its details. It is admitted by all that Barbara Frietchie was no myth, but a worthy and highly esteemed gentlewoman, intensely loyal and a hater of the Slavery Rebellion, holding her Union flag sacred and keeping it with her Bible; that when the Confederates halted before her house, and entered her dooryard, she denounced them in vigorous language, shook her cane in their faces, and drove them out; and when General Burnside's troops followed close upon Jackson's, she waved her flag and cheered them. It is stated that May Qnantrell, a brave and loyal lady in another part of the city, did wave her flag in sight of the Confederates. It is possible that there has been a blending of the two incidents.

Up from the meadows rich with corn,
Clear in the cool September morn.

The clustered spires of Frederick stand
Green-walled by the hills of Maryland.

Round about them orchards sweep,
Apple and peach tree fruited deep,

Fair as the garden of the Lord
To the eyes of the famished rebel horde,

On that pleasant morn of the early fall
When Lee marched over the mountain-wall;

Over the mountains winding down,
Horse and foot, into Frederick town.

Forty flags with their silver stars,

Forty flags with their crimson bars,

Flapped in the morning wind: the sun
Of noon looked down, and saw not one.

Up rose old Barbara Frietchie then,
Bowed with her fourscore years and ten;

Bravest of all in Frederick town,
She took up the flag the men hauled down;

In her attic window the staff she set,
To show that one heart was loyal yet.

Up the street came the rebel tread,
Stonewall Jackson riding ahead.

Under his slouched hat left and right
He glanced; the old flag met his sight.

"Halt!"—the dust-brown ranks stood fast.
"Fire!"—out blazed the rifle-blast.
It shivered the window, pane and sash;
It rent the banner with seam and gash.

Quick, as it fell, from the broken staff
Dame Barbara snatched the silken scarf.

She leaned far out on the window-sill,

And shook it forth with a royal will.

"Shoot, if you must, this old gray head,
But spare your country's flag," she said.

A shade of sadness, a blush of shame,
Over the face of the leader came;

The nobler nature within him stirred
To life at that woman's deed and word.

"Who touches a hair of yon gray head
Dies like a dog! March on!" he said.

All day long through Frederick street
Sounded the tread of marching feet.

All day long that free flag tost
Over the heads of the rebel host.

Ever its torn folds rose and fell
On the loyal winds that loved it well;
And through the hill-gaps sunset light
Shone over it with a warm good-night.

Barbara Frietchie's work is o'er,
And the Rebel rides on his raids no more.

Honor to her! and let a tear

Fall, for her sake, on Stonewall's bier.

Over Barbara Frietchie's grave,
Flag of Freedom and Union, wave!

Peace and order and beauty draw
Round thy symbol of light and law;

And ever the stars above look down
On thy stars below in Frederick town!

1863.

WHAT THE BIRDS SAID.

THE birds against the April wind
Flew northward, singing as they flew;
They sang, "The land we leave behind
Has swords for corn-blades, blood for dew."

"O wild-birds, flying from the South,
What saw and heard ye, gazing down?"
"We saw the mortar's upturned mouth,
The sickened camp, the blazing town!

"Beneath the bivouac's starry lamps,
We saw your march-worn children die;
In shrouds of moss, in cypress swamps,
We saw your dead uncoffined lie.

"We heard the starving prisoner's sighs,
And saw, from line and trench, your sons
Follow our flight with home-sick eyes
Beyond the battery's smoking guns."

"And heard and saw ye only wrong
And pain," I cried, "O wing-worn flocks?"
"We heard," they sang, "the freedman's song,
The crash of Slavery's broken locks!

"We saw from new, uprising States
The treason-nursing mischief spurned,
As, crowding Freedom's ample gates,

The long estranged and lost returned.

"O'er dusky faces, seamed and old,
And hands horn-hard with unpaid toil,
With hope in every rustling fold,
We saw your star-dropt flag uncoil.

"And struggling up through sounds accursed,
A grateful murmur clomb the air;
A whisper scarcely heard at first,
It filled the listening heavens with prayer.

"And sweet and far, as from a star,
Replied a voice which shall not cease,
Till, drowning all the noise of war,
It sings the blessed song of peace!"

So to me, in a doubtful day
Of chill and slowly greening spring,
Low stooping from the cloudy gray,
The wild-birds sang or seemed to sing.

They vanished in the misty air,
The song went with them in their flight;
But lo! they left the sunset fair,
And in the evening there was light.
April, 1864.

THE MANTLE OF ST. JOHN DE MATHA.

A LEGEND OF "THE RED, WHITE, AND BLUE," A. D. 1154-1864.

A STRONG and mighty Angel,
Calm, terrible, and bright,
The cross in blended red and blue
Upon his mantle white.

Two captives by him kneeling,
Each on his broken chain,
Sang praise to God who raiseth
The dead to life again!

Dropping his cross-wrought mantle,
"Wear this," the Angel said;
"Take thou, O Freedom's priest, its sign,
The white, the blue, and red."

Then rose up John de Matha
In the strength the Lord Christ gave,
And begged through all the land of France
The ransom of the slave.

The gates of tower and castle
Before him open flew,
The drawbridge at his coming fell,
The door-bolt backward drew.

For all men owned his errand,

And paid his righteous tax;
And the hearts of lord and peasant
Were in his hands as wax.

At last, outbound from Tunis,
His bark her anchor weighed,
Freighted with seven-score Christian souls
Whose ransom he had paid.
But, torn by Paynim hatred,
Her sails in tatters hung;
And on the wild waves, rudderless,
A shattered hulk she swung.

"God save us!" cried the captain,
"For naught can man avail;
Oh, woe betide the ship that lacks
Her rudder and her sail!

"Behind us are the Moormen;
At sea we sink or strand
There's death upon the water,
There's death upon the land!"

Then up spake John de Matha
"God's errands never fail!
Take thou the mantle which I wear,
And make of it a sail."

They raised the cross-wrought mantle,

The blue, the white, the red;
And straight before the wind off-shore
The ship of Freedom sped.

"God help us!" cried the seamen,
"For vain is mortal skill
The good ship on a stormy sea
Is drifting at its will."
Then up spake John de Matha
"My mariners, never fear
The Lord whose breath has filled her sail
May well our vessel steer!"

So on through storm and darkness
They drove for weary hours;
And lo! the third gray morning shone
On Ostia's friendly towers.

And on the walls the watchers
The ship of mercy knew,
They knew far off its holy cross,
The red, the white, and blue.

And the bells in all the steeples
Rang out in glad accord,
To welcome home to Christian soil
The ransomed of the Lord.

So runs the ancient legend

By bard and painter told;
And lo! the cycle rounds again,
The new is as the old!

With rudder foully broken,
And sails by traitors torn,
Our country on a midnight sea
Is waiting for the morn.
Before her, nameless terror;
Behind, the pirate foe;
The clouds are black above her,
The sea is white below.

The hope of all who suffer,
The dread of all who wrong,
She drifts in darkness and in storm,
How long, O Lord I how long?

But courage, O my mariners
Ye shall not suffer wreck,
While up to God the freedman's prayers
Are rising from your deck.

Is not your sail the banner
Which God hath blest anew,
The mantle that De Matha wore,
The red, the white, the blue?

Its hues are all of heaven,

The red of sunset's dye,
The whiteness of the moon-lit cloud,
The blue of morning's sky.

Wait cheerily, then, O mariners,
For daylight and for land;
The breath of God is in your sail,
Your rudder is His hand.
Sail on, sail on, deep-freighted
With blessings and with hopes;
The saints of old with shadowy hands
Are pulling at your ropes.

Behind ye holy martyrs
Uplift the palm and crown;
Before ye unborn ages send
Their benedictions down.

Take heart from John de Matha!—
God's errands never fail!
Sweep on through storm and darkness,
The thunder and the hail!

Sail on! The morning cometh,
The port ye yet shall win;
And all the bells of God shall ring
The good ship bravely in!

1865.

LAUS DEO!

On hearing the bells ring on the passage of the constitutional amendment abolishing slavery. The resolution was adopted by Congress, January 31, 1865. The ratification by the requisite number of states was announced December 18, 1865.

IT is done!
Clang of bell and roar of gun
Send the tidings up and down.
How the belfries rock and reel!
How the great guns, peal on peal,
Fling the joy from town to town!

Ring, O bells!
Every stroke exulting tells
Of the burial hour of crime.
Loud and long, that all may hear,
Ring for every listening ear
Of Eternity and Time!

Let us kneel
God's own voice is in that peal,
And this spot is holy ground.
Lord, forgive us! What are we,
That our eyes this glory see,
That our ears have heard the sound!

For the Lord
On the whirlwind is abroad;
In the earthquake He has spoken;
He has smitten with His thunder

The iron walls asunder,
And the gates of brass are broken.

Loud and long
Lift the old exulting song;
Sing with Miriam by the sea,
He has cast the mighty down;
Horse and rider sink and drown;
"He hath triumphed gloriously!"

Did we dare,
In our agony of prayer,
Ask for more than He has done?
When was ever His right hand
Over any time or land
Stretched as now beneath the sun?

How they pale,
Ancient myth and song and tale,
In this wonder of our days,
When the cruel rod of war
Blossoms white with righteous law,
And the wrath of man is praise!

Blotted out
All within and all about
Shall a fresher life begin;
Freer breathe the universe
As it rolls its heavy curse

On the dead and buried sin!

It is done!
In the circuit of the sun
Shall the sound thereof go forth.
It shall bid the sad rejoice,
It shall give the dumb a voice,
It shall belt with joy the earth!

Ring and swing,
Bells of joy! On morning's wing
Send the song of praise abroad!
With a sound of broken chains
Tell the nations that He reigns,
Who alone is Lord and God!

1865.

HYMN FOR THE CELEBRATION OF EMANCIPATION AT NEWBURYPORT.

NOT unto us who did but seek
The word that burned within to speak,
Not unto us this day belong
The triumph and exultant song.

Upon us fell in early youth
The burden of unwelcome truth,
And left us, weak and frail and few,
The censor's painful work to do.

Thenceforth our life a fight became,
The air we breathed was hot with blame;
For not with gauged and softened tone
We made the bondman's cause our own.
We bore, as Freedom's hope forlorn,
The private hate, the public scorn;
Yet held through all the paths we trod
Our faith in man and trust in God.

We prayed and hoped; but still, with awe,
The coming of the sword we saw;
We heard the nearing steps of doom,
We saw the shade of things to come.

In grief which they alone can feel
Who from a mother's wrong appeal,
With blended lines of fear and hope

We cast our country's horoscope.

For still within her house of life
We marked the lurid sign of strife,
And, poisoning and imbittering all,
We saw the star of Wormwood fall.

Deep as our love for her became
Our hate of all that wrought her shame,
And if, thereby, with tongue and pen
We erred,—we were but mortal men.

We hoped for peace; our eyes survey
The blood-red dawn of Freedom's day
We prayed for love to loose the chain;
'T is shorn by battle's axe in twain!
Nor skill nor strength nor zeal of ours
Has mined and heaved the hostile towers;
Not by our hands is turned the key
That sets the sighing captives free.

A redder sea than Egypt's wave
Is piled and parted for the slave;
A darker cloud moves on in light;
A fiercer fire is guide by night.

The praise, O Lord! is Thine alone,
In Thy own way Thy work is done!

Our poor gifts at Thy feet we cast,
  To whom be glory, first and last!

  1865.

AFTER THE WAR.

THE PEACE AUTUMN.

Written for the Essex County Agricultural Festival, 1865.

THANK God for rest, where none molest,
And none can make afraid;
For Peace that sits as Plenty's guest
Beneath the homestead shade!

Bring pike and gun, the sword's red scourge,
The negro's broken chains,
And beat them at the blacksmith's forge
To ploughshares for our plains.

Alike henceforth our hills of snow,
And vales where cotton flowers;
All streams that flow, all winds that blow,
Are Freedom's motive-powers.

Henceforth to Labor's chivalry
Be knightly honors paid;
For nobler than the sword's shall be
The sickle's accolade.

Build up an altar to the Lord,
O grateful hearts of ours
And shape it of the greenest sward
That ever drank the showers.

Lay all the bloom of gardens there,
And there the orchard fruits;
Bring golden grain from sun and air,
From earth her goodly roots.

There let our banners droop and flow,
The stars uprise and fall;
Our roll of martyrs, sad and slow,
Let sighing breezes call.
Their names let hands of horn and tan
And rough-shod feet applaud,
Who died to make the slave a man,
And link with toil reward.

There let the common heart keep time
To such an anthem sung
As never swelled on poet's rhyme,
Or thrilled on singer's tongue.

Song of our burden and relief,
Of peace and long annoy;
The passion of our mighty grief
And our exceeding joy!

A song of praise to Him who filled
The harvests sown in tears,
And gave each field a double yield
To feed our battle-years.

A song of faith that trusts the end
To match the good begun,
Nor doubts the power of Love to blend
The hearts of men as one!

TO THE THIRTY-NINTH CONGRESS.

The thirty-ninth congress was that which met in 1865 after the close of the war, when it was charged with the great question of reconstruction; the uppermost subject in men's minds was the standing of those who had recently been in arms against the Union and their relations to the freedmen.

O PEOPLE-CHOSEN! are ye not
Likewise the chosen of the Lord,
To do His will and speak His word?

From the loud thunder-storm of war
Not man alone hath called ye forth,
But He, the God of all the earth!

The torch of vengeance in your hands
He quenches; unto Him belongs
The solemn recompense of wrongs.

Enough of blood the land has seen,
And not by cell or gallows-stair
Shall ye the way of God prepare.

Say to the pardon-seekers: Keep
Your manhood, bend no suppliant knees,
Nor palter with unworthy pleas.

Above your voices sounds the wail
Of starving men; we shut in vain *
Our eyes to Pillow's ghastly stain. **

What words can drown that bitter cry?

What tears wash out the stain of death?
What oaths confirm your broken faith?

From you alone the guaranty
Of union, freedom, peace, we claim;
We urge no conqueror's terms of shame.

Alas! no victor's pride is ours;
We bend above our triumphs won
Like David o'er his rebel son.

Be men, not beggars. Cancel all
By one brave, generous action; trust
Your better instincts, and be just.

Make all men peers before the law,
Take hands from off the negro's throat,
Give black and white an equal vote.

Keep all your forfeit lives and lands,
But give the common law's redress
To labor's utter nakedness.

Revive the old heroic will;
Be in the right as brave and strong
As ye have proved yourselves in wrong.

Defeat shall then be victory,
Your loss the wealth of full amends,

And hate be love, and foes be friends.

Then buried be the dreadful past,
Its common slain be mourned, and let
All memories soften to regret.

Then shall the Union's mother-heart
Her lost and wandering ones recall,
Forgiving and restoring all,—

And Freedom break her marble trance
Above the Capitolian dome,
Stretch hands, and bid ye welcome home
November, 1865.

* *Andersonville prison.*
** *The massacre of Negro troops at Fort Pillow.*

THE HIVE AT GETTYSBURG.

IN the old Hebrew myth the lion's frame,
So terrible alive,
Bleached by the desert's sun and wind, became
The wandering wild bees' hive;
And he who, lone and naked-handed, tore
Those jaws of death apart,
In after time drew forth their honeyed store
To strengthen his strong heart.

Dead seemed the legend: but it only slept
To wake beneath our sky;
Just on the spot whence ravening Treason crept
Back to its lair to die,
Bleeding and torn from Freedom's mountain bounds,
A stained and shattered drum
Is now the hive where, on their flowery rounds,
The wild bees go and come.

Unchallenged by a ghostly sentinel,
They wander wide and far,
Along green hillsides, sown with shot and shell,
Through vales once choked with war.
The low reveille of their battle-drum
Disturbs no morning prayer;
With deeper peace in summer noons their hum
Fills all the drowsy air.

And Samson's riddle is our own to-day,

*Of sweetness from the strong,
Of union, peace, and freedom plucked away
From the rent jaws of wrong.
From Treason's death we draw a purer life,
As, from the beast he slew,
A sweetness sweeter for his bitter strife
The old-time athlete drew!
1868.*

HOWARD AT ATLANTA.

RIGHT in the track where Sherman
Ploughed his red furrow,
Out of the narrow cabin,
Up from the cellar's burrow,
Gathered the little black people,
With freedom newly dowered,
Where, beside their Northern teacher,
Stood the soldier, Howard.

He listened and heard the children
Of the poor and long-enslaved
Reading the words of Jesus,
Singing the songs of David.
Behold!—the dumb lips speaking,
The blind eyes seeing!
Bones of the Prophet's vision
Warmed into being!

Transformed he saw them passing
Their new life's portal
Almost it seemed the mortal
Put on the immortal.
No more with the beasts of burden,
No more with stone and clod,
But crowned with glory and honor
In the image of God!

There was the human chattel

Its manhood taking;
There, in each dark, bronze statue,
A soul was waking!
The man of many battles,
With tears his eyelids pressing,
Stretched over those dusky foreheads
His one-armed blessing.

And he said: "Who hears can never
Fear for or doubt you;
What shall I tell the children
Up North about you?"
Then ran round a whisper, a murmur,
Some answer devising:
And a little boy stood up: "General,
Tell 'em we're rising!"

O black boy of Atlanta!
But half was spoken
The slave's chain and the master's
Alike are broken.
The one curse of the races
Held both in tether
They are rising,—all are rising,
The black and white together!

O brave men and fair women!
Ill comes of hate and scorning
Shall the dark faces only

Be turned to mourning?—
Make Time your sole avenger,
All-healing, all-redressing;
Meet Fate half-way, and make it
A joy and blessing!

1869.

THE EMANCIPATION GROUP.

Moses Kimball, a citizen of Boston, presented to the city a duplicate of the Freedman's Memorial statue erected in Lincoln Square, Washington. The group, which stands in Park Square, represents the figure of a slave, from whose limbs the broken fetters have fallen, kneeling in gratitude at the feet of Lincoln. The group was designed by Thomas Ball, and was unveiled December 9, 1879. These verses were written for the occasion.

AMIDST thy sacred effigies
Of old renown give place,
O city, Freedom-loved! to his
Whose hand unchained a race.

Take the worn frame, that rested not
Save in a martyr's grave;
The care-lined face, that none forgot,
Bent to the kneeling slave.

Let man be free! The mighty word
He spake was not his own;
An impulse from the Highest stirred
These chiselled lips alone.

The cloudy sign, the fiery guide,
Along his pathway ran,
And Nature, through his voice, denied
The ownership of man.
We rest in peace where these sad eyes
Saw peril, strife, and pain;
His was the nation's sacrifice,
And ours the priceless gain.

O symbol of God's will on earth
As it is done above!
Bear witness to the cost and worth
Of justice and of love.

Stand in thy place and testify
To coming ages long,
That truth is stronger than a lie,
And righteousness than wrong.

THE JUBILEE SINGERS.

A number of students of Fisk University, under the direction of one of the officers, gave a series of concerts in the Northern States, for the purpose of establishing the college on a firmer financial foundation. Their hymns and songs, mostly in a minor key, touched the hearts of the people, and were received as peculiarly expressive of a race delivered from bondage.

VOICE of a people suffering long,
The pathos of their mournful song,
The sorrow of their night of wrong!

Their cry like that which Israel gave,
A prayer for one to guide and save,
Like Moses by the Red Sea's wave!

The stern accord her timbrel lent
To Miriam's note of triumph sent
O'er Egypt's sunken armament!

The tramp that startled camp and town,
And shook the walls of slavery down,
The spectral march of old John Brown!

The storm that swept through battle-days,
The triumph after long delays,
The bondmen giving God the praise!

Voice of a ransomed race, sing on
Till Freedom's every right is won,

And slavery's every wrong undone
   1880.

GARRISON.

The earliest poem in this division was my youthful tribute to the great reformer when himself a young man he was first sounding his trumpet in Essex County. I close with the verses inscribed to him at the end of his earthly career, May 24, 1879. My poetical service in the cause of freedom is thus almost synchronous with his life of devotion to the same cause.

THE storm and peril overpast,
The hounding hatred shamed and still,
Go, soul of freedom! take at last
The place which thou alone canst fill.

Confirm the lesson taught of old—
Life saved for self is lost, while they
Who lose it in His service hold
The lease of God's eternal day.

Not for thyself, but for the slave
Thy words of thunder shook the world;
No selfish griefs or hatred gave
The strength wherewith thy bolts were hurled.

From lips that Sinai's trumpet blew
We heard a tender under song;
Thy very wrath from pity grew,
From love of man thy hate of wrong.

Now past and present are as one;
The life below is life above;
Thy mortal years have but begun
Thy immortality of love.

*With somewhat of thy lofty faith
We lay thy outworn garment by,
Give death but what belongs to death,
And life the life that cannot die!*

*Not for a soul like thine the calm
Of selfish ease and joys of sense;
But duty, more than crown or palm,
Its own exceeding recompense.*

*Go up and on thy day well done,
Its morning promise well fulfilled,
Arise to triumphs yet unwon,
To holier tasks that God has willed.*

*Go, leave behind thee all that mars
The work below of man for man;
With the white legions of the stars
Do service such as angels can.*

*Wherever wrong shall right deny
Or suffering spirits urge their plea,
Be thine a voice to smite the lie,
A hand to set the captive free!*

SONGS OF LABOR AND REFORM

THE QUAKER OF THE OLDEN TIME.

THE Quaker of the olden time!
How calm and firm and true,
Unspotted by its wrong and crime,
He walked the dark earth through.
The lust of power, the love of gain,
The thousand lures of sin
Around him, had no power to stain
The purity within.
With that deep insight which detects
All great things in the small,
And knows how each man's life affects
The spiritual life of all,
He walked by faith and not by sight,
By love and not by law;
The presence of the wrong or right
He rather felt than saw.

He felt that wrong with wrong partakes,
That nothing stands alone,
That whoso gives the motive, makes
His brother's sin his own.
And, pausing not for doubtful choice
Of evils great or small,
He listened to that inward voice
Which called away from all.

O Spirit of that early day,
So pure and strong and true,
Be with us in the narrow way
Our faithful fathers knew.
Give strength the evil to forsake,
The cross of Truth to bear,
And love and reverent fear to make
Our daily lives a prayer!

1838.

DEMOCRACY.

All things whatsoever ye would that men should do to you, do ye even so to them.—MATTHEW vii. 12.

BEARER of Freedom's holy light,
Breaker of Slavery's chain and rod,
The foe of all which pains the sight,
Or wounds the generous ear of God!

Beautiful yet thy temples rise,
Though there profaning gifts are thrown;
And fires unkindled of the skies
Are glaring round thy altar-stone.

Still sacred, though thy name be breathed
By those whose hearts thy truth deride;
And garlands, plucked from thee, are wreathed
Around the haughty brows of Pride.

Oh, ideal of my boyhood's time!
The faith in which my father stood,
Even when the sons of Lust and Crime
Had stained thy peaceful courts with blood!

Still to those courts my footsteps turn,
For through the mists which darken there,
I see the flame of Freedom burn,—
The Kebla of the patriot's prayer!

The generous feeling, pure and warm,

Which owns the right of all divine;
The pitying heart, the helping arm,
The prompt self-sacrifice, are thine.

Beneath thy broad, impartial eye,
How fade the lines of caste and birth!
How equal in their suffering lie
The groaning multitudes of earth!

Still to a stricken brother true,
Whatever clime hath nurtured him;
As stooped to heal the wounded Jew
The worshipper of Gerizim.

By misery unrepelled, unawed
By pomp or power, thou seest a Man
In prince or peasant, slave or lord,
Pale priest, or swarthy artisan.

Through all disguise, form, place, or name,
Beneath the flaunting robes of sin,
Through poverty and squalid shame,
Thou lookest on the man within.

On man, as man, retaining yet,
Howe'er debased, and soiled, and dim,
The crown upon his forehead set,
The immortal gift of God to him.

And there is reverence in thy look;
For that frail form which mortals wear
The Spirit of the Holiest took,
And veiled His perfect brightness there.

Not from the shallow babbling fount
Of vain philosophy thou art;
He who of old on Syria's Mount
Thrilled, warmed, by turns, the listener's heart,

In holy words which cannot die,
In thoughts which angels leaned to know,
Proclaimed thy message from on high,
Thy mission to a world of woe.

That voice's echo hath not died!
From the blue lake of Galilee,
And Tabor's lonely mountain-side,
It calls a struggling world to thee.

Thy name and watchword o'er this land
I hear in every breeze that stirs,
And round a thousand altars stand
Thy banded party worshippers.

Not, to these altars of a day,
At party's call, my gift I bring;
But on thy olden shrine I lay
A freeman's dearest offering.

The voiceless utterance of his will,—
His pledge to Freedom and to Truth,
That manhood's heart remembers still
The homage of his generous youth.

Election Day, 1841

THE GALLOWS.

Written on reading pamphlets published by clergymen against the abolition of the gallows.

I.

THE suns of eighteen centuries have shone
Since the Redeemer walked with man, and made
The fisher's boat, the cavern's floor of stone,
And mountain moss, a pillow for His head;
And He, who wandered with the peasant Jew,
And broke with publicans the bread of shame,
And drank with blessings, in His Father's name,
The water which Samaria's outcast drew,
Hath now His temples upon every shore,
Altar and shrine and priest; and incense dim
Evermore rising, with low prayer and hymn,
From lips which press the temple's marble floor,
Or kiss the gilded sign of the dread cross He bore.

II.

Yet as of old, when, meekly "doing good,"
He fed a blind and selfish multitude,
And even the poor companions of His lot
With their dim earthly vision knew Him not,
How ill are His high teachings understood
Where He hath spoken Liberty, the priest
At His own altar binds the chain anew;
Where He hath bidden to Life's equal feast,
The starving many wait upon the few;
Where He hath spoken Peace, His name hath been
The loudest war-cry of contending men;

*Priests, pale with vigils, in His name have blessed
The unsheathed sword, and laid the spear in rest,
Wet the war-banner with their sacred wine,
And crossed its blazon with the holy sign;
Yea, in His name who bade the erring live,
And daily taught His lesson, to forgive!
Twisted the cord and edged the murderous steel;
And, with His words of mercy on their lips,
Hung gloating o'er the pincer's burning grips,
And the grim horror of the straining wheel;
Fed the slow flame which gnawed the victim's limb,
Who saw before his searing eyeballs swim
The image of their Christ in cruel zeal,
Through the black torment-smoke, held mockingly to him!*

III.

*The blood which mingled with the desert sand,
And beaded with its red and ghastly dew
The vines and olives of the Holy Land;
The shrieking curses of the hunted Jew;
The white-sown bones of heretics, where'er
They sank beneath the Crusade's holy spear;
Goa's dark dungeons, Malta's sea-washed cell,
Where with the hymns the ghostly fathers sung
Mingled the groans by subtle torture wrung,
Heaven's anthem blending with the shriek of hell!
The midnight of Bartholomew, the stake
Of Smithfield, and that thrice-accursed flame
Which Calvin kindled by Geneva's lake;
New England's scaffold, and the priestly sneer*

Which mocked its victims in that hour of fear,
When guilt itself a human tear might claim,—
Bear witness, O Thou wronged and merciful One!
That Earth's most hateful crimes have in Thy name been done!

IV.

Thank God! that I have lived to see the time
When the great truth begins at last to find
An utterance from the deep heart of mankind,
Earnest and clear, that all Revenge is Crime,
That man is holier than a creed, that all
Restraint upon him must consult his good,
Hope's sunshine linger on his prison wall,
And Love look in upon his solitude.
The beautiful lesson which our Saviour taught
Through long, dark centuries its way hath wrought
Into the common mind and popular thought;
And words, to which by Galilee's lake shore
The humble fishers listened with hushed oar,
Have found an echo in the general heart,
And of the public faith become a living part.

V.

Who shall arrest this tendency? Bring back
The cells of Venice and the bigot's rack?
Harden the softening human heart again
To cold indifference to a brother's pain?
Ye most unhappy men! who, turned away
From the mild sunshine of the Gospel day,
Grope in the shadows of Man's twilight time,

What mean ye, that with ghoul-like zest ye brood,
O'er those foul altars streaming with warm blood,
Permitted in another age and clime?
Why cite that law with which the bigot Jew
Rebuked the Pagan's mercy, when he knew
No evil in the Just One? Wherefore turn
To the dark, cruel past? Can ye not learn
From the pure Teacher's life how mildly free
Is the great Gospel of Humanity?
The Flamen's knife is bloodless, and no more
Mexitli's altars soak with human gore,
No more the ghastly sacrifices smoke
Through the green arches of the Druid's oak;
And ye of milder faith, with your high claim
Of prophet-utterance in the Holiest name,
Will ye become the Druids of our time
Set up your scaffold-altars in our land,
And, consecrators of Law's darkest crime,
Urge to its loathsome work the hangman's hand?
Beware, lest human nature, roused at last,
From its peeled shoulder your encumbrance cast,
And, sick to loathing of your cry for blood,
Rank ye with those who led their victims round
The Celt's red altar and the Indian's mound,
Abhorred of Earth and Heaven, a pagan brotherhood!

1842.

SEED-TIME AND HARVEST.

As o'er his furrowed fields which lie
Beneath a coldly dropping sky,
Yet chill with winter's melted snow,
The husbandman goes forth to sow,

Thus, Freedom, on the bitter blast
The ventures of thy seed we cast,
And trust to warmer sun and rain
To swell the germs and fill the grain.

Who calls thy glorious service hard?
Who deems it not its own reward?
Who, for its trials, counts it less.
A cause of praise and thankfulness?

It may not be our lot to wield
The sickle in the ripened field;
Nor ours to hear, on summer eves,
The reaper's song among the sheaves.

Yet where our duty's task is wrought
In unison with God's great thought,
The near and future blend in one,
And whatsoe'er is willed, is done!

And ours the grateful service whence
Comes day by day the recompense;
The hope, the trust, the purpose stayed,

The fountain and the noonday shade.

And were this life the utmost span,
The only end and aim of man,
Better the toil of fields like these
Than waking dream and slothful ease.

But life, though falling like our grain,
Like that revives and springs again;
And, early called, how blest are they
Who wait in heaven their harvest-day!

1843.

TO THE REFORMERS OF ENGLAND.

This poem was addressed to those who like Richard Cobden and John Bright were seeking the reform of political evils in Great Britain by peaceful and Christian means. It will be remembered that the Anti-Corn Law League was in the midst of its labors at this time.

GOD bless ye, brothers! in the fight
Ye 're waging now, ye cannot fail,
For better is your sense of right
Than king-craft's triple mail.

Than tyrant's law, or bigot's ban,
More mighty is your simplest word;
The free heart of an honest man
Than crosier or the sword.

Go, let your blinded Church rehearse
The lesson it has learned so well;
It moves not with its prayer or curse
The gates of heaven or hell.

Let the State scaffold rise again;
Did Freedom die when Russell died?
Forget ye how the blood of Vane
From earth's green bosom cried?

The great hearts of your olden time
Are beating with you, full and strong;
All holy memories and sublime
And glorious round ye throng.

The bluff, bold men of Runnymede
Are with ye still in times like these;
The shades of England's mighty dead,
Your cloud of witnesses!

The truths ye urge are borne abroad
By every wind and every tide;
The voice of Nature and of God
Speaks out upon your side.

The weapons which your hands have found
Are those which Heaven itself has wrought,
Light, Truth, and Love; your battle-ground
The free, broad field of Thought.

No partial, selfish purpose breaks
The simple beauty of your plan,
Nor lie from throne or altar shakes
Your steady faith in man.

The languid pulse of England starts
And bounds beneath your words of power,
The beating of her million hearts
Is with you at this hour!

O ye who, with undoubting eyes,
Through present cloud and gathering storm,
Behold the span of Freedom's skies,
And sunshine soft and warm;

Press bravely onward! not in vain
Your generous trust in human-kind;
The good which bloodshed could not gain
Your peaceful zeal shall find.

Press on! the triumph shall be won
Of common rights and equal laws,
The glorious dream of Harrington,
And Sidney's good old cause.

Blessing the cotter and the crown,
Sweetening worn Labor's bitter cup;
And, plucking not the highest down,
Lifting the lowest up.

Press on! and we who may not share
The toil or glory of your fight
May ask, at least, in earnest prayer,
God's blessing on the right!

1843.

THE HUMAN SACRIFICE.

Some leading sectarian papers had lately published the letter of a clergyman, giving an account of his attendance upon a criminal (who had committed murder during a fit of intoxication), at the time of his execution, in western New York. The writer describes the agony of the wretched being, his abortive attempts at prayer, his appeal for life, his fear of a violent death; and, after declaring his belief that the poor victim died without hope of salvation, concludes with a warm eulogy upon the gallows, being more than ever convinced of its utility by the awful dread and horror which it inspired.

I.

FAR from his close and noisome cell,
By grassy lane and sunny stream,
Blown clover field and strawberry dell,
And green and meadow freshness, fell
The footsteps of his dream.
Again from careless feet the dew
Of summer's misty morn he shook;
Again with merry heart he threw
His light line in the rippling brook.
Back crowded all his school-day joys;
He urged the ball and quoit again,
And heard the shout of laughing boys
Come ringing down the walnut glen.
Again he felt the western breeze,
With scent of flowers and crisping hay;
And down again through wind-stirred trees
He saw the quivering sunlight play.
An angel in home's vine-hung door,
He saw his sister smile once more;
Once more the truant's brown-locked head
Upon his mother's knees was laid,

And sweetly lulled to slumber there,
With evening's holy hymn and prayer!

II.
He woke. At once on heart and brain
The present Terror rushed again;
Clanked on his limbs the felon's chain
He woke, to hear the church-tower tell
Time's footfall on the conscious bell,
And, shuddering, feel that clanging din
His life's last hour had ushered in;
To see within his prison-yard,
Through the small window, iron barred,
The gallows shadow rising dim
Between the sunrise heaven and him;
A horror in God's blessed air;
A blackness in his morning light;
Like some foul devil-altar there
Built up by demon hands at night.
And, maddened by that evil sight,
Dark, horrible, confused, and strange,
A chaos of wild, weltering change,
All power of check and guidance gone,
Dizzy and blind, his mind swept on.
In vain he strove to breathe a prayer,
In vain he turned the Holy Book,
He only heard the gallows-stair
Creak as the wind its timbers shook.
No dream for him of sin forgiven,

While still that baleful spectre stood,
With its hoarse murmur, "Blood for Blood!"
Between him and the pitying Heaven.

III.

Low on his dungeon floor he knelt,
And smote his breast, and on his chain,
Whose iron clasp he always felt,
His hot tears fell like rain;
And near him, with the cold, calm look
And tone of one whose formal part,
Unwarmed, unsoftened of the heart,
Is measured out by rule and book,
With placid lip and tranquil blood,
The hangman's ghostly ally stood,
Blessing with solemn text and word
The gallows-drop and strangling cord;
Lending the sacred Gospel's awe
And sanction to the crime of Law.

IV.

He saw the victim's tortured brow,
The sweat of anguish starting there,
The record of a nameless woe
In the dim eye's imploring stare,
Seen hideous through the long, damp hair,—
Fingers of ghastly skin and bone
Working and writhing on the stone!
And heard, by mortal terror wrung

From heaving breast and stiffened tongue,
The choking sob and low hoarse prayer;
As o'er his half-crazed fancy came
A vision of the eternal flame,
Its smoking cloud of agonies,
Its demon-worm that never dies,
The everlasting rise and fall
Of fire-waves round the infernal wall;
While high above that dark red flood,
Black, giant-like, the gallows stood;
Two busy fiends attending there
One with cold mocking rite and prayer,
The other with impatient grasp,
Tightening the death-rope's strangling clasp.

V.

The unfelt rite at length was done,
The prayer unheard at length was said,
An hour had passed: the noonday sun
Smote on the features of the dead!
And he who stood the doomed beside,
Calm gauger of the swelling tide
Of mortal agony and fear,
Heeding with curious eye and ear
Whate'er revealed the keen excess
Of man's extremest wretchedness
And who in that dark anguish saw
An earnest of the victim's fate,
The vengeful terrors of God's law,

The kindlings of Eternal hate,
The first drops of that fiery rain
Which beats the dark red realm of pain,
Did he uplift his earnest cries
Against the crime of Law, which gave
His brother to that fearful grave,
Whereon Hope's moonlight never lies,
And Faith's white blossoms never wave
To the soft breath of Memory's sighs;
Which sent a spirit marred and stained,
By fiends of sin possessed, profaned,
In madness and in blindness stark,
Into the silent, unknown dark?
No, from the wild and shrinking dread,
With which he saw the victim led
Beneath the dark veil which divides
Ever the living from the dead,
And Nature's solemn secret hides,
The man of prayer can only draw
New reasons for his bloody law;
New faith in staying Murder's hand
By murder at that Law's command;
New reverence for the gallows-rope,
As human nature's latest hope;
Last relic of the good old time,
When Power found license for its crime,
And held a writhing world in check
By that fell cord about its neck;
Stifled Sedition's rising shout,

Choked the young breath of Freedom out,
And timely checked the words which sprung
From Heresy's forbidden tongue;
While in its noose of terror bound,
The Church its cherished union found,
Conforming, on the Moslem plan,
The motley-colored mind of man,
Not by the Koran and the Sword,
But by the Bible and the Cord.

VI.
O Thou at whose rebuke the grave
Back to warm life its sleeper gave,
Beneath whose sad and tearful glance
The cold and changed countenance
Broke the still horror of its trance,
And, waking, saw with joy above,
A brother's face of tenderest love;
Thou, unto whom the blind and lame,
The sorrowing and the sin-sick came,
And from Thy very garment's hem
Drew life and healing unto them,
The burden of Thy holy faith
Was love and life, not hate and death;
Man's demon ministers of pain,
The fiends of his revenge, were sent
From thy pure Gospel's element
To their dark home again.
Thy name is Love! What, then, is he,

Who in that name the gallows rears,
An awful altar built to Thee,
With sacrifice of blood and tears?
Oh, once again Thy healing lay
On the blind eyes which knew Thee not,
And let the light of Thy pure day
Melt in upon his darkened thought.
Soften his hard, cold heart, and show
The power which in forbearance lies,
And let him feel that mercy now
Is better than old sacrifice.

VII.

As on the White Sea's charmed shore,
The Parsee sees his holy hill (10)
With dunnest smoke-clouds curtained o'er,
Yet knows beneath them, evermore,
The low, pale fire is quivering still;
So, underneath its clouds of sin,
The heart of man retaineth yet
Gleams of its holy origin;
And half-quenched stars that never set,
Dim colors of its faded bow,
And early beauty, linger there,
And o'er its wasted desert blow
Faint breathings of its morning air.
Oh, never yet upon the scroll
Of the sin-stained, but priceless soul,
Hath Heaven inscribed "Despair!"
Cast not the clouded gem away,

Quench not the dim but living ray,—
My brother man, Beware!
With that deep voice which from the skies
Forbade the Patriarch's sacrifice,
God's angel cries, Forbear.

1843

SONGS OF LABOR.

DEDICATION.

Prefixed to the volume of which the group of six poems following this prelude constituted the first portion.

I WOULD the gift I offer here
Might graces from thy favor take,
And, seen through Friendship's atmosphere,
On softened lines and coloring, wear
The unaccustomed light of beauty, for thy sake.

Few leaves of Fancy's spring remain
But what I have I give to thee,
The o'er-sunned bloom of summer's plain,
And paler flowers, the latter rain
Calls from the westering slope of life's autumnal lea.

Above the fallen groves of green,
Where youth's enchanted forest stood,
Dry root and mossed trunk between,
A sober after-growth is seen,
As springs the pine where falls the gay-leafed maple wood!

Yet birds will sing, and breezes play
Their leaf-harps in the sombre tree;
And through the bleak and wintry day
It keeps its steady green alway,—
So, even my after-thoughts may have a charm for thee.

Art's perfect forms no moral need,

And beauty is its own excuse;
But for the dull and flowerless weed
Some healing virtue still must plead,
And the rough ore must find its honors in its use.

So haply these, my simple lays
Of homely toil, may serve to show
The orchard bloom and tasselled maize
That skirt and gladden duty's ways,
The unsung beauty hid life's common things below.

Haply from them the toiler, bent
Above his forge or plough, may gain,
A manlier spirit of content,
And feel that life is wisest spent
Where the strong working hand makes strong the working brain.

The doom which to the guilty pair
Without the walls of Eden came,
Transforming sinless ease to care
And rugged toil, no more shall bear
The burden of old crime, or mark of primal shame.

A blessing now, a curse no more;
Since He, whose name we breathe with awe,
The coarse mechanic vesture wore,

A poor man toiling with the poor,

In labor, as in prayer, fulfilling the same law.

1850.

THE SHOEMAKERS.

Ho! workers of the old time styled
The Gentle Craft of Leather
Young brothers of the ancient guild,
Stand forth once more together!
Call out again your long array,
In the olden merry manner
Once more, on gay St. Crispin's day,
Fling out your blazoned banner!

Rap, rap! upon the well-worn stone
How falls the polished hammer
Rap, rap I the measured sound has grown
A quick and merry clamor.
Now shape the sole! now deftly curl
The glossy vamp around it,
And bless the while the bright-eyed girl
Whose gentle fingers bound it!

For you, along the Spanish main
A hundred keels are ploughing;
For you, the Indian on the plain
His lasso-coil is throwing;
For you, deep glens with hemlock dark
The woodman's fire is lighting;
For you, upon the oak's gray bark,
The woodman's axe is smiting.

For you, from Carolina's pine

The rosin-gum is stealing;
For you, the dark-eyed Florentine
Her silken skein is reeling;
For you, the dizzy goatherd roams
His rugged Alpine ledges;
For you, round all her shepherd homes,
Bloom England's thorny hedges.

The foremost still, by day or night,
On moated mound or heather,
Where'er the need of trampled right
Brought toiling men together;
Where the free burghers from the wall
Defied the mail-clad master,
Than yours, at Freedom's trumpet-call,
No craftsmen rallied faster.

Let foplings sneer, let fools deride,
Ye heed no idle scorner;
Free hands and hearts are still your pride,
And duty done, your honor.
Ye dare to trust, for honest fame,
The jury Time empanels,
And leave to truth each noble name
Which glorifies your annals.

Thy songs, Hans Sachs, are living yet,
In strong and hearty German;
And Bloomfield's lay, and Gifford's wit,

And patriot fame of Sherman;
Still from his book, a mystic seer,
The soul of Behmen teaches,
And England's priestcraft shakes to hear
Of Fox's leathern breeches.

The foot is yours; where'er it falls,
It treads your well-wrought leather,
On earthen floor, in marble halls,
On carpet, or on heather.
Still there the sweetest charm is found
Of matron grace or vestal's,
As Hebe's foot bore nectar round
Among the old celestials.

Rap, rap!—your stout and bluff brogan,
With footsteps slow and weary,
May wander where the sky's blue span
Shuts down upon the prairie.
On Beauty's foot your slippers glance,
By Saratoga's fountains,
Or twinkle down the summer dance
Beneath the Crystal Mountains!

The red brick to the mason's hand,
The brown earth to the tiller's,
The shoe in yours shall wealth command,
Like fairy Cinderella's!
As they who shunned the household maid

Beheld the crown upon her,
So all shall see your toil repaid
With hearth and home and honor.

Then let the toast be freely quaffed,
In water cool and brimming,—
"All honor to the good old Craft,
Its merry men and women!"
Call out again your long array,
In the old time's pleasant manner
Once more, on gay St. Crispin's day,
Fling out his blazoned banner!

1845.

THE FISHERMEN.

HURRAH! the seaward breezes
Sweep down the bay amain;
Heave up, my lads, the anchor!
Run up the sail again
Leave to the lubber landsmen
The rail-car and the steed;
The stars of heaven shall guide us,
The breath of heaven shall speed.

From the hill-top looks the steeple,
And the lighthouse from the sand;
And the scattered pines are waving
Their farewell from the land.
One glance, my lads, behind us,
For the homes we leave one sigh,
Ere we take the change and chances
Of the ocean and the sky.

Now, brothers, for the icebergs
Of frozen Labrador,
Floating spectral in the moonshine,
Along the low, black shore!
Where like snow the gannet's feathers
On Brador's rocks are shed,
And the noisy murr are flying,
Like black scuds, overhead;

Where in mist tie rock is hiding,

And the sharp reef lurks below,
And the white squall smites in summer,
And the autumn tempests blow;
Where, through gray and rolling vapor,
From evening unto morn,
A thousand boats are hailing,
Horn answering unto horn.

Hurrah! for the Red Island,
With the white cross on its crown
Hurrah! for Meccatina,
And its mountains bare and brown!
Where the Caribou's tall antlers
O'er the dwarf-wood freely toss,
And the footstep of the Mickmack
Has no sound upon the moss.

There we'll drop our lines, and gather
Old Ocean's treasures in,
Where'er the mottled mackerel
Turns up a steel-dark fin.
The sea's our field of harvest,
Its scaly tribes our grain;
We'll reap the teeming waters
As at home they reap the plain.

Our wet hands spread the carpet,
And light the hearth of home;
From our fish, as in the old time,

The silver coin shall come.
As the demon fled the chamber
Where the fish of Tobit lay,
So ours from all our dwellings
Shall frighten Want away.

Though the mist upon our jackets
In the bitter air congeals,
And our lines wind stiff and slowly
From off the frozen reels;
Though the fog be dark around us,
And the storm blow high and loud,
We will whistle down the wild wind,
And laugh beneath the cloud!

In the darkness as in daylight,
On the water as on land,
God's eye is looking on us,
And beneath us is His hand!
Death will find us soon or later,
On the deck or in the cot;
And we cannot meet him better
Than in working out our lot.

Hurrah! hurrah! the west-wind
Comes freshening down the bay,
The rising sails are filling;
Give way, my lads, give way!
Leave the coward landsman clinging

To the dull earth, like a weed;
The stars of heaven shall guide us,
The breath of heaven shall speed!

1845.

THE LUMBERMEN.

WILDLY round our woodland quarters
Sad-voiced Autumn grieves;
Thickly down these swelling waters
Float his fallen leaves.
Through the tall and naked timber,
Column-like and old,
Gleam the sunsets of November,
From their skies of gold.

O'er us, to the southland heading,
Screams the gray wild-goose;
On the night-frost sounds the treading
Of the brindled moose.
Noiseless creeping, while we're sleeping,
Frost his task-work plies;
Soon, his icy bridges heaping,
Shall our log-piles rise.

When, with sounds of smothered thunder,
On some night of rain,
Lake and river break asunder
Winter's weakened chain,
Down the wild March flood shall bear them
To the saw-mill's wheel,
Or where Steam, the slave, shall tear them
With his teeth of steel.

Be it starlight, be it moonlight,

In these vales below,
When the earliest beams of sunlight
Streak the mountain's snow,
Crisps the hoar-frost, keen and early,
To our hurrying feet,
And the forest echoes clearly
All our blows repeat.

Where the crystal Ambijejis
Stretches broad and clear,
And Millnoket's pine-black ridges
Hide the browsing deer;
Where, through lakes and wide morasses,
Or through rocky walls,
Swift and strong, Penobscot passes
White with foamy falls;

Where, through clouds, are glimpses given
Of Katahdin's sides,—
Rock and forest piled to heaven,
Torn and ploughed by slides!
Far below, the Indian trapping,
In the sunshine warm;
Far above, the snow-cloud wrapping
Half the peak in storm!

Where are mossy carpets better
Than the Persian weaves,
And than Eastern perfumes sweeter

Seem the fading leaves;
And a music wild and solemn,
From the pine-tree's height,
Rolls its vast and sea-like volume
On the wind of night;

Make we here our camp of winter;
And, through sleet and snow,
Pitchy knot and beechen splinter
On our hearth shall glow.
Here, with mirth to lighten duty,
We shall lack alone
Woman's smile and girlhood's beauty,
Childhood's lisping tone.

But their hearth is brighter burning
For our toil to-day;
And the welcome of returning
Shall our loss repay,
When, like seamen from the waters,
From the woods we come,
Greeting sisters, wives, and daughters,
Angels of our home!

Not for us the measured ringing
From the village spire,
Not for us the Sabbath singing
Of the sweet-voiced choir,
Ours the old, majestic temple,

*Where God's brightness shines
Down the dome so grand and ample,
Propped by lofty pines!*

*Through each branch-enwoven skylight,
Speaks He in the breeze,
As of old beneath the twilight
Of lost Eden's trees!
For His ear, the inward feeling
Needs no outward tongue;
He can see the spirit kneeling
While the axe is swung.*

*Heeding truth alone, and turning
From the false and dim,
Lamp of toil or altar burning
Are alike to Him.
Strike, then, comrades! Trade is waiting
On our rugged toil;
Far ships waiting for the freighting
Of our woodland spoil.*

*Ships, whose traffic links these highlands,
Bleak and cold, of ours,
With the citron-planted islands
Of a clime of flowers;
To our frosts the tribute bringing
Of eternal heats;
In our lap of winter flinging*

Tropic fruits and sweets.

Cheerly, on the axe of labor,
Let the sunbeams dance,
Better than the flash of sabre
Or the gleam of lance!
Strike! With every blow is given
Freer sun and sky,
And the long-hid earth to heaven
Looks, with wondering eye!

Loud behind us grow the murmurs
Of the age to come;
Clang of smiths, and tread of farmers,
Bearing harvest home!
Here her virgin lap with treasures
Shall the green earth fill;
Waving wheat and golden maize-ears
Crown each beechen hill.

Keep who will the city's alleys
Take the smooth-shorn plain';
Give to us the cedarn valleys,
Rocks and hills of Maine!
In our North-land, wild and woody,
Let us still have part
Rugged nurse and mother sturdy,
Hold us to thy heart!

*Oh, our free hearts beat the warmer
For thy breath of snow;
And our tread is all the firmer
For thy rocks below.
Freedom, hand in hand with labor,
Walketh strong and brave;
On the forehead of his neighbor
No man writeth Slave!*

*Lo, the day breaks! old Katahdin's
Pine-trees show its fires,
While from these dim forest gardens
Rise their blackened spires.
Up, my comrades! up and doing!
Manhood's rugged play
Still renewing, bravely hewing
Through the world our way!*

1845.

THE SHIP-BUILDERS

THE sky is ruddy in the east,
The earth is gray below,
And, spectral in the river-mist,
The ship's white timbers show.
Then let the sounds of measured stroke
And grating saw begin;
The broad-axe to the gnarled oak,
The mallet to the pin!

Hark! roars the bellows, blast on blast,
The sooty smithy jars,
And fire-sparks, rising far and fast,
Are fading with the stars.
All day for us the smith shall stand
Beside that flashing forge;
All day for us his heavy hand
The groaning anvil scourge.

From far-off hills, the panting team
For us is toiling near;
For us the raftsmen down the stream
Their island barges steer.
Rings out for us the axe-man's stroke
In forests old and still;
For us the century-circled oak
Falls crashing down his hill.

Up! up! in nobler toil than ours

No craftsmen bear a part
We make of Nature's giant powers
The slaves of human Art.
Lay rib to rib and beam to beam,
And drive the treenails free;
Nor faithless joint nor yawning seam
Shall tempt the searching sea.

Where'er the keel of our good ship
The sea's rough field shall plough;
Where'er her tossing spars shall drip
With salt-spray caught below;
That ship must heed her master's beck,
Her helm obey his hand,
And seamen tread her reeling deck
As if they trod the land.

Her oaken ribs the vulture-beak
Of Northern ice may peel;
The sunken rock and coral peak
May grate along her keel;
And know we well the painted shell
We give to wind and wave,
Must float, the sailor's citadel,
Or sink, the sailor's grave.

Ho! strike away the bars and blocks,
And set the good ship free!
Why lingers on these dusty rocks

The young bride of the sea?
Look! how she moves adown the grooves,
In graceful beauty now!
How lowly on the breast she loves
Sinks down her virgin prow.

God bless her! wheresoe'er the breeze
Her snowy wing shall fan,
Aside the frozen Hebrides,
Or sultry Hindostan!
Where'er, in mart or on the main,
With peaceful flag unfurled,
She helps to wind the silken chain
Of commerce round the world!

Speed on the ship! But let her bear
No merchandise of sin,
No groaning cargo of despair
Her roomy hold within;
No Lethean drug for Eastern lands,
Nor poison-draught for ours;
But honest fruits of toiling hands
And Nature's sun and showers.

Be hers the Prairie's golden grain,
The Desert's golden sand,
The clustered fruits of sunny Spain,
The spice of Morning-land!
Her pathway on the open main

May blessings follow free,
And glad hearts welcome back again
Her white sails from the sea
1846.

THE DROVERS.

THROUGH heat and cold, and shower and sun,
Still onward cheerly driving
There's life alone in duty done,
And rest alone in striving.
But see! the day is closing cool,
The woods are dim before us;
The white fog of the wayside pool
Is creeping slowly o'er us.

The night is falling, comrades mine,
Our footsore beasts are weary,
And through yon elms the tavern sign
Looks out upon us cheery.
The landlord beckons from his door,
His beechen fire is glowing;
These ample barns, with feed in store,
Are filled to overflowing.

From many a valley frowned across
By brows of rugged mountains;
From hillsides where, through spongy moss,
Gush out the river fountains;
From quiet farm-fields, green and low,
And bright with blooming clover;
From vales of corn the wandering crow
No richer hovers over;

Day after day our way has been

O'er many a hill and hollow;
By lake and stream, by wood and glen,
Our stately drove we follow.
Through dust-clouds rising thick and dun,
As smoke of battle o'er us,
Their white horns glisten in the sun,
Like plumes and crests before us.

We see them slowly climb the hill,
As slow behind it sinking;
Or, thronging close, from roadside rill,
Or sunny lakelet, drinking.
Now crowding in the narrow road,
In thick and struggling masses,
They glare upon the teamster's load,
Or rattling coach that passes.

Anon, with toss of horn and tail,
And paw of hoof, and bellow,
They leap some farmer's broken pale,
O'er meadow-close or fallow.
Forth comes the startled goodman; forth
Wife, children, house-dog, sally,
Till once more on their dusty path
The baffled truants rally.

We drive no starvelings, scraggy grown,
Loose-legged, and ribbed and bony,
Like those who grind their noses down

On pastures bare and stony,—
Lank oxen, rough as Indian dogs,
And cows too lean for shadows,
Disputing feebly with the frogs
The crop of saw-grass meadows!

In our good drove, so sleek and fair,
No bones of leanness rattle;
No tottering hide-bound ghosts are there,
Or Pharaoh's evil cattle.
Each stately beeve bespeaks the hand
That fed him unrepining;
The fatness of a goodly land
In each dun hide is shining.

We've sought them where, in warmest nooks,
The freshest feed is growing,
By sweetest springs and clearest brooks
Through honeysuckle flowing;
Wherever hillsides, sloping south,
Are bright with early grasses,
Or, tracking green the lowland's drouth,
The mountain streamlet passes.

But now the day is closing cool,
The woods are dim before us,
The white fog of the wayside pool
Is creeping slowly o'er us.
The cricket to the frog's bassoon

His shrillest time is keeping;
The sickle of yon setting moon
The meadow-mist is reaping.

The night is falling, comrades mine,
Our footsore beasts are weary,
And through yon elms the tavern sign
Looks out upon us cheery.
To-morrow, eastward with our charge
We'll go to meet the dawning,
Ere yet the pines of Kearsarge
Have seen the sun of morning.

When snow-flakes o'er the frozen earth,
Instead of birds, are flitting;
When children throng the glowing hearth,
And quiet wives are knitting;
While in the fire-light strong and clear
Young eyes of pleasure glisten,
To tales of all we see and hear
The ears of home shall listen.

By many a Northern lake and hill,
From many a mountain pasture,
Shall Fancy play the Drover still,
And speed the long night faster.
Then let us on, through shower and sun,
And heat and cold, be driving;

There 's life alone in duty done,
    And rest alone in striving.

   1847.

THE HUSKERS.

IT was late in mild October, and the long autumnal rain
Had left the summer harvest-fields all green with grass again;
The first sharp frosts had fallen, leaving all the woodlands gay
With the hues of summer's rainbow, or the meadow-flowers of May.

Through a thin, dry mist, that morning, the sun rose broad and red,
At first a rayless disk of fire, he brightened as he sped;
Yet, even his noontide glory fell chastened and subdued,
On the cornfields and the orchards, and softly pictured wood.

And all that quiet afternoon, slow sloping to the night,
He wove with golden shuttle the haze with yellow light;
Slanting through the painted beeches, he glorified the hill;
And, beneath it, pond and meadow lay brighter, greener still.

And shouting boys in woodland haunts caught glimpses of that sky,
Flecked by the many-tinted leaves, and laughed, they knew not why;
And school-girls, gay with aster-flowers, beside the meadow brooks,
Mingled the glow of autumn with the sunshine of sweet looks.

From spire and barn looked westerly the patient weathercocks;
But even the birches on the hill stood motionless as rocks.
No sound was in the woodlands, save the squirrel's dropping shell,
And the yellow leaves among the boughs, low rustling as they fell.

The summer grains were harvested; the stubble-fields lay dry,
Where June winds rolled, in light and shade, the pale green waves
of rye;

But still, on gentle hill-slopes, in valleys fringed with wood,
Ungathered, bleaching in the sun, the heavy corn crop stood.

Bent low, by autumn's wind and rain, through husks that, dry and sere,
Unfolded from their ripened charge, shone out the yellow ear;
Beneath, the turnip lay concealed, in many a verdant fold,
And glistened in the slanting light the pumpkin's sphere of gold.

There wrought the busy harvesters; and many a creaking wain
Bore slowly to the long barn-floor its load of husk and grain;
Till broad and red, as when he rose, the sun sank down, at last,
And like a merry guest's farewell, the day in brightness passed.

And lo! as through the western pines, on meadow, stream, and pond,
Flamed the red radiance of a sky, set all afire beyond,
Slowly o'er the eastern sea-bluffs a milder glory shone,
And the sunset and the moonrise were mingled into one!

As thus into the quiet night the twilight lapsed away,
And deeper in the brightening moon the tranquil shadows lay;
From many a brown old farm-house, and hamlet without name,
Their milking and their home-tasks done, the merry huskers came.

Swung o'er the heaped-up harvest, from pitchforks in the mow,
Shone dimly down the lanterns on the pleasant scene below;
The growing pile of husks behind, the golden ears before,
And laughing eyes and busy hands and brown cheeks glimmering o'er.

Half hidden, in a quiet nook, serene of look and heart,

Talking their old times over, the old men sat apart;
While up and down the unhusked pile, or nestling in its shade,
At hide-and-seek, with laugh and shout, the happy children played.

Urged by the good host's daughter, a maiden young and fair,
Lifting to light her sweet blue eyes and pride of soft brown hair,
The master of the village school, sleek of hair and smooth of tongue,
To the quaint tune of some old psalm, a husking ballad sung.

THE CORN-SONG.

Heap high the farmer's wintry hoard
Heap high the golden corn
No richer gift has Autumn poured
From out her lavish horn!

Let other lands, exulting, glean
The apple from the pine,
The orange from its glossy green,
The cluster from the vine;

We better love the hardy gift
Our rugged vales bestow,
To cheer us when the storm shall drift
Our harvest-fields with snow.

Through vales of grass and mends of flowers
Our ploughs their furrows made,
While on the hills the sun and showers
Of changeful April played.

We dropped the seed o'er hill and plain
Beneath the sun of May,
And frightened from our sprouting grain
The robber crows away.

All through the long, bright days of June
Its leaves grew green and fair,
And waved in hot midsummer's noon

Its soft and yellow hair.

And now, with autumn's moonlit eves,
Its harvest-time has come,
We pluck away the frosted leaves,
And bear the treasure home.

There, when the snows about us drift,
And winter winds are cold,
Fair hands the broken grain shall sift,
And knead its meal of gold.

Let vapid idlers loll in silk
Around their costly board;
Give us the bowl of samp and milk,
By homespun beauty poured!

Where'er the wide old kitchen hearth
Sends up its smoky curls,
Who will not thank the kindly earth,
And bless our farmer girls!

Then shame on all the proud and vain,
Whose folly laughs to scorn
The blessing of our hardy grain,
Our wealth of golden corn.

Let earth withhold her goodly root,
Let mildew blight the rye,

Give to the worm the orchard's fruit,
The wheat-field to the fly.

But let the good old crop adorn
The hills our fathers trod;
Still let us, for his golden corn,
Send up our thanks to God!

1847.

THE REFORMER.

*ALL grim and soiled and brown with tan,
I saw a Strong One, in his wrath,
Smiting the godless shrines of man
Along his path.*

*The Church, beneath her trembling dome,
Essayed in vain her ghostly charm
Wealth shook within his gilded home
With strange alarm.*

*Fraud from his secret chambers fled
Before the sunlight bursting in
Sloth drew her pillow o'er her head
To drown the din.*

*"Spare," Art implored, "yon holy pile;
That grand, old, time-worn turret spare;"
Meek Reverence, kneeling in the aisle,
Cried out, "Forbear!"*

*Gray-bearded Use, who, deaf and blind,
Groped for his old accustomed stone,
Leaned on his staff, and wept to find
His seat o'erthrown.*

*Young Romance raised his dreamy eyes,
O'erhung with paly locks of gold,—
"Why smite," he asked in sad surprise,*

"The fair, the old?"

Yet louder rang the Strong One's stroke,
Yet nearer flashed his axe's gleam;
Shuddering and sick of heart I woke,
As from a dream.

I looked: aside the dust-cloud rolled,
The Waster seemed the Builder too;
Upspringing from the ruined Old
I saw the New.

'T was but the ruin of the bad,—
The wasting of the wrong and ill;
Whate'er of good the old time had
Was living still.

Calm grew the brows of him I feared;
The frown which awed me passed away,
And left behind a smile which cheered
Like breaking day.

The grain grew green on battle-plains,
O'er swarded war-mounds grazed the cow;
The slave stood forging from his chains
The spade and plough.

Where frowned the fort, pavilions gay
And cottage windows, flower-entwined,

Looked out upon the peaceful bay
And hills behind.

Through vine-wreathed cups with wine once red,
The lights on brimming crystal fell,
Drawn, sparkling, from the rivulet head
And mossy well.

Through prison walls, like Heaven-sent hope,
Fresh breezes blew, and sunbeams strayed,
And with the idle gallows-rope
The young child played.

Where the doomed victim in his cell
Had counted o'er the weary hours,
Glad school-girls, answering to the bell,
Came crowned with flowers.

Grown wiser for the lesson given,
I fear no longer, for I know
That, where the share is deepest driven,
The best fruits grow.

The outworn rite, the old abuse,
The pious fraud transparent grown,
The good held captive in the use
Of wrong alone,—

These wait their doom, from that great law

Which makes the past time serve to-day;
And fresher life the world shall draw
From their decay.

Oh, backward-looking son of time!
The new is old, the old is new,
The cycle of a change sublime
Still sweeping through.

So wisely taught the Indian seer;
Destroying Seva, forming Brahm,
Who wake by turns Earth's love and fear,
Are one, the same.

Idly as thou, in that old day
Thou mournest, did thy sire repine;
So, in his time, thy child grown gray
Shall sigh for thine.

But life shall on and upward go;
Th' eternal step of Progress beats
To that great anthem, calm and slow,
Which God repeats.

Take heart! the Waster builds again,
A charmed life old Goodness hath;
The tares may perish, but the grain
Is not for death.

God works in all things; all obey
His first propulsion from the night
Wake thou and watch! the world is gray
With morning light!

1848.

THE PEACE CONVENTION AT BRUSSELS.

STILL in thy streets, O Paris! doth the stain
Of blood defy the cleansing autumn rain;
Still breaks the smoke Messina's ruins through,
And Naples mourns that new Bartholomew,
When squalid beggary, for a dole of bread,
At a crowned murderer's beck of license, fed
The yawning trenches with her noble dead;
Still, doomed Vienna, through thy stately halls
The shell goes crashing and the red shot falls,
And, leagued to crush thee, on the Danube's side,
The bearded Croat and Bosniak spearman ride;
Still in that vale where Himalaya's snow
Melts round the cornfields and the vines below,
The Sikh's hot cannon, answering ball for ball,
Flames in the breach of Moultan's shattered wall;
On Chenab's side the vulture seeks the slain,
And Sutlej paints with blood its banks again.

"What folly, then," the faithless critic cries,
With sneering lip, and wise world-knowing eyes,
"While fort to fort, and post to post, repeat
The ceaseless challenge of the war-drum's beat,
And round the green earth, to the church-bell's chime,
The morning drum-roll of the camp keeps time,
To dream of peace amidst a world in arms,
Of swords to ploughshares changed by Scriptural charms,
Of nations, drunken with the wine of blood,
Staggering to take the Pledge of Brotherhood,

Like tipplers answering Father Matthew's call;
The sullen Spaniard, and the mad-cap Gaul,
The bull-dog Briton, yielding but with life,
The Yankee swaggering with his bowie-knife,
The Russ, from banquets with the vulture shared,
The blood still dripping from his amber beard,
Quitting their mad Berserker dance to hear
The dull, meek droning of a drab-coat seer;
Leaving the sport of Presidents and Kings,
Where men for dice each titled gambler flings,
To meet alternate on the Seine and Thames,
For tea and gossip, like old country dames
No! let the cravens plead the weakling's cant,
Let Cobden cipher, and let Vincent rant,
Let Sturge preach peace to democratic throngs,
And Burritt, stammering through his hundred tongues,
Repeat, in all, his ghostly lessons o'er,
Timed to the pauses of the battery's roar;
Check Ban or Kaiser with the barricade
Of "Olive-leaves" and Resolutions made,
Spike guns with pointed Scripture-texts, and hope
To capsize navies with a windy trope;
Still shall the glory and the pomp of War
Along their train the shouting millions draw;
Still dusty Labor to the passing Brave
His cap shall doff, and Beauty's kerchief wave;
Still shall the bard to Valor tune his song,
Still Hero-worship kneel before the Strong;
Rosy and sleek, the sable-gowned divine,

O'er his third bottle of suggestive wine,
To plumed and sworded auditors, shall prove
Their trade accordant with the Law of Love;
And Church for State, and State for Church, shall fight,
And both agree, that "Might alone is Right!"
Despite of sneers like these, O faithful few,
Who dare to hold God's word and witness true,
Whose clear-eyed faith transcends our evil time,
And o'er the present wilderness of crime
Sees the calm future, with its robes of green,
Its fleece-flecked mountains, and soft streams between,—
Still keep the path which duty bids ye tread,
Though worldly wisdom shake the cautious head;
No truth from Heaven descends upon our sphere,
Without the greeting of the skeptic's sneer;
Denied and mocked at, till its blessings fall,
Common as dew and sunshine, over all."

Then, o'er Earth's war-field, till the strife shall cease,
Like Morven's harpers, sing your song of peace;
As in old fable rang the Thracian's lyre,
Midst howl of fiends and roar of penal fire,
Till the fierce din to pleasing murmurs fell,
And love subdued the maddened heart of hell.
Lend, once again, that holy song a tongue,
Which the glad angels of the Advent sung,
Their cradle-anthem for the Saviour's birth,
Glory to God, and peace unto the earth
Through the mad discord send that calming word

Which wind and wave on wild Genesareth heard,
Lift in Christ's name his Cross against the Sword!
Not vain the vision which the prophets saw,
Skirting with green the fiery waste of war,
Through the hot sand-gleam, looming soft and calm
On the sky's rim, the fountain-shading palm.
Still lives for Earth, which fiends so long have trod,
The great hope resting on the truth of God,—
Evil shall cease and Violence pass away,
And the tired world breathe free through a long Sabbath day.

11th mo., 1848.

THE PRISONER FOR DEBT.

Before the law authorizing imprisonment for debt had been abolished in Massachusetts, a revolutionary pensioner was confined in Charlestown jail for a debt of fourteen dollars, and on the fourth of July was seen waving a handkerchief from the bars of his cell in honor of the day.

Look on him! through his dungeon grate,
Feebly and cold, the morning light
Comes stealing round him, dim and late,
As if it loathed the sight.
Reclining on his strawy bed,
His hand upholds his drooping head;
His bloodless cheek is seamed and hard,
Unshorn his gray, neglected beard;
And o'er his bony fingers flow
His long, dishevelled locks of snow.
No grateful fire before him glows,
And yet the winter's breath is chill;
And o'er his half-clad person goes
The frequent ague thrill!
Silent, save ever and anon,
A sound, half murmur and half groan,
Forces apart the painful grip
Of the old sufferer's bearded lip;
Oh, sad and crushing is the fate
Of old age chained and desolate!

Just God! why lies that old man there?
A murderer shares his prison bed,
Whose eyeballs, through his horrid hair,
Gleam on him, fierce and red;

And the rude oath and heartless jeer
Fall ever on his loathing ear,
And, or in wakefulness or sleep,
Nerve, flesh, and pulses thrill and creep
Whene'er that ruffian's tossing limb,
Crimson with murder, touches him!

What has the gray-haired prisoner done?
Has murder stained his hands with gore?
Not so; his crime's a fouler one;
God made the old man poor!
For this he shares a felon's cell,
The fittest earthly type of hell
For this, the boon for which he poured
His young blood on the invader's sword,
And counted light the fearful cost;
His blood-gained liberty is lost!

And so, for such a place of rest,
Old prisoner, dropped thy blood as rain
On Concord's field, and Bunker's crest,
And Saratoga's plain?
Look forth, thou man of many scars,
Through thy dim dungeon's iron bars;
It must be joy, in sooth, to see
Yon monument upreared to thee;
Piled granite and a prison cell,
The land repays thy service well!

Go, ring the bells and fire the guns,
And fling the starry banner out;
Shout "Freedom!" till your lisping ones
Give back their cradle-shout;
Let boastful eloquence declaim
Of honor, liberty, and fame;
Still let the poet's strain be heard,
With glory for each second word,
And everything with breath agree
To praise "our glorious liberty!"

But when the patron cannon jars
That prison's cold and gloomy wall,
And through its grates the stripes and stars
Rise on the wind, and fall,
Think ye that prisoner's aged ear
Rejoices in the general cheer?
Think ye his dim and failing eye
Is kindled at your pageantry?
Sorrowing of soul, and chained of limb,
What is your carnival to him?

Down with the law that binds him thus!
Unworthy freemen, let it find
No refuge from the withering curse
Of God and human-kind
Open the prison's living tomb,
And usher from its brooding gloom
The victims of your savage code

To the free sun and air of God;
No longer dare as crime to brand
The chastening of the Almighty's hand.

1849.

THE CHRISTIAN TOURISTS.

The reader of the biography of William Allen, the philanthropic associate of Clarkson and Romilly, cannot fail to admire his simple and beautiful record of a tour through Europe, in the years 1818 and 1819, in the company of his American friend, Stephen Grellett.

No aimless wanderers, by the fiend Unrest
Goaded from shore to shore;
No schoolmen, turning, in their classic quest,
The leaves of empire o'er.
Simple of faith, and bearing in their hearts
The love of man and God,
Isles of old song, the Moslem's ancient marts,
And Scythia's steppes, they trod.

Where the long shadows of the fir and pine
In the night sun are cast,
And the deep heart of many a Norland mine
Quakes at each riving blast;
Where, in barbaric grandeur, Moskwa stands,
A baptized Scythian queen,
With Europe's arts and Asia's jewelled hands,
The North and East between!

Where still, through vales of Grecian fable, stray
The classic forms of yore,
And beauty smiles, new risen from the spray,
And Dian weeps once more;
Where every tongue in Smyrna's mart resounds;
And Stamboul from the sea
Lifts her tall minarets over burial-grounds

Black with the cypress-tree.

From Malta's temples to the gates of Rome,
Following the track of Paul,
And where the Alps gird round the Switzer's home
Their vast, eternal wall;
They paused not by the ruins of old time,
They scanned no pictures rare,
Nor lingered where the snow-locked mountains climb
The cold abyss of air!

But unto prisons, where men lay in chains,
To haunts where Hunger pined,
To kings and courts forgetful of the pains
And wants of human-kind,
Scattering sweet words, and quiet deeds of good,
Along their way, like flowers,
Or pleading, as Christ's freemen only could,
With princes and with powers;

Their single aim the purpose to fulfil
Of Truth, from day to day,
Simply obedient to its guiding will,
They held their pilgrim way.
Yet dream not, hence, the beautiful and old
Were wasted on their sight,
Who in the school of Christ had learned to hold
All outward things aright.

Not less to them the breath of vineyards blown
From off the Cyprian shore,
Not less for them the Alps in sunset shone,
That man they valued more.
A life of beauty lends to all it sees
The beauty of its thought;
And fairest forms and sweetest harmonies
Make glad its way, unsought.

In sweet accordancy of praise and love,
The singing waters run;
And sunset mountains wear in light above
The smile of duty done;
Sure stands the promise,—ever to the meek
A heritage is given;
Nor lose they Earth who, single-hearted, seek
The righteousness of Heaven!

1849.

THE MEN OF OLD.

"WELL speed thy mission, bold Iconoclast!
Yet all unworthy of its trust thou art,
If, with dry eye, and cold, unloving heart,
Thou tread'st the solemn Pantheon of the Past,
By the great Future's dazzling hope made blind
To all the beauty, power, and truth behind.
Not without reverent awe shouldst thou put by
The cypress branches and the amaranth blooms,
Where, with clasped hands of prayer, upon their tombs
The effigies of old confessors lie,
God's witnesses; the voices of His will,
Heard in the slow march of the centuries still
Such were the men at whose rebuking frown,
Dark with God's wrath, the tyrant's knee went down;
Such from the terrors of the guilty drew
The vassal's freedom and the poor man's due."

St. Anselm (may he rest forevermore
In Heaven's sweet peace!) forbade, of old, the sale
Of men as slaves, and from the sacred pale
Hurled the Northumbrian buyers of the poor.
To ransom souls from bonds and evil fate
St. Ambrose melted down the sacred plate,—
Image of saint, the chalice, and the pix,
Crosses of gold, and silver candlesticks.
"Man is worth more than temples!" he replied
To such as came his holy work to chide.
And brave Cesarius, stripping altars bare,

And coining from the Abbey's golden hoard
The captive's freedom, answered to the prayer
Or threat of those whose fierce zeal for the Lord
Stifled their love of man,—"An earthen dish
The last sad supper of the Master bore
Most miserable sinners! do ye wish
More than your Lord, and grudge His dying poor
What your own pride and not His need requires?
Souls, than these shining gauds, He values more
Mercy, not sacrifice, His heart desires!"
O faithful worthies! resting far behind
In your dark ages, since ye fell asleep,
Much has been done for truth and human-kind;
Shadows are scattered wherein ye groped blind;
Man claims his birthright, freer pulses leap
Through peoples driven in your day like sheep;
Yet, like your own, our age's sphere of light,
Though widening still, is walled around by night;
With slow, reluctant eye, the Church has read,
Skeptic at heart, the lessons of its Head;
Counting, too oft, its living members less
Than the wall's garnish and the pulpit's dress;
World-moving zeal, with power to bless and feed
Life's fainting pilgrims, to their utter need,
Instead of bread, holds out the stone of creed;
Sect builds and worships where its wealth and pride
And vanity stand shrined and deified,
Careless that in the shadow of its walls

*God's living temple into ruin falls.
We need, methinks, the prophet-hero still,
Saints true of life, and martyrs strong of will,
To tread the land, even now, as Xavier trod
The streets of Goa, barefoot, with his bell,
Proclaiming freedom in the name of God,
And startling tyrants with the fear of hell
Soft words, smooth prophecies, are doubtless well;
But to rebuke the age's popular crime,
We need the souls of fire, the hearts of that old time!*

1849.

TO PIUS IX.

The writer of these lines is no enemy of Catholics. He has, on more than one occasion, exposed himself to the censures of his Protestant brethren, by his strenuous endeavors to procure indemnification for the owners of the convent destroyed near Boston. He defended the cause of the Irish patriots long before it had become popular in this country; and he was one of the first to urge the most liberal aid to the suffering and starving population of the Catholic island. The severity of his language finds its ample apology in the reluctant confession of one of the most eminent Romish priests, the eloquent and devoted Father Ventura.

THE cannon's brazen lips are cold;
No red shell blazes down the air;
And street and tower, and temple old,
Are silent as despair.

The Lombard stands no more at bay,
Rome's fresh young life has bled in vain;
The ravens scattered by the day
Come back with night again.

Now, while the fratricides of France
Are treading on the neck of Rome,
Hider at Gaeta, seize thy chance!
Coward and cruel, come!
Creep now from Naples' bloody skirt;
Thy mummer's part was acted well,
While Rome, with steel and fire begirt,
Before thy crusade fell!

Her death-groans answered to thy prayer;
Thy chant, the drum and bugle-call;

Thy lights, the burning villa's glare;
Thy beads, the shell and ball!

Let Austria clear thy way, with hands
Foul from Ancona's cruel sack,
And Naples, with his dastard bands
Of murderers, lead thee back!

Rome's lips are dumb; the orphan's wail,
The mother's shriek, thou mayst not hear
Above the faithless Frenchman's hail,
The unsexed shaveling's cheer!

Go, bind on Rome her cast-off weight,
The double curse of crook and crown,
Though woman's scorn and manhood's hate
From wall and roof flash down!

Nor heed those blood-stains on the wall,
Not Tiber's flood can wash away,
Where, in thy stately Quirinal,
Thy mangled victims lay!
Let the world murmur; let its cry
Of horror and disgust be heard;
Truth stands alone; thy coward lie
Is backed by lance and sword!

The cannon of St. Angelo,
And chanting priest and clanging bell,

And beat of drum and bugle blow,
Shall greet thy coming well!

Let lips of iron and tongues of slaves
Fit welcome give thee; for her part,
Rome, frowning o'er her new-made graves,
Shall curse thee from her heart!

No wreaths of sad Campagna's flowers
Shall childhood in thy pathway fling;
No garlands from their ravaged bowers
Shall Terni's maidens bring;

But, hateful as that tyrant old,
The mocking witness of his crime,
In thee shall loathing eyes behold
The Nero of our time!

Stand where Rome's blood was freest shed,
Mock Heaven with impious thanks, and call
Its curses on the patriot dead,
Its blessings on the Gaul!
Or sit upon thy throne of lies,
A poor, mean idol, blood-besmeared,
Whom even its worshippers despise,
Unhonored, unrevered!

Yet, Scandal of the World! from thee
One needful truth mankind shall learn

That kings and priests to Liberty
And God are false in turn.

Earth wearies of them; and the long
Meek sufferance of the Heavens doth fail;
Woe for weak tyrants, when the strong
Wake, struggle, and prevail!

Not vainly Roman hearts have bled
To feed the Crosier and the Crown,
If, roused thereby, the world shall tread
The twin-born vampires down.

1849.

CALEF IN BOSTON.

1692.

IN *the solemn days of old,*
Two men met in Boston town,
One a tradesman frank and bold,
One a preacher of renown.
Cried the last, in bitter tone:
"Poisoner of the wells of truth
Satan's hireling, thou hast sown
With his tares the heart of youth!"

Spake the simple tradesman then,
"God be judge 'twixt thee and me;
All thou knowed of truth hath been
Once a lie to men like thee.

"Falsehoods which we spurn to-day
Were the truths of long ago;
Let the dead boughs fall away,
Fresher shall the living grow.

"God is good and God is light,
In this faith I rest secure;
Evil can but serve the right,
Over all shall love endure.

"Of your spectral puppet play
I have traced the cunning wires;
Come what will, I needs must say,

God is true, and ye are liars."

When the thought of man is free,
Error fears its lightest tones;
So the priest cried, "Sadducee!"
And the people took up stones.
In the ancient burying-ground,
Side by side the twain now lie;
One with humble grassy mound,
One with marbles pale and high.

But the Lord hath blest the seed
Which that tradesman scattered then,
And the preacher's spectral creed
Chills no more the blood of men.

Let us trust, to one is known
Perfect love which casts out fear,
While the other's joys atone
For the wrong he suffered here.

1849.

OUR STATE.

THE South-land boasts its teeming cane,
The prairied West its heavy grain,
And sunset's radiant gates unfold
On rising marts and sands of gold.

Rough, bleak, and hard, our little State
Is scant of soil, of limits strait;
Her yellow sands are sands alone,
Her only mines are ice and stone!

From Autumn frost to April rain,
Too long her winter woods complain;
From budding flower to falling leaf,
Her summer time is all too brief.

Yet, on her rocks, and on her sands,
And wintry hills, the school-house stands,
And what her rugged soil denies,
The harvest of the mind supplies.

The riches of the Commonwealth
Are free, strong minds, and hearts of health;
And more to her than gold or grain,
The cunning hand and cultured brain.

For well she keeps her ancient stock,
The stubborn strength of Pilgrim Rock;
And still maintains, with milder laws,

And clearer light, the Good Old Cause.

Nor heeds the skeptic's puny hands,
While near her school the church-spire stands;
Nor fears the blinded bigot's rule,
While near her church-spire stands the school.

1849.

THE PRISONERS OF NAPLES.

I HAVE been thinking of the victims bound
In Naples, dying for the lack of air
And sunshine, in their close, damp cells of pain,
Where hope is not, and innocence in vain
Appeals against the torture and the chain!
Unfortunates! whose crime it was to share
Our common love of freedom, and to dare,
In its behalf, Rome's harlot triple-crowned,
And her base pander, the most hateful thing
Who upon Christian or on Pagan ground
Makes vile the old heroic name of king.
O God most merciful! Father just and kind
Whom man hath bound let thy right hand unbind.
Or, if thy purposes of good behind
Their ills lie hidden, let the sufferers find
Strong consolations; leave them not to doubt
Thy providential care, nor yet without
The hope which all thy attributes inspire,
That not in vain the martyr's robe of fire
Is worn, nor the sad prisoner's fretting chain;
Since all who suffer for thy truth send forth,
Electrical, with every throb of pain,
Unquenchable sparks, thy own baptismal rain
Of fire and spirit over all the earth,
Making the dead in slavery live again.
Let this great hope be with them, as they lie
Shut from the light, the greenness, and the sky;
From the cool waters and the pleasant breeze,

The smell of flowers, and shade of summer trees;
Bound with the felon lepers, whom disease
And sins abhorred make loathsome; let them share
Pellico's faith, Foresti's strength to bear
Years of unutterable torment, stern and still,
As the chained Titan victor through his will!
Comfort them with thy future; let them see
The day-dawn of Italian liberty;
For that, with all good things, is hid with Thee,
And, perfect in thy thought, awaits its time to be.

I, who have spoken for freedom at the cost
Of some weak friendships, or some paltry prize
Of name or place, and more than I have lost
Have gained in wider reach of sympathies,
And free communion with the good and wise;
May God forbid that I should ever boast
Such easy self-denial, or repine
That the strong pulse of health no more is mine;
That, overworn at noonday, I must yield
To other hands the gleaning of the field;
A tired on-looker through the day's decline.
For blest beyond deserving still, and knowing
That kindly Providence its care is showing
In the withdrawal as in the bestowing,
Scarcely I dare for more or less to pray.
Beautiful yet for me this autumn day
Melts on its sunset hills; and, far away,
For me the Ocean lifts its solemn psalm,

To me the pine-woods whisper; and for me
Yon river, winding through its vales of calm,
By greenest banks, with asters purple-starred,
And gentian bloom and golden-rod made gay,
Flows down in silent gladness to the sea,
Like a pure spirit to its great reward!

Nor lack I friends, long-tried and near and dear,
Whose love is round me like this atmosphere,
Warm, soft, and golden. For such gifts to me
What shall I render, O my God, to thee?
Let me not dwell upon my lighter share
Of pain and ill that human life must bear;
Save me from selfish pining; let my heart,
Drawn from itself in sympathy, forget
The bitter longings of a vain regret,
The anguish of its own peculiar smart.
Remembering others, as I have to-day,
In their great sorrows, let me live alway
Not for myself alone, but have a part,
Such as a frail and erring spirit may,
In love which is of Thee, and which indeed Thou art!

1851.

THE PEACE OF EUROPE.

"GREAT peace in Europe! Order reigns
From Tiber's hills to Danube's plains!"
So say her kings and priests; so say
The lying prophets of our day.

Go lay to earth a listening ear;
The tramp of measured marches hear;
The rolling of the cannon's wheel,
The shotted musket's murderous peal,
The night alarm, the sentry's call,
The quick-eared spy in hut and hall!
From Polar sea and tropic fen
The dying-groans of exiled men!
The bolted cell, the galley's chains,
The scaffold smoking with its stains!
Order, the hush of brooding slaves
Peace, in the dungeon-vaults and graves!

O Fisher! of the world-wide net,
With meshes in all waters set,
Whose fabled keys of heaven and hell
Bolt hard the patriot's prison-cell,
And open wide the banquet-hall,
Where kings and priests hold carnival!
Weak vassal tricked in royal guise,
Boy Kaiser with thy lip of lies;
Base gambler for Napoleon's crown,
Barnacle on his dead renown!

Thou, Bourbon Neapolitan,
Crowned scandal, loathed of God and man
And thou, fell Spider of the North!
Stretching thy giant feelers forth,
Within whose web the freedom dies
Of nations eaten up like flies!
Speak, Prince and Kaiser, Priest and Czar !
If this be Peace, pray what is War?

White Angel of the Lord! unmeet
That soil accursed for thy pure feet.
Never in Slavery's desert flows
The fountain of thy charmed repose;
No tyrant's hand thy chaplet weaves
Of lilies and of olive-leaves;
Not with the wicked shalt thou dwell,
Thus saith the Eternal Oracle;
Thy home is with the pure and free!
Stern herald of thy better day,
Before thee, to prepare thy way,
The Baptist Shade of Liberty,
Gray, scarred and hairy-robed, must press
With bleeding feet the wilderness!
Oh that its voice might pierces the ear
Of princes, trembling while they hear
A cry as of the Hebrew seer
Repent! God's kingdom draweth near!

1852.

ASTRAEA.

> *"Jove means to settle*
> *Astraea in her seat again,*
> *And let down from his golden chain*
> *An age of better metal."*
>   BEN JONSON, 1615.

O POET rare and old!
Thy words are prophecies;
Forward the age of gold,
The new Saturnian lies.

The universal prayer
And hope are not in vain;
Rise, brothers! and prepare
The way for Saturn's reign.

Perish shall all which takes
From labor's board and can;
Perish shall all which makes
A spaniel of the man!

Free from its bonds the mind,
The body from the rod;
Broken all chains that bind
The image of our God.

Just men no longer pine
Behind their prison-bars;
Through the rent dungeon shine

*The free sun and the stars.
Earth own, at last, untrod
By sect, or caste, or clan,
The fatherhood of God,
The brotherhood of man!*

*Fraud fail, craft perish, forth
The money-changers driven,
And God's will done on earth,
As now in heaven.*

1852.

THE DISENTHRALLED.

HE had bowed down to drunkenness,
An abject worshipper
The pride of manhood's pulse had grown
Too faint and cold to stir;
And he had given his spirit up
To the unblessed thrall,
And bowing to the poison cup,
He gloried in his fall!

There came a change—the cloud rolled off,
And light fell on his brain—
And like the passing of a dream
That cometh not again,
The shadow of the spirit fled.
He saw the gulf before,
He shuddered at the waste behind,
And was a man once more.

He shook the serpent folds away,
That gathered round his heart,
As shakes the swaying forest-oak
Its poison vine apart;
He stood erect; returning pride
Grew terrible within,
And conscience sat in judgment, on
His most familiar sin.

The light of Intellect again

Along his pathway shone;
And Reason like a monarch sat
Upon his olden throne.
The honored and the wise once more
Within his presence came;
And lingered oft on lovely lips
His once forbidden name.

There may be glory in the might,
That treadeth nations down;
Wreaths for the crimson conqueror,
Pride for the kingly crown;
But nobler is that triumph hour,
The disenthralled shall find,
When evil passion boweth down,
Unto the Godlike mind.

THE POOR VOTER ON ELECTION DAY.

THE proudest now is but my peer,
The highest not more high;
To-day, of all the weary year,
A king of men am I.
To-day, alike are great and small,
The nameless and the known;
My palace is the people's hall,
The ballot-box my throne!

Who serves to-day upon the list
Beside the served shall stand;
Alike the brown and wrinkled fist,
The gloved and dainty hand!
The rich is level with the poor,
The weak is strong to-day;
And sleekest broadcloth counts no more
Than homespun frock of gray.

To-day let pomp and vain pretence
My stubborn right abide;
I set a plain man's common sense
Against the pedant's pride.
To-day shall simple manhood try
The strength of gold and land;
The wide world has not wealth to buy
The power in my right hand!

While there's a grief to seek redress,

Or balance to adjust,
Where weighs our living manhood less
Than Mammon's vilest dust,—
While there's a right to need my vote,
A wrong to sweep away,
Up! clouted knee and ragged coat
A man's a man to-day.

1848.

THE DREAM OF PIO NONO.

IT chanced that while the pious troops of France
Fought in the crusade Pio Nono preached,
What time the holy Bourbons stayed his hands
(The Hun and Aaron meet for such a Moses),
Stretched forth from Naples towards rebellious Rome
To bless the ministry of Oudinot,
And sanctify his iron homilies
And sharp persuasions of the bayonet,
That the great pontiff fell asleep, and dreamed.

He stood by Lake Tiberias, in the sun
Of the bight Orient; and beheld the lame,
The sick, and blind, kneel at the Master's feet,
And rise up whole. And, sweetly over all,
Dropping the ladder of their hymn of praise
From heaven to earth, in silver rounds of song,
He heard the blessed angels sing of peace,
Good-will to man, and glory to the Lord.

Then one, with feet unshod, and leathern face
Hardened and darkened by fierce summer suns
And hot winds of the desert, closer drew
His fisher's haick, and girded up his loins,
And spake, as one who had authority
"Come thou with me."

Lakeside and eastern sky
And the sweet song of angels passed away,

And, with a dream's alacrity of change,
The priest, and the swart fisher by his side,
Beheld the Eternal City lift its domes
And solemn fanes and monumental pomp
Above the waste Campagna. On the hills
The blaze of burning villas rose and fell,
And momently the mortar's iron throat
Roared from the trenches; and, within the walls,
Sharp crash of shells, low groans of human pain,
Shout, drum beat, and the clanging larum-bell,
And tramp of hosts, sent up a mingled sound,
Half wail and half defiance. As they passed
The gate of San Pancrazio, human blood
Flowed ankle-high about them, and dead men
Choked the long street with gashed and gory piles,—
A ghastly barricade of mangled flesh,
From which at times, quivered a living hand,
And white lips moved and moaned. A father tore
His gray hairs, by the body of his son,
In frenzy; and his fair young daughter wept
On his old bosom. Suddenly a flash
Clove the thick sulphurous air, and man and maid
Sank, crushed and mangled by the shattering shell.

Then spake the Galilean: "Thou hast seen
The blessed Master and His works of love;
Look now on thine! Hear'st thou the angels sing
Above this open hell? Thou God's high-priest!
Thou the Vicegerent of the Prince of Peace!

Thou the successor of His chosen ones!
I, Peter, fisherman of Galilee,
In the dear Master's name, and for the love
Of His true Church, proclaim thee Antichrist,
Alien and separate from His holy faith,
Wide as the difference between death and life,
The hate of man and the great love of God!
Hence, and repent!"

Thereat the pontiff woke,
Trembling, and muttering o'er his fearful dream.
"What means he?" cried the Bourbon, "Nothing more
Than that your majesty hath all too well
Catered for your poor guests, and that, in sooth,
The Holy Father's supper troubleth him,"
Said Cardinal Antonelli, with a smile.

1853.

THE VOICES.

WHY urge the long, unequal fight,
Since Truth has fallen in the street,
Or lift anew the trampled light,
Quenched by the heedless million's feet?

"Give o'er the thankless task; forsake
The fools who know not ill from good
Eat, drink, enjoy thy own, and take
Thine ease among the multitude.

"Live out thyself; with others share
Thy proper life no more; assume
The unconcern of sun and air,
For life or death, or blight or bloom.

"The mountain pine looks calmly on
The fires that scourge the plains below,
Nor heeds the eagle in the sun
The small birds piping in the snow!

"The world is God's, not thine; let Him
Work out a change, if change must be
The hand that planted best can trim
And nurse the old unfruitful tree."

So spake the Tempter, when the light
Of sun and stars had left the sky;
I listened, through the cloud and night,

And beard, methought, a voice reply:

"Thy task may well seem over-hard,
Who scatterest in a thankless soil
Thy life as seed, with no reward
Save that which Duty gives to Toil.

"Not wholly is thy heart resigned
To Heaven's benign and just decree,
Which, linking thee with all thy kind,
Transmits their joys and griefs to thee.

"Break off that sacred chain, and turn
Back on thyself thy love and care;
Be thou thine own mean idol, burn
Faith, Hope, and Trust, thy children, there.

"Released from that fraternal law
Which shares the common bale and bliss,
No sadder lot could Folly draw,
Or Sin provoke from Fate, than this.

"The meal unshared is food unblest
Thou hoard'st in vain what love should spend;
Self-ease is pain; thy only rest
Is labor for a worthy end;

"A toil that gains with what it yields,
And scatters to its own increase,

*And hears, while sowing outward fields,
The harvest-song of inward peace.*

*"Free-lipped the liberal streamlets run,
Free shines for all the healthful ray;
The still pool stagnates in the sun,
The lurid earth-fire haunts decay.*

*"What is it that the crowd requite
Thy love with hate, thy truth with lies?
And but to faith, and not to sight,
The walls of Freedom's temple rise?*

*"Yet do thy work; it shall succeed
In thine or in another's day;
And, if denied the victor's meed,
Thou shalt not lack the toiler's pay.*

*"Faith shares the future's promise; Love's
Self-offering is a triumph won;
And each good thought or action moves
The dark world nearer to the sun.*

*"Then faint not, falter not, nor plead
Thy weakness; truth itself is strong;
The lion's strength, the eagle's speed,
Are not alone vouchsafed to wrong.*

"Thy nature, which, through fire and flood,

To place or gain finds out its way,
Hath power to seek the highest good,
And duty's holiest call obey!

"Strivest thou in darkness?—Foes without
In league with traitor thoughts within;
Thy night-watch kept with trembling Doubt
And pale Remorse the ghost of Sin?

"Hast thou not, on some week of storm,
Seen the sweet Sabbath breaking fair,
And cloud and shadow, sunlit, form
The curtains of its tent of prayer?

"So, haply, when thy task shall end,
The wrong shall lose itself in right,
And all thy week-day darkness blend
With the long Sabbath of the light!"

1854.

THE NEW EXODUS.

Written upon hearing that slavery had been formally abolished in Egypt. Unhappily, the professions and pledges of the vacillating government of Egypt proved unreliable.

BY fire and cloud, across the desert sand,
And through the parted waves,
From their long bondage, with an outstretched hand,
God led the Hebrew slaves!

Dead as the letter of the Pentateuch,
As Egypt's statues cold,
In the adytum of the sacred book
Now stands that marvel old.

"Lo, God is great!" the simple Moslem says.
We seek the ancient date,
Turn the dry scroll, and make that living phrase
A dead one: "God was great!"

And, like the Coptic monks by Mousa's wells,
We dream of wonders past,
Vague as the tales the wandering Arab tells,
Each drowsier than the last.

O fools and blind! Above the Pyramids
Stretches once more that hand,
And tranced Egypt, from her stony lids,
Flings back her veil of sand.

And morning-smitten Memnon, singing, wakes;
And, listening by his Nile,
O'er Ammon's grave and awful visage breaks
A sweet and human smile.

Not, as before, with hail and fire, and call
Of death for midnight graves,
But in the stillness of the noonday, fall
The fetters of the slaves.

No longer through the Red Sea, as of old,
The bondmen walk dry shod;
Through human hearts, by love of Him controlled,
Runs now that path of God.

1856.

THE CONQUEST OF FINLAND.

"Joseph Sturge, with a companion, Thomas Harvey, has been visiting the shores of Finland, to ascertain the amount of mischief and loss to poor and peaceable sufferers, occasioned by the gun-boats of the allied squadrons in the late war, with a view to obtaining relief for them."— Friends' Review.

ACROSS the frozen marshes
The winds of autumn blow,
And the fen-lands of the Wetter
Are white with early snow.

But where the low, gray headlands
Look o'er the Baltic brine,
A bark is sailing in the track
Of England's battle-line.

No wares hath she to barter
For Bothnia's fish and grain;
She saileth not for pleasure,
She saileth not for gain.

But still by isle or mainland
She drops her anchor down,
Where'er the British cannon
Rained fire on tower and town.

Outspake the ancient Amtman,
At the gate of Helsingfors
"Why comes this ship a-spying
In the track of England's wars?"

"God bless her," said the coast-guard,—
"God bless the ship, I say.
The holy angels trim the sails
That speed her on her way!

"Where'er she drops her anchor,
The peasant's heart is glad;
Where'er she spreads her parting sail,
The peasant's heart is sad.

"Each wasted town and hamlet
She visits to restore;
To roof the shattered cabin,
And feed the starving poor.

"The sunken boats of fishers,
The foraged beeves and grain,
The spoil of flake and storehouse,
The good ship brings again.

"And so to Finland's sorrow
The sweet amend is made,
As if the healing hand of Christ
Upon her wounds were laid!"

Then said the gray old Amtman,
"The will of God be done!
The battle lost by England's hate,
By England's love is won!

*"We braved the iron tempest
That thundered on our shore;
But when did kindness fail to find
The key to Finland's door?*

*"No more from Aland's ramparts
Shall warning signal come,
Nor startled Sweaborg hear again
The roll of midnight drum.*

*"Beside our fierce Black Eagle
The Dove of Peace shall rest;
And in the mouths of cannon
The sea-bird make her nest.*

*"For Finland, looking seaward,
No coming foe shall scan;
And the holy bells of Abo
Shall ring, 'Good-will to man!'*

*"Then row thy boat, O fisher!
In peace on lake and bay;
And thou, young maiden, dance again
Around the poles of May!*

*"Sit down, old men, together,
Old wives, in quiet spin;
Henceforth the Anglo-Saxon*

Is the brother of the Finn!"

   1856.

THE EVE OF ELECTION.

FROM gold to gray
Our mild sweet day
Of Indian Summer fades too soon;
But tenderly
Above the sea
Hangs, white and calm, the hunter's moon.

In its pale fire,
The village spire
Shows like the zodiac's spectral lance;
The painted walls
Whereon it falls
Transfigured stand in marble trance!

O'er fallen leaves
The west-wind grieves,
Yet comes a seed-time round again;
And morn shall see
The State sown free
With baleful tares or healthful grain.

Along the street
The shadows meet
Of Destiny, whose hands conceal
The moulds of fate
That shape the State,
And make or mar the common weal.

Around I see
The powers that be;
I stand by Empire's primal springs;
And princes meet,
In every street,
And hear the tread of uncrowned kings!

Hark! through the crowd
The laugh runs loud,
Beneath the sad, rebuking moon.
God save the land
A careless hand
May shake or swerve ere morrow's noon!

No jest is this;
One cast amiss
May blast the hope of Freedom's year.
Oh, take me where
Are hearts of prayer,
And foreheads bowed in reverent fear!

Not lightly fall
Beyond recall
The written scrolls a breath can float;
The crowning fact
The kingliest act
Of Freedom is the freeman's vote!

For pearls that gem

A diedem

The diver in the deep sea dies;
The regal right
We boast to-night
Is ours through costlier sacrifice;

The blood of Vane,
His prison pain
Who traced the path the Pilgrim trod,
And hers whose faith
Drew strength from death,
And prayed her Russell up to God!

Our hearts grow cold,
We lightly hold
A right which brave men died to gain;
The stake, the cord,
The axe, the sword,
Grim nurses at its birth of pain.

The shadow rend,
And o'er us bend,
O martyrs, with your crowns and palms;
Breathe through these throngs
Your battle songs,
Your scaffold prayers, and dungeon psalms.

Look from the sky,
Like God's great eye,

Thou solemn moon, with searching beam,
Till in the sight
Of thy pure light
Our mean self-seekings meaner seem.

Shame from our hearts
Unworthy arts,
The fraud designed, the purpose dark;
And smite away
The hands we lay
Profanely on the sacred ark.

To party claims
And private aims,
Reveal that august face of Truth,
Whereto are given
The age of heaven,
The beauty of immortal youth.

So shall our voice
Of sovereign choice
Swell the deep bass of duty done,
And strike the key
Of time to be,
When God and man shall speak as one!

1858.

FROM PERUGIA.

"The thing which has the most dissevered the people from the Pope,—the unforgivable thing,—the breaking point between him and them,—has been the encouragement and promotion he gave to the officer under whom were executed the slaughters of Perugia. That made the breaking point in many honest hearts that had clung to him before."—HARRIET BEECHER STOWE'S Letters from Italy.

The tall, sallow guardsmen their horsetails have spread,
Flaming out in their violet, yellow, and red;
And behind go the lackeys in crimson and buff,
And the chamberlains gorgeous in velvet and ruff;
Next, in red-legged pomp, come the cardinals forth,
Each a lord of the church and a prince of the earth.

What's this squeak of the fife, and this batter of drum
Lo! the Swiss of the Church from Perugia come;
The militant angels, whose sabres drive home
To the hearts of the malcontents, cursed and abhorred,
The good Father's missives, and "Thus saith the Lord!"
And lend to his logic the point of the sword!

O maids of Etruria, gazing forlorn
O'er dark Thrasymenus, dishevelled and torn!
O fathers, who pluck at your gray beards for shame!
O mothers, struck dumb by a woe without name!
Well ye know how the Holy Church hireling behaves,
And his tender compassion of prisons and graves!

There they stand, the hired stabbers, the blood-stains yet fresh,
That splashed like red wine from the vintage of flesh;

Grim instruments, careless as pincers and rack
How the joints tear apart, and the strained sinews crack;
But the hate that glares on them is sharp as their swords,
And the sneer and the scowl print the air with fierce words!

Off with hats, down with knees, shout your vivas like mad!
Here's the Pope in his holiday righteousness clad,
From shorn crown to toe-nail, kiss-worn to the quick,
Of sainthood in purple the pattern and pick,
Who the role of the priest and the soldier unites,
And, praying like Aaron, like Joshua fights!

Is this Pio Nono the gracious, for whom
We sang our hosannas and lighted all Rome;
With whose advent we dreamed the new era began
When the priest should be human, the monk be a man?
Ah, the wolf's with the sheep, and the fox with the fowl,
When freedom we trust to the crosier and cowl!

Stand aside, men of Rome! Here's a hangman-faced Swiss—
(A blessing for him surely can't go amiss)—
Would kneel down the sanctified slipper to kiss.
Short shrift will suffice him,—he's blest beyond doubt;
But there 's blood on his hands which would scarcely wash out,
Though Peter himself held the baptismal spout!

Make way for the next! Here's another sweet son
What's this mastiff-jawed rascal in epaulets done?
He did, whispers rumor, (its truth God forbid!)

At Perugia what Herod at Bethlehem did.
And the mothers? Don't name them! these humors of war
They who keep him in service must pardon him for.

Hist! here's the arch-knave in a cardinal's hat,
With the heart of a wolf, and the stealth of a cat
(As if Judas and Herod together were rolled),
Who keeps, all as one, the Pope's conscience and gold,

Mounts guard on the altar, and pilfers from thence,
And flatters St. Peter while stealing his pence!
Who doubts Antonelli? Have miracles ceased
When robbers say mass, and Barabbas is priest?
When the Church eats and drinks, at its mystical board,
The true flesh and blood carved and shed by its sword,
When its martyr, unsinged, claps the crown on his head,
And roasts, as his proxy, his neighbor instead!

There! the bells jow and jangle the same blessed way
That they did when they rang for Bartholomew's day.
Hark! the tallow-faced monsters, nor women nor boys,
Vex the air with a shrill, sexless horror of noise.
Te Deum laudamus! All round without stint
The incense-pot swings with a taint of blood in 't!

And now for the blessing! Of little account,
You know, is the old one they heard on the Mount.
Its giver was landless, His raiment was poor,
No jewelled tiara His fishermen wore;

No incense, no lackeys, no riches, no home,
No Swiss guards! We order things better at Rome.

So bless us the strong hand, and curse us the weak;
Let Austria's vulture have food for her beak;
Let the wolf-whelp of Naples play Bomba again,
With his death-cap of silence, and halter, and chain;
Put reason, and justice, and truth under ban;

For the sin unforgiven is freedom for man!

1858.

ITALY.

ACROSS the sea I heard the groans
Of nations in the intervals
Of wind and wave. Their blood and bones
Cried out in torture, crushed by thrones,
And sucked by priestly cannibals.

I dreamed of Freedom slowly gained
By martyr meekness, patience, faith,
And lo! an athlete grimly stained,
With corded muscles battle-strained,
Shouting it from the fields of death!

I turn me, awe-struck, from the sight,
Among the clamoring thousands mute,
I only know that God is right,
And that the children of the light
Shall tread the darkness under foot.

I know the pent fire heaves its crust,
That sultry skies the bolt will form
To smite them clear; that Nature must
The balance of her powers adjust,
Though with the earthquake and the storm.
God reigns, and let the earth rejoice!
I bow before His sterner plan.
Dumb are the organs of my choice;
He speaks in battle's stormy voice,
His praise is in the wrath of man!

Yet, surely as He lives, the day
Of peace He promised shall be ours,
To fold the flags of war, and lay
Its sword and spear to rust away,
And sow its ghastly fields with flowers!

1860.

FREEDOM IN BRAZIL.

WITH clearer light, Cross of the South, shine forth
In blue Brazilian skies;
And thou, O river, cleaving half the earth
From sunset to sunrise,

From the great mountains to the Atlantic waves
Thy joy's long anthem pour.
Yet a few years (God make them less!) and slaves
Shall shame thy pride no more.
No fettered feet thy shaded margins press;
But all men shall walk free
Where thou, the high-priest of the wilderness,
Hast wedded sea to sea.
And thou, great-hearted ruler, through whose mouth
The word of God is said,
Once more, "Let there be light!"—Son of the South,
Lift up thy honored head,
Wear unashamed a crown by thy desert
More than by birth thy own,
Careless of watch and ward; thou art begirt
By grateful hearts alone.
The moated wall and battle-ship may fail,
But safe shall justice prove;
Stronger than greaves of brass or iron mail
The panoply of love.

Crowned doubly by man's blessing and God's grace,
Thy future is secure;

Who frees a people makes his statue's place
In Time's Valhalla sure.
Lo! from his Neva's banks the Scythian Czar
Stretches to thee his hand,
Who, with the pencil of the Northern star,
Wrote freedom on his land.
And he whose grave is holy by our calm
And prairied Sangamon,
From his gaunt hand shall drop the martyr's palm
To greet thee with "Well done!"

And thou, O Earth, with smiles thy face make sweet,
And let thy wail be stilled,
To hear the Muse of prophecy repeat
Her promise half fulfilled.
The Voice that spake at Nazareth speaks still,
No sound thereof hath died;
Alike thy hope and Heaven's eternal will
Shall yet be satisfied.
The years are slow, the vision tarrieth long,
And far the end may be;
But, one by one, the fiends of ancient wrong
Go out and leave thee free.

1867.

AFTER ELECTION.

THE day's sharp strife is ended now,
Our work is done, God knoweth how!
As on the thronged, unrestful town
The patience of the moon looks down,
I wait to hear, beside the wire,
The voices of its tongues of fire.

Slow, doubtful, faint, they seem at first
Be strong, my heart, to know the worst!
Hark! there the Alleghanies spoke;
That sound from lake and prairie broke,
That sunset-gun of triumph rent
The silence of a continent!

That signal from Nebraska sprung,
This, from Nevada's mountain tongue!
Is that thy answer, strong and free,
O loyal heart of Tennessee?
What strange, glad voice is that which calls
From Wagner's grave and Sumter's walls?

From Mississippi's fountain-head
A sound as of the bison's tread!
There rustled freedom's Charter Oak
In that wild burst the Ozarks spoke!
Cheer answers cheer from rise to set
Of sun. We have a country yet!

The praise, O God, be thine alone!
Thou givest not for bread a stone;
Thou hast not led us through the night
To blind us with returning light;
Not through the furnace have we passed,
To perish at its mouth at last.

O night of peace, thy flight restrain!
November's moon, be slow to wane!
Shine on the freedman's cabin floor,
On brows of prayer a blessing pour;
And give, with full assurance blest,
The weary heart of Freedom rest!

1868.

DISARMAMENT.

"PUT up the sword!" The voice of Christ once more
Speaks, in the pauses of the cannon's roar,
O'er fields of corn by fiery sickles reaped
And left dry ashes; over trenches heaped
With nameless dead; o'er cities starving slow
Under a rain of fire; through wards of woe
Down which a groaning diapason runs
From tortured brothers, husbands, lovers, sons
Of desolate women in their far-off homes,
Waiting to hear the step that never comes!
O men and brothers! let that voice be heard.
War fails, try peace; put up the useless sword!

Fear not the end. There is a story told
In Eastern tents, when autumn nights grow cold,
And round the fire the Mongol shepherds sit
With grave responses listening unto it
Once, on the errands of his mercy bent,
Buddha, the holy and benevolent,
Met a fell monster, huge and fierce of look,
Whose awful voice the hills and forests shook.
"O son of peace!" the giant cried, "thy fate
Is sealed at last, and love shall yield to hate."
The unarmed Buddha looking, with no trace
Of fear or anger, in the monster's face,
In pity said: "Poor fiend, even thee I love."
Lo! as he spake the sky-tall terror sank
To hand-breadth size; the huge abhorrence shrank

Into the form and fashion of a dove;
And where the thunder of its rage was heard,
Circling above him sweetly sang the bird
"Hate hath no harm for love," so ran the song;
"And peace unweaponed conquers every wrong!"

1871.

THE PROBLEM.

I.

NOT without envy Wealth at times must look
On their brown strength who wield the reaping-hook
And scythe, or at the forge-fire shape the plough
Or the steel harness of the steeds of steam;
All who, by skill and patience, anyhow
Make service noble, and the earth redeem
From savageness. By kingly accolade
Than theirs was never worthier knighthood made.
Well for them, if, while demagogues their vain
And evil counsels proffer, they maintain
Their honest manhood unseduced, and wage
No war with Labor's right to Labor's gain
Of sweet home-comfort, rest of hand and brain,
And softer pillow for the head of Age.

II.

And well for Gain if it ungrudging yields
Labor its just demand; and well for Ease
If in the uses of its own, it sees
No wrong to him who tills its pleasant fields
And spreads the table of its luxuries.
The interests of the rich man and the poor
Are one and same, inseparable evermore;
And, when scant wage or labor fail to give
Food, shelter, raiment, wherewithal to live,
Need has its rights, necessity its claim.
Yea, even self-wrought misery and shame

Test well the charity suffering long and kind.
The home-pressed question of the age can find
No answer in the catch-words of the blind
Leaders of blind. Solution there is none
Save in the Golden Rule of Christ alone.

1877.

OUR COUNTRY.

Read at Woodstock, Conn., July 4, 1883.

WE give thy natal day to hope,
O Country of our love and prayer!
Thy way is down no fatal slope,
But up to freer sun and air.

Tried as by furnace-fires, and yet
By God's grace only stronger made,
In future tasks before thee set
Thou shalt not lack the old-time aid.
The fathers sleep, but men remain
As wise, as true, and brave as they;
Why count the loss and not the gain?
The best is that we have to-day.

Whate'er of folly, shame, or crime,
Within thy mighty bounds transpires,
With speed defying space and time
Comes to us on the accusing wires;

While of thy wealth of noble deeds,
Thy homes of peace, thy votes unsold,
The love that pleads for human needs,
The wrong redressed, but half is told!

We read each felon's chronicle,
His acts, his words, his gallows-mood;
We know the single sinner well

And not the nine and ninety good.

Yet if, on daily scandals fed,
We seem at times to doubt thy worth,
We know thee still, when all is said,
The best and dearest spot on earth.

From the warm Mexic Gulf, or where
Belted with flowers Los Angeles
Basks in the semi-tropic air,
To where Katahdin's cedar trees
Are dwarfed and bent by Northern winds,
Thy plenty's horn is yearly filled;
Alone, the rounding century finds
Thy liberal soil by free hands tilled.

A refuge for the wronged and poor,
Thy generous heart has borne the blame
That, with them, through thy open door,
The old world's evil outcasts came.

But, with thy just and equal rule,
And labor's need and breadth of lands,
Free press and rostrum, church and school,
Thy sure, if slow, transforming hands

Shall mould even them to thy design,
Making a blessing of the ban;
And Freedom's chemistry combine

The alien elements of man.

The power that broke their prison bar
And set the dusky millions free,
And welded in the flame of war
The Union fast to Liberty,

Shall it not deal with other ills,
Redress the red man's grievance, break
The Circean cup which shames and kills,
And Labor full requital make?
Alone to such as fitly bear
Thy civic honors bid them fall?
And call thy daughters forth to share
The rights and duties pledged to all?

Give every child his right of school,
Merge private greed in public good,
And spare a treasury overfull
The tax upon a poor man's food?

No lack was in thy primal stock,
No weakling founders builded here;
Thine were the men of Plymouth Rock,
The Huguenot and Cavalier;

And they whose firm endurance gained
The freedom of the souls of men,
Whose hands, unstained with blood, maintained

The swordless commonwealth of Penn.

And thine shall be the power of all
To do the work which duty bids,
And make the people's council hall
As lasting as the Pyramids!

Well have thy later years made good
Thy brave-said word a century back,
The pledge of human brotherhood,
The equal claim of white and black.
That word still echoes round the world,
And all who hear it turn to thee,
And read upon thy flag unfurled
The prophecies of destiny.

Thy great world-lesson all shall learn,
The nations in thy school shall sit,
Earth's farthest mountain-tops shall burn
With watch-fires from thy own uplit.

Great without seeking to be great
By fraud or conquest, rich in gold,
But richer in the large estate
Of virtue which thy children hold,

With peace that comes of purity
And strength to simple justice due,
So runs our loyal dream of thee;

God of our fathers! make it true.

O Land of lands! to thee we give
Our prayers, our hopes, our service free;
For thee thy sons shall nobly live,
And at thy need shall die for thee!

ON THE BIG HORN.

In the disastrous battle on the Big Horn River, in which General Custer and his entire force were slain, the chief Rain-in-the-Face was one of the fiercest leaders of the Indians. In Longfellow's poem on the massacre, these lines will be remembered:—

> *"Revenge!" cried Rain-in-the-Face,*
>
> *"Revenge upon all the race*
>
> *Of the White Chief with yellow hair!"*
>
> *And the mountains dark and high*
>
> *From their crags reechoed the cry*
>
> *Of his anger and despair.*

He is now a man of peace; and the agent at Standing Rock, Dakota, writes, September 28, 1886: "Rain-in-the-Face is very anxious to go to Hampton. I fear he is too old, but he desires very much to go." The Southern Workman, the organ of General Armstrong's Industrial School at Hampton, Va., says in a late number:—

"Rain-in-the-Face has applied before to come to Hampton, but his age would exclude him from the school as an ordinary student. He has shown himself very much in earnest about it, and is anxious, all say, to learn the better ways of life. It is as unusual as it is striking to see a man of his age, and one who has had such an experience, willing to give up the old way, and put himself in the position of a boy and a student."

> *THE years are but half a score,*
>
> *And the war-whoop sounds no more*
>
> *With the blast of bugles, where*
>
> *Straight into a slaughter pen,*
>
> *With his doomed three hundred men,*
>
> *Rode the chief with the yellow hair.*
>
>
> *O Hampton, down by the sea!*
>
> *What voice is beseeching thee*
>
> *For the scholar's lowliest place?*
>
> *Can this be the voice of him*

*Who fought on the Big Horn's rim?
Can this be Rain-in-the-Face?*

*His war-paint is washed away,
His hands have forgotten to slay;
He seeks for himself and his race
The arts of peace and the lore
That give to the skilled hand more
Than the spoils of war and chase.*

*O chief of the Christ-like school!
Can the zeal of thy heart grow cool
When the victor scarred with fight
Like a child for thy guidance craves,
And the faces of hunters and braves
Are turning to thee for light?*

*The hatchet lies overgrown
With grass by the Yellowstone,
Wind River and Paw of Bear;
And, in sign that foes are friends,
Each lodge like a peace-pipe sends
Its smoke in the quiet air.*

*The hands that have done the wrong
To right the wronged are strong,
And the voice of a nation saith
"Enough of the war of swords,
Enough of the lying words*

And shame of a broken faith!"

The hills that have watched afar
The valleys ablaze with war
Shall look on the tasselled corn;
And the dust of the grinded grain,
Instead of the blood of the slain,
Shall sprinkle thy banks, Big Horn!

The Ute and the wandering Crow
Shall know as the white men know,
And fare as the white men fare;
The pale and the red shall be brothers,
One's rights shall be as another's,
Home, School, and House of Prayer!

O mountains that climb to snow,
O river winding below,
Through meadows by war once trod,
O wild, waste lands that await
The harvest exceeding great,
Break forth into praise of God!

1887.

NOTES

Note 1, page 18. The reader may, perhaps, call to mind the beautiful sonnet of William Wordsworth, addressed to Toussaint L'Ouverture, during his confinement in France.

"Toussaint!—thou most unhappy man of men
Whether the whistling rustic tends his plough
Within thy hearing, or thou liest now
Buried in some deep dungeon's earless den;
O miserable chieftain!—where and when
Wilt thou find patience?—Yet, die not, do thou
Wear rather in thy bonds a cheerful brow;
Though fallen thyself, never to rise again,
Live and take comfort. Thou hast left behind
Powers that will work for thee; air, earth, and skies,—
There's not a breathing of the common wind
That will forget thee; thou hast great allies.
Thy friends are exultations, agonies,
And love, and man's unconquerable mind."

Note 2, page 67. The Northern author of the Congressional rule against receiving petitions of the people on the subject of Slavery.

Note 3, page 88. There was at the time when this poem was written an Association in Liberty County, Georgia, for the religious instruction of negroes. One of their annual reports contains an address by the Rev. Josiah Spry Law, in which the following passage occurs: "There is a growing interest in this community in the religious instruction of negroes. There is a conviction that religious instruction promotes the quiet and order of the people, and the pecuniary interest of the owners."

Note 4, page 117. The book-establishment of the Free-Will Baptists in Dover was refused the act of incorporation by the New Hampshire Legislature, for the reason that the newspaper organ of that sect and its leading preachers favored abolition.

Note 5, page 118. The senatorial editor of the Belknap Gazette all along manifested a peculiar horror of "niggers" and "nigger parties."

Note 6, page 118. The justice before whom Elder Storrs was brought for preaching abolition on a writ drawn by Hon. M. N., Jr., of Pittsfield. The sheriff served the writ while the elder was praying.

Note 7, page 118. The academy at Canaan, N. H., received one or two colored scholars, and was in consequence dragged off into a swamp by Democratic teams.

Note 8, page 119. "Papers and memorials touching the subject of slavery shall be laid on the table without reading, debate, or reference." So read the gag-law, as it was called, introduced in the House by Mr. Atherton.

Note 9, page 120. The Female Anti-Slavery Society, at its first meeting in Concord, was assailed with stones and brickbats.

Note 10, page 168. The election of Charles Sumner to the United States Senate "followed hard upon" the rendition of the fugitive Sims by the United States officials and the armed police of Boston.

Note 11, page 290. For the idea of this line, I am indebted to Emerson, in his inimitable sonnet to the Rhodora,—

"If eyes were made for seeing,

Then Beauty is its own excuse for being."